Horoscope Handbook:

a Rudolf Steiner Approach

A practical manual for the
professional astrologer and counsellor

Adrian Anderson Ph. D.

Also available by this author:

The Rudolf Steiner Handbook
The Foundation Stone Meditation: a new commentary
The Way to the Sacred
The Hellenistic Mysteries & Christianity
Two Gems from Rudolf Steiner
Dramatic Anthroposophy: Identification and contextualization of primary features of Rudolf Steiner's anthroposophy. (Ph.D. thesis)
Living a Spiritual year: seasonal festivals in both hemispheres

See also as Damien Pryor:

The nature & origin of the Tropical Zodiac
Stonehenge
The Externsteine
Lalibela
The Great Pyramid & the Sphinx

© Threshold Publishing, Australia, 2015

The author reserves the moral right to be regarded as the author of this book.

www.rudolfsteinerstudies.com

ISBN 978-0-9941602-2-5

ACKNOWLEDGEMENT

The author has the very pleasant task here of acknowledging the generous support for this project given to him by the Ligsma Kirpe Trust. Without this support, the task of writing this book would not have been possible.

I would also like to thank Andrew of Port Campbell Press for his assistance and my colleagues for their insights.

Introduction

Chapter One   Basic Principles   2
The value of horoscope interpretation. The difference between the zodiac signs and the zodiac constellations (the 'tropical' or 'sidereal' zodiacs). What is a tropical zodiac really? What is the new perspective that Rudolf Steiner brings to horoscope interpretation ? What are the Houses? What about fatalism, karma and free-will? The four pillars of the personality in the horoscope. The south lunar node and the north lunar node

Chapter Two   The Sun signs and the Moon Signs   22
The sun-signs: their primary spiritual-psychological qualities. The moon in the signs: their spiritual-psychological qualities.

Chapter Three   New perspectives on the planets   42
Beyond myths: the spiritual influences from the seven classical planets on the various facets of human consciousness.

Chapter Four   Interpreting the Planetary Aspects   53
New insights into all the major 'aspects' or angles between the planets. Correlating the planetary aspects to the ego-sense, the life-forces/temperament, the intellect, emotions, will, the Spiritual-self, and the lower-self (or the Double).

Chapter Five   The Planets in the Houses   178
What a planet's position in a house means.

Chapter Six   Planets in the Signs   219
What a planet's position in a sign means.

Chapter Seven   House Cusps
The Rising Sign and zodiac signs on the house cusps.   240

Chapter Eight   More features of the Horoscope   282
& how to interpret a horoscope
Where to start, how to integrate all the information; the four main features, the planetary aspects, zodiac ruler of planets and houses, planets in houses, the lunar nodes, retrograding planets, intercepted houses, the Part of Fortune, etc.
Horoscopes for the Arctic Circle. Mean lunar nodes or true nodes? The two hemispheres and the lunar nodes

Books and software recommended as additional help.

Appendix   p. 319
The Life and work of Rudolf Steiner

INDEX

Copyright acknowledgments

Illustrations
1:	The tropical and sidereal zodiacs	p. 9
2:	The Inherent Zodiac	p. 11
3:	The four quadrants & the 12 Houses	p. 15
4:	The lunar nodes	p. 17
5:	The sigils & pictures of the 12 zodiac signs	p. 20
6:	The ancient Dendera zodiac	p. 22
7:	The planetary symbols	p. 41
8:	The Blanchini Planisphere	p. 42
9:	Symbols for the Aspects	p. 57
10:	Z odiac signs and parts of the body	p. 301
11:	t he 12 Themes of the Houses	p. 302
12:	The Archetypal Zodiac	p. 303
13:	An intercepted chart	p. 304

Foreword

Self-knowledge is a very important goal, both for people seeking personal development and for people who are undergoing counselling. It is my experience that when a horoscope is skilfully assessed, it provides a degree of self-knowledge which is hard to acquire from any other source. The capacity of a counsellor to assist a client, is enormously enhanced, if they can interpret the horoscope. For parents there is no better way to understand the personality of a child than to have the child's chart interpreted. For those who are seeking to find an appropriate life-partner, knowledge of the other person's chart is a reliable guide to their personality. It is also possible to have a 'relationship analysis' process, based on a comparison of the two horoscopes.

It is also my experience that when the extensive teachings of Rudolf Steiner about the influence of the zodiac signs and of the planets in the soul are integrated into modern astrological knowledge, then horoscope interpretation is given an invaluable deepening.

At some time in the future the interpretation of a person's horoscope, to a professional standard, may well become a highly valued tool for psychiatrists, psychologists, therapists and people involved in spirituality. I hope this book will help to make that time arrive more quickly !

Chapter One   Basic Principles

The intention of this book is to provide a practical guide to interpreting the horoscope, incorporating the additional insights that the renowned spiritual teacher and pioneer of genius in many fields of life, Rudolf Steiner (1861-1925), has provided. See the Appendix for a brief biographical sketch of his life and work. Before we explore Steiner's contributions and become acquainted with the main features of a horoscope, we need to have an overview of the historical background of astrology. The interpretation of a horoscope carried out today, builds on knowledge gained over some 2,500 years. Astrological wisdom started to accumulate even further back in time, about 3,000 BC, with the ancient Sumerians. But as far as documentary evidence is concerned, personal horoscope interpretations started about 410 BC, in Babylonia. This became more widespread in the Hellenistic age, as the Greeks worked further with what they learnt from Babylonian astrological wisdom.

This work became enriched throughout the following centuries, in the Middle Ages, the Renaissance, and then into the 20th century, when a new phase of intense research was undertaken. This research is often carried out by researchers with academic qualifications. These people can see that the horoscope yields the most detailed and accurate psychological profile of a person available today.

However it is well-established that today's "sun-sign" astrology, which puts the sun-sign at the centre of the horoscope's value, was not practiced in earlier times. The sun-sign was not so prominent because the horoscope was viewed as an organic entirety, consisting of many equal parts. It was only at the beginning of the 20th century that the emphasis was placed so strongly on the sun-sign. This arose from more spiritually aware astrologers, in particular, from theosophists, especially Alan Leo.

For example, in the 19th century, even two of the most prominent astrologers of that century, Sepharial (Harry Old) and Raphael (Robert Smith) placed the sun as just one factor amongst equals, in their books. This was also the case back in the Middle Ages with such famous astrologers as Agrippa von Nettesheim and Girolamo Cardano. In the Renaissance this was also the usual procedure with prominent astrologers, such as Johannes Stöffler and Jakob Pflaum. Their horoscope interpretation work reported to some extent on the nature of the person, but equally it reported on the destiny that awaited them as the years went by. So horoscope interpretation also involved forecasting the future of the client. However, these earlier astrologers did view the sun as slightly prominent if the birth-hour was in the daytime, otherwise the moon was seen as more important. The sun itself was seen as part of triple dynamic, (called a triplicity) which was inextricably linked to two other planets and hence to the nature of their dynamics. With a 'triplicity' the question was, are these planets located in a house that is strengthening or weakening to themselves, and did those dynamics support or weaken that of the sun? This complex assessment method was particularly prevalent in the Hellenistic era, from which these later astrologers borrowed.

Though a few modern astrologers are interested in this system, professional astrologers today find that interpreting the horoscope with an emphasis upon the sun-sign, but embedded within a series of other sophisticated and complex features in the chart, is the most satisfactory method. This is because it meets more fully the conscious needs and queries of the individual.

It is however true that in earlier times the sun's movement through the zodiac was considered very important. For example in the Latin world, the poet Virgil wrote in his 'First Georgic', "The golden sun rules the great firmament through the twelve constellations."[1] And of course ancient cultures built temples (such as the temple of Khafre at the Giza plateau) or megalithic sites (Stonehenge, etc) to experience this. But in these early times this focus on the zodiac was not on the sun-sign in the individual's birth chart, it was about life on Earth in a larger sense, especially the passage of the sun underlying seasonal dynamics or on a larger timescale, creating zodiac ages.

The role of the sun-sign has become very important in today's world, because the sense of self, of being an individual, is very powerfully affected by the sun-sign, and this sense of self has become much stronger in recent times. On this topic, Rudolf Steiner indicated that the influence of the sun-sign is very important in our personality. He also taught that in the far future every person will be permanently linked in the core of their being (their spirit) to a particular zodiac sign.[2]

The reason that a person is – only as from recent times – called "a Gemini" or "a Cancerian" is precisely because **the sun** was in that sign when they were born, and not one of the planets ! We are not called "a Gemini" or "an Aries", or whatever, because Mercury or

---

1. Translated by Robert Fitzgerald.
2 Rudolf Steiner's fascinating new series of symbols for the zodiac and our link to them will be presented in a forthcoming book, "Zodiac Images of Rudolf Steiner".

Saturn, or another planet, is in Gemini or Aries when we were born. What counts is where the sun is located when a person is born.

The zodiac sign located at the eastern point of the chart where the sun rises, a point called the Ascendant, also has a powerful influence on the ego of the human being. The more prominent the ego-sense is, the more important are these two signs for that person. However it remains the case that a horoscope is not properly interpreted if many other factors are not included as well. Rudolf Steiner's perspective on the evolving of humanity is very useful here. He taught that the sense of ego was very weak amongst people in times before the time of the ancient Greeks. It was amongst these people that a personal sense of self began to emerge.

So, before the Hellenistic Age, a personalized, ego-oriented horoscope would have been a rarity. A clue to understanding this pivotal theme, that the sense of self was weaker in previous millennia, comes from a comment by a great Hellenistic astrologer, Vettius Valens, who wrote late in the 2nd century AD. He stated in his Anthologies, that the sun "...is the light of the mind, the organ for mental perception of the soul". Yet even so, the sun's role was not prominent in the horoscope interpretation of the time ! This is because for it to be prominent there would need to have been a strong sense of self.

Rudolf Steiner's contributions
Early in the 20th century Rudolf Steiner presented research based on his ability to spiritually experience and assess the influence of the zodiac and the planets on humanity. His work resulted in insights perhaps unequalled in the literature of the western world. In his teachings, which fill nearly 400 volumes, he gave approximately 2,000 lectures on the cosmos, and its significance for humanity. Steiner almost never used the word 'astrology', apparently because he wanted to differentiate his direct, first-hand knowledge about the cosmos from the inherited astrological principles used by astrologers early in the 20th century.

He viewed that kind of astrology as limited and formulaic. However many of his lectures offer invaluable perspectives on the horoscope, without directly referring to astrology as such. I have sought to integrate Steiner's views on the influence of the cosmos, with the best of modern astrological knowledge. It is my experience that this provides invaluable new insights for the interpretation of the horoscope.

In the only lecture Steiner ever gave specifically on horoscopes, he affirmed the remarkable power of horoscope interpretation as carried out over the last two millennia or so to delineate the human personality,

> The horoscope which has been cast for thousands of years for the individual corresponded with infallible exactitude to the soul ....[3]

His taught that the practice of horoscope analysis is a very valuable process, provided that the practitioner has real wisdom, "...it demands from those who practise it, a higher spiritual faculty of cognition."[4] This in effect means, a capacity for wisdom, for being spiritually intuitive.

The primary question facing anyone who considers astrology is; how can the planets actually structure our personality? Steiner's research provides an answer to this fundamental question, which is really asking, how can a horoscope be accurate? That is, how can the positions of the planets at birth determine the personality? The answer is that the planets at birth don't really cause or create the personality, but rather they **activate** it. For on the journey down to birth the soul develops a new personality which forms its new aura.[5]

This aura is formed from the energies raying out from the planets. This is the new personality, and it is determined by the kind of energies flowing in from the planets on a spiritual level. Now, at the time of birth, and at the place of birth, the planets will be in particular positions with regard to each other, to the zodiac signs and to the horizon (and also the 12 Houses).

This situation invokes a particular dynamic, or rather collection of dynamics, in the atmosphere of our planet, such as negative or positive qualities of planets. But these qualities are in effect, soul qualities too, of course. For example, if the Moon is close to Venus (that is, 'in conjunction') this creates a gracefulness, charm and affectionate qualities.

The dynamics that are present in the Earth's aura, at the time and over the local place of birth, are breathed-in by the baby with its first breath, and these dynamics then become activated in that person. Those dynamics should be the same dynamics or soul

---

3. From an archive lecture, not in the German Complete Works, from Feb. 2nd 1911
4. The Complete Works, volume 162 p. 20.
5. Actually on the way down to re-birth.

qualities that already existed in that baby's soul or aura when it was formed on the pathway down to birth. A more substantial exploration of this question is available in my book the *Rudolf Steiner Handbook.*

Fatalism, karma and free-will
There are also philosophical questions underlying astrology to do with fatalism, karma and free-will. There is no need for anything superstitious or fatalistic to be in a horoscope analysis which is intended to yield a spiritual-psychological profile of the person. The perspective gained through astrology is experience-based, not theoretical superstition. With regard to being fatalistic – where one thinks that everything is predetermined and hence we are unfree beings – Rudolf Steiner points out that the personality is the outcome of our previous life, and that is our karma, and indeed that is fixed or predetermined; it can't be changed. However a person is actually quite free to determine how they shall respond to the challenges and opportunities given by their own personality and life experiences.

Furthermore from Steiner's wisdom, called anthroposophy, it is clear that the negative or challenging traits of the person are not determined by the accident of birth so to speak, but are decided upon by that person before re-birth. This is done in conjunction with the wisdom of higher Powers before conception, and these traits become activated by the time and place of the birth.

Furthermore, these negative traits do not have to remain for all of one's life. They can be greatly reduced, even removed, by making effort at personal development. So to me, this means that a horoscope for a person of mature age, who has made an effort to improve their nature, could actually have the negative angles between various planets specifically altered by the astrologer in a new horoscope, so that they are removed.

Rudolf Steiner provides a very useful new perspective on the fourfold-ness of the horoscope, one that relates the 'fourfold human being' to the four quadrants of the chart (see below for more about this). His research also allows the influence of the seven classical planets to be related to human consciousness in a very illuminating way, greatly deepening the interpretation of the chart.

In addition, he provides an understanding of the twelve zodiac influences from his insights into the way these same forces have been active in creating the human life-wave, over vast periods of time. When one has an understanding of Steiner's teachings on karma, then it is possible to see the chart in a profound context; namely that of the evolving of the human personality over lifetimes. We shall be exploring these insights in this book.

The angles between planets
A major feature of astrology is that the angles formed between two planets activate specific qualities of those planets in the personality. To someone new to astrology, this sounds really strange, but it is the case that if two planets are in a sharp angle to each other (a square or opposition) then unpleasant, unethical qualities in one or both of those planets will be activated. But if the angles formed are 'soft' (30° or 60°) then good qualities of those planets are activated. (This is discussed further in Chapter Six.) This mysterious phenomenon is completely substantiated by millennia of astrological experience, but why this happens, is unknown.

What is the tropical zodiac and the sidereal zodiac ?
It is important to briefly mention now that there are two kinds of zodiac systems. One is called the tropical zodiac, the other the sidereal zodiac. Those remarks mentioned above by Steiner, "The horoscope which has been cast for thousands of years for the individual corresponded with infallible exactitude to the person...", refer to the tropical zodiac. The term, 'tropical zodiac' is simply a technical (and vague) way of referring to the zodiac signs. The term 'sidereal zodiac' is a technical way of referring to the zodiac constellations. Steiner, along with virtually every astrologer in the western world, uses the tropical zodiac for the interpretation of the horoscope, never the sidereal zodiac.

So what is the tropical zodiac actually? Few people know that their zodiac sign is not the same thing as the zodiac constellation of the same name. Few astrologers speak about this subject because in fact, surprising as this sounds, they themselves are quite unclear as to just what the tropical zodiac is. The actual nature of the so-called tropical zodiac, which is the basis of horoscopes, has remained a complete mystery to everyone for some 2,000 years, until very recently.

In the modern scientific era, this awkward fact has socially placed the practice of astrology on a very insecure footing. Clearly, this zodiac is a division of the heavens into 12 parts, just like the twelve constellations. But unlike them, these signs are all of the same size or length, each being 30° of the 360° circle of the heavens, so the sun takes the same time, namely 30 days, to go through them. Whereas the zodiac constellations are each of different sizes, and so the sun takes a varying number of days to go through them.

Furthermore, very significantly, the zodiac signs are not in the same part of the heavens as the constellations of the same name. These two zodiacs cannot be aligned, because the constellations are of varying sizes. Because of astronomical motions in our solar system, these two zodiacs will drift ever further apart as the centuries pass by, see illustration One. The fact that the zodiac signs are not in the same sector of the sky as the constellation they are named after has caused a lot of doubt about their validity in recent times. The signs have even been dismissed by some as an empty theoretical zodiac.

But the tropical zodiac is not an abstract man-made theory; it is a factual thing. However there is only one book that can explain just what the zodiac signs are, out there in space, it is *The Origin and Nature Of The Tropical Zodiac* by Damien Pryor.[6] The tropical zodiac, and therefore the zodiac signs, are shown to be valid, and this is confirmed by the great authority on astrology, Claudius Ptolemy in the 2nd century AD. It is also confirmed of course by thousands of astrologers over several millennia.

As Pryor demonstrates, this inherent zodiac exists in an energy form around the upper atmosphere of the Earth, see illustration Two. Each of the sectors or signs in this 12-fold circle in the heavens receive the energies from whatever zodiac constellation they are so wisely named after – regardless of the spatial distance between them. So the tropical zodiac is not a theoretical construct, even if it is not physically visible amongst the stars of the night sky. The term 'tropical zodiac' is quite wrong, and directly leads to confusion. It is better to call it the "inherent zodiac", as Pryor's book suggests.

Some examples of how Steiner validated the zodiac signs or tropical zodiac include the occasion when he analyzed the horoscopes of two albino people in a lecture cycle about special educational needs. For this purpose, the tropical zodiac signs were used.[7] Likewise, when he established the cosmic setting for the crucial and pivotal event in his life of laying the foundation stone of the huge Goetheanum building in 1913, he specifically pointed out in writing that Mercury was in

---

6. A small book, it is published by Port Campbell Press, and available on Amazon and the Book Depository and book stores.

7 A false analysis of this horoscope as sidereal was put forward by a sidereal enthusiast, see my ebooklet: Rudolf Steiner & the Tropical Zodiac.

1 The tropical zodiac signs and the sidereal constellations.

The Signs (pink) are not aligned with the constellations. Thus a 'Cancerian' person for example is born when the sun is amidst the stars of the Twins (Gemini); that is, in the sidereal zodiac the sun is located in Gemini.

the sign of Libra (although at that time it was in the constellation of Virgo).[8] Whereas in explaining the bio-dynamic agricultural approach to farming, he showed how the movement of the moon through the actual stars or constellations of the zodiac, the sidereal zodiac, is a pivotal factor. Steiner also provided a series of twelve meditations on the zodiac signs or tropical zodiac, and worked with an astrologer, doing hundreds of charts over about ten years. It is an experiential reality for astrologers that, if they were to use the sidereal zodiac when drawing up a horoscope, this would provide the client with with a character analysis that does not match their personality.

The validity of the tropical Zodiac
An example of the validity of the zodiac signs from my own work is that of a four-year-old boy, whose severely indrawn, anti-sociable disposition resulted in him being brought to the psychiatrist's office, where he was diagnosed as having broad-spectrum autism. He was about to commence a course of potent drugs that would alter his brain-function.

However, his grand-parents consulted with me first, and I was able to give my opinion that this child was not autistic, but rather had a number of intense anxieties and fears that would enormously inhibit his confidence socially in any situation other than his home. The horoscope showed precisely that he had a communication impediment with regard to his own feelings, as well as a distorted world-view with regard to both his own life and the external world.

In addition it was clear from the birth chart that he was very insecure emotionally, easily becoming a 'victim' whenever opposition to him arose. The chart also showed that he had an inherent dislike of being cuddled by the mother. Crucially he had a huge total of seven of these emotionally destabilizing influences from the sign of Cancer the crab – the most emotionally vulnerable of all twelve signs. (He also had several other factors that tend to distort perception of reality.)

But the main point here is that if the chart had been drawn up as a sidereal chart, he would have been assessed as a happy-go-lucky, emotionally stable boy with seven Gemini influences, with no Cancerian traits. This is because the Sign of Cancer lies in the general area of the constellation of Gemini.

---

8. Steiner's use of, and affirmation of, the tropical zodiac is found in my ebooklet, Rudolf Steiner and the Tropical Zodiac, www.rudolfsteinerstudies.com

2: The Inherent Zodiac

Shown here in pink, the Inherent Zodiac which is situated above the Earth's atmosphere. Further out, in green, is the ancient Babylonian zodiac (the BES zodiac), dividing the star constellations into 12 equal sectors. The Inherent zodiac sectors or 'signs' each receive and activate the influences from the corresponding zodiac constellations.

So a sidereal chart would falsely indicate seven Gemini influences, and with these, he should have been an irrepressible, sanguine, outgoing free spirit (even over-active), and so no inherent cause for his behaviour would have been discernible. He would have ended up on psychiatric drugs. In view of his emotional vulnerabilities, I consequently suggested that the parents request a delay in commencing drug treatment. A delay of no more than 3 months was agreed to by the psychiatrist. I suggested a new way to parent the child, designed to enhance his confidence with his own skills and with himself when placed in an unfamiliar social setting. This technique was successful, within a few months the boy could be placed in a kindergarten. He is now enjoying a normal schooling and normal social life.

The fourfold-ness of the horoscope
There is a fourfold-ness to the horoscope in various ways: amongst these are the four quadrants, and the four elements of fire, air, water, earth, and the four distinct types of houses and also what I call the four pillars of the personality. These will be explored later.

But before we go further into the theme of one of these fourfold elements, called the quadrants, we need to note that the horoscope consists of twelve sections called Houses. Each house governs a particular feature or theme of human existence, such as career, friends, daily work, romance, life-goals, etc.

There are various systems of houses used, because the division of the circle of the heavens, shown within every horoscope as twelve sectors, is actually difficult to mathematically devise, owing to various difficulties. A particular difficulty is that the curvature of the Earth, intersecting with the straight horizon, as you attempt to divide the circle of the heavens into 12 sectors, distorts all the orderly, straight lines that one is accustomed to using in any kind of diagram. But the Placidus house system is the system that I use and recommend, as it results in a chart which, in my experience, corresponds to the client's life and personality most accurately. In Chapter Five the significance of the planets in the houses is explored, and in Chapter Eight more is said about the different House systems. Here we just need to note what themes or dynamics in life each house governs.

These themes have been defined since Hellenistic times, although not always uniformly. Here I am slightly re-defining these themes based on my experience and the implications of Rudolf Steiner's world-view.

Table of The Houses

House One: the sense of self (the ego).

House Two: talents & abilities and our life-values. These together help form our sense of our self-worth.

House Three: the mind (thinking & speech), also siblings and the local neighbourhood.

House Four: the core feelings and the home.

House Five: romance, children and one's energies, as used in romance or work or in creative interests.

House Six: daily work and health.

House Seven: marriage, and other long-term significant people.

House Eight: intimations from spirit realities (consciously or subconsciously influencing the soul), also sexuality, the partner's income, and the end of life.[9]

House Nine: one's attitude to religious-spiritual ideas & values, to relationships and also travel.

House Ten: one's social reality: usually career and marital status.

House Eleven: life-goals and groups of friends.

House Twelve: the subconscious soul-life (wishes, ideas, or intentions, etc)

Rudolf Steiner pointed out that, when one assesses a horoscope, the four quadrants of the horoscope represent the fourfold human being, see illustration Three. What he means by the fourfold human being is a fourfold structure underlying the human being. These are

---

9. The 8th House acts as a threshold, through which spiritual influences flow into humanity.

the physical body, the life-forces, the soul and finally, the 'I' or sense of self. With regard to the houses and the fourfold human being, the quadrants are arranged like this,

Quadrant One: = the ego or sense of self
                                (Houses 3,2,1)

Quadrant Two: = the soul, or personality
                                (Houses 12,11,10)

Quadrant Three: = the life-forces
                                (Houses 9,8,7)

Quadrant Four: = the body or physical life
                                (Houses 6,5,4)

Exploring further this view of the four quadrants, we can see that in quadrant One is the house of the mind, which is the a prime manifestation of the ego. Secondly the house of one's abilities and capacities, through which the self manifests directly. Then thirdly the house of the actual sense of self. So quadrant One tells the astrologer about the ego or sense of self of the client.

Whereas in quadrant Two are houses that relate to the subconscious wishes and fears, secondly of one's friends (and goals) and thirdly of one's marital and career inclinations. So quadrant Two tells us about the soul or personality as a reality amongst other people. We shall consider the four hemispheres and the four elements and four types of houses later.

Quadrant Three contains the house of one's attitude to religious-spiritual values, to relationships and also travel. Secondly it has the house of spirit intimations, partner's income, desires, the end of life; and thirdly the house of marriage, and other significant people. These all have a common thread, namely of life-forces; by this I mean the subtle energies that interconnect people.[10] (The experiencing of psychic intimations is dependent upon the nature of our etheric energies or life-forces.[11]) This energy link exists also within a shared religious/spiritual belief, and with desires, and with the psychic

---
10. This interlinking medium of energy is referred to as the 'etheric body' in esoteric terms.
11. This is explained in the Rudolf Steiner Handbook. Basically if the life-forces flow out more than usual, or have a weak link to the physical body, a psychic state arises.

3: **The Four Quadrants of the Horoscope** and
the 12 Houses or themes of human life

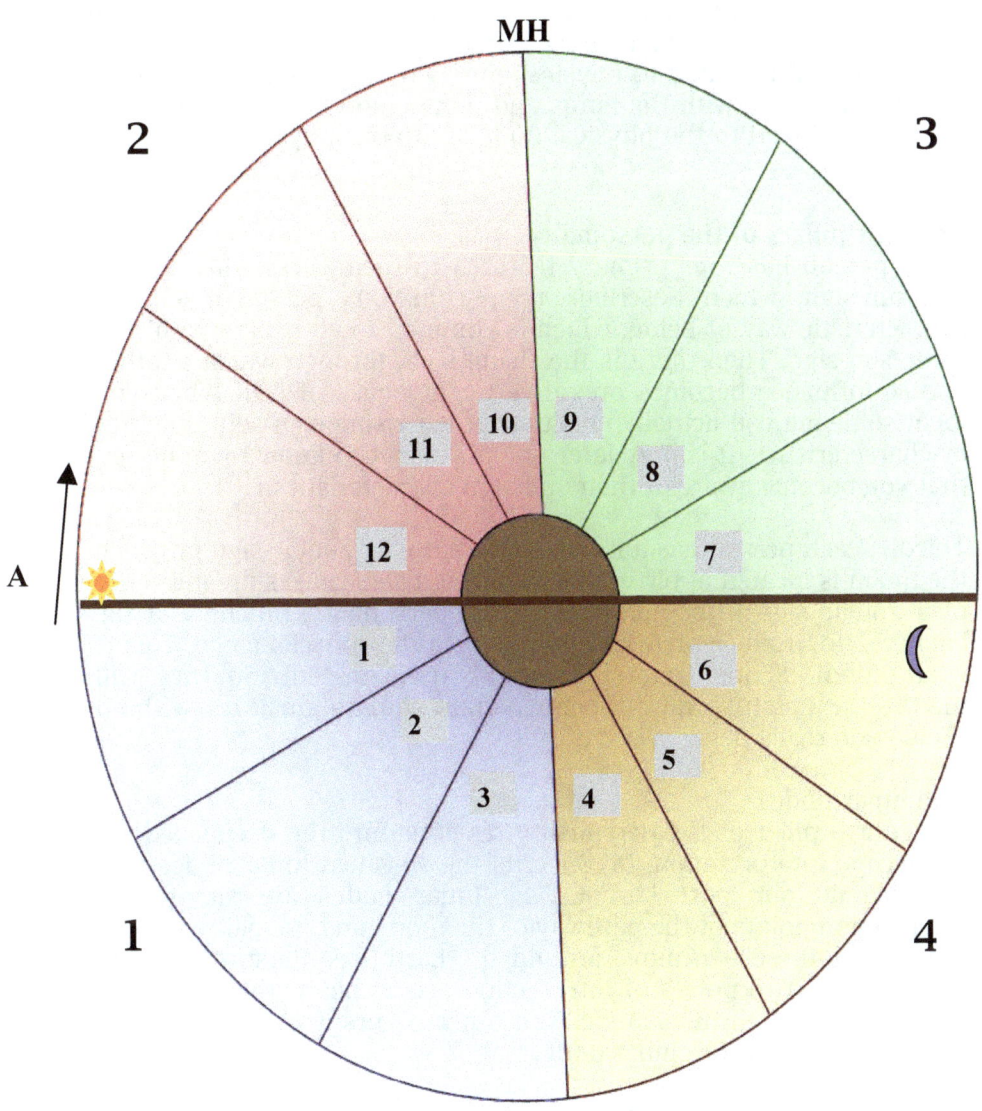

━━━ = the horizon. What is below this line is not seen (has not risen) at the birth time; here the sun has just risen in the east, so the birth took place at sunrise, the moon had already set in the west.

Quadrant 1 (blue)   : The Ego or sense-of-self (self/abilities/mind)
Quadrant 2 (red)   : The soul or personality (vocation/life-goals/subconscious)
Quadrant 3 (green) : The life-forces (social interaction energies)
Quadrant 4 (brown) : The body or physical life (home/recreation/work)

A = the Ascendant point: the planets & stars ascend from below the horizon.
MH = the Midheaven point (or 'medium coeli', MC)

sensitivity that results in spirit intimations, also there are life-forces involved in marital life and in long-term work-place interaction. Then in quadrant Four we have houses firstly to do with daily work and health, secondly related to physical energy used in leisure activities, and thirdly to do with the home and core emotions. These themes are mainly linked to the physical body and to our physical life.

The four pillars of the personality

Every person has four primary features to their personality. Firstly the sun-sign, which describes their conscious personal self, its characteristic way of being, which is common to all people with that same sun-sign. Then there is the rising sign, through which another zodiac influence becomes operative in the sense of self. When you meet someone you actually encounter their rising sign soul qualities or characteristics. It is only later on, as you get to know them better, that you become aware of their sun-sign characteristics.

Thirdly, each person has a moon-sign, that is, a zodiac sign in which the moon is located at birth. The moon-sign also causes the influence of a zodiac sign to be activated in the personality, but now in the background, in their predisposition, not in the conscious ego. This is what Rudolf Steiner refers to as the temperament. So they will manifest as habitual ways of being certain zodiacal qualities, without the person really being aware of this.

The lunar nodes

The fourth pillar of the personality takes us into the deeper side of horoscope interpretation. It concerns the so-called lunar nodes, and it concerns our past karma. The lunar nodes are simply the intersection points of the pathway of the moon and the pathway of the sun as these two move around the Earth, see illustration Four. One of these two points of intersection occurs below the equator, it is called the south lunar node. The other occurs above the equator, and is called the north lunar node.

Behind these two intersection points there lies of course, the band of the zodiac signs. So each node will have a zodiac sign behind it, and this is linked to a number of psychological dynamics which function in the personality, but in the subconscious. With regard to the south lunar node these are mainly negative qualities, qualities that can seriously impede the life of the person. The zodiac sign involved may not have any other significant role in the chart at all. If this nodal point is close to planets and those planets have negative aspects to them, then the negative influences from the south node will be all the more potent.

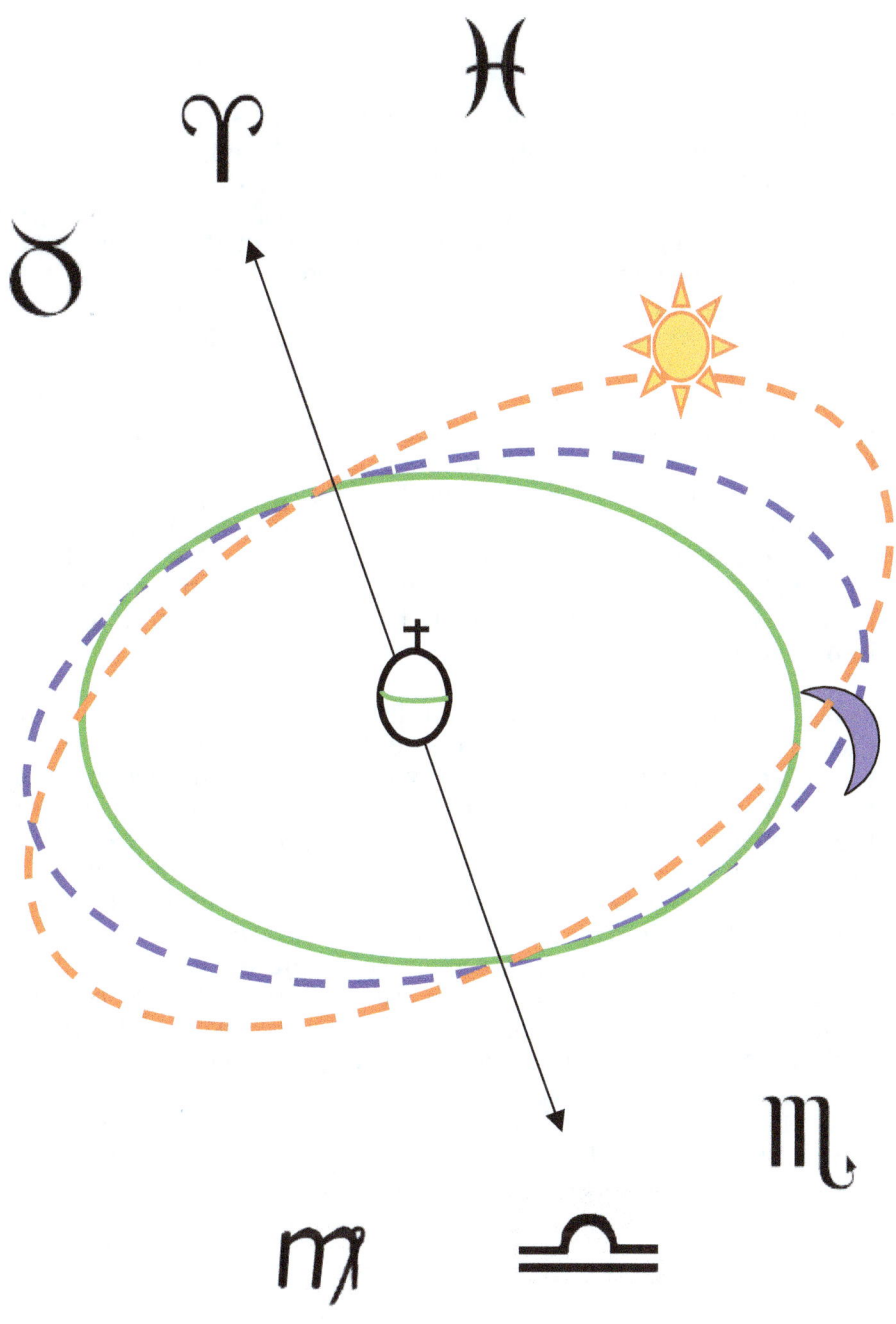

4: **The lunar nodes:** The meeting point of the sun & moon's pathways with the Earth's equator, projected out into space. Here Aries is at the north node and Libra at the south node.

So where do these influences come from, what are they? It is commonly concluded amongst astrologers, that they are the residue of the past life's primary soul qualities. From my decades of work in astrology I agree with this conclusion. That is, they are the more persistent, and usually the more negative, soul qualities belonging to the zodiac sun-sign or rising-sign from your last lifetime. These qualities are still persisting on, to some extent, in one's new personality.[12] We shall explore this further in the last chapter.

We also need to note that each person has a north lunar node, and the cosmos is so created that the soul qualities of the zodiac sign in which it is placed, is a perfect counter-balance to the zodiac sign of the south lunar node ! So this north lunar node zodiac sign has qualities that directly help to counter-act the negative qualities in the south lunar node sign.[13] But these qualities, which are the very finest of that sign, are not actually placed in the person's aura or soul. They hover above it so to speak, asking to be taken hold of, and integrated into the personality.

In other words, the person needs to learn about these qualities, and then to strive to manifest them. The north lunar node, its zodiac sign, is not necessarily the future zodiac sign of the person. That person may not be intended to receive that north lunar node sign as their sun-sign in the future life. But in order to have a better future generally, the person needs to learn the lesson of that sign. The importance of the north lunar node sign is weak, if the person does not have a lot of impeding factors in their soul from the south lunar node. However the importance of learning the lesson of the north node is very strong indeed, if the south node influence is really prominent and there are negative influences weakening the north node, such as several planets in square or opposition to it.

Once these four pillars of the personality have been assessed, then the influence of the planets in terms of how they are nuanced from the zodiac sign that they are in, need to be considered.

---

12. They are, it seems, the negative part of what the Buddhists refer to as 'skhandas'.

13 See the Appendix for the question of whether in the southern hemisphere the lunar nodes are reversed in terms of their spiritual significance.

Chapter Two   The Sun signs and the Moon signs

The sun-signs and their symbols: their primary spiritual-psychological qualities. The moon in the zodiac signs: the main spiritual-psychological qualities it creates.

The influence of each planet in its zodiac sign is clearly discernible, and needs to be noted when a horoscope is interpreted. But the core of the soul, the sense of self, is far more influenced by the sun's position than by a planet's position. That is, as we noted earlier, the sense of self, or the core nature of the personality, is determined by the sun-sign, not by a "planetary sign". The self, or what Steiner terms 'the ego', manifests as our mind, our attitudes and ideas, and hence as our responses to life.

We shall now consider the influence of the sun on the personality in each zodiac sign, and also the symbols, (or more accurately, the pictorial 'sigils') for each sign. These graphics arose from the spiritual vision of priests in ancient Mesopotamian times (the Sumerians and the later Babylonians). These graphics bear no resemblance to the shapes of the zodiac constellations (excerpt for Scorpio). The sigils profoundly symbolize the inner significance for humanity of the zodiac energies.

Illustration Five shows the modern sigils for each zodiac sign and to which of the four elements of fire, air, water and earth these belong. We can also note that there are the three 'elements' of the zodiac signs. These three are the Cardinal, Fixed or Mutable. I find it is better to refer to these as 'modalities'. These modalities are quite subtle, and of unclear significance in today's astrology. For most therapists and counsellors, they can be ignored.

5:   The symbols of the zodiac signs & their 4 elements

Illustration Six is taken from an ancient Egyptian zodiac carving, from the town of Dendera. In this the reader can see the images used to represent the twelve zodiac energies. It is a valuable exercise for the astrologer to contemplate these images, as they hint at the profound insights of the ancient Sumerian astrologers who create them. The Dendera zodiac is carved in the ceiling of a building which is only about 2,000 years old; but I conclude that this zodiac derives from the much more ancient zodiac of the Sumerians.

For there are other sigils here which clearly have their origin in the Sumerian-Babylonian peoples. It appears to me that this carving was re-copied on to this relatively recent building, from a much more ancient building which was replaced in the Hellenistic Age. The 12 zodiac images carved here are quite similar to what is used today. But other images of constellations in this carving are drawn from ancient Sumerian descriptions of the heavens.

Both academic and astrological writers confirm that the Dendera zodiac has its origins in the ancient Mesopotamian world.[14] For example, under the feet of the Sagittarius figure of Dendera is a tiny boat; this is called Pabilsag, a Babylonian cargo-boat star-group. And between the two fishes (see Illustration 6), there is a rectangle image with zig-zag lines inside it. As Gavin White suggests, this is a way of showing the regularly shaped plots of irrigated land that was a hallmark of the Mesopotamian agricultural system.

This complex situation is no doubt the reason that the carving at Dendra was at first defined by Egyptologists as about 4,000 years old, but in recent decades re-defined as only about 2,000 years old.
They were correct in essence the first time; the images do go back about 5,000 years. But the current version is much more recent. The earliest buildings at the Dendera site are dated back to a time long before the current building was erected. The site has remains of buildings going back to the time of Pharaoh Khufu, which is the time of the ancient Sumerians (about 2800-2900 BC). My conclusions here are confirmed by two other ancient Egyptian zodiacs; they were found in a grave in a place called Athribis. These zodiacs, from 300 years before the current Dendera zodiac, show Aries as a Ram looking straight ahead. This is the normal Hellenistic Age drawing of Aries, where the older, deeply esoteric knowledge is absent.

More is said about each of the zodiac sigils in the following pages.

---

14 See, J.H. Rogers, Origins of the ancient constellations, Brit. Astronomical Assoc. vol. 108; and Gavin White, Babylonian Star-lore.

6: The Dendera Zodiac : part of an ancient Egyptian star map

Although the temple is only about 2000 years old, the zodiac design appears to faithfully preserve a much more ancient astrological view, with Babylonian elements.

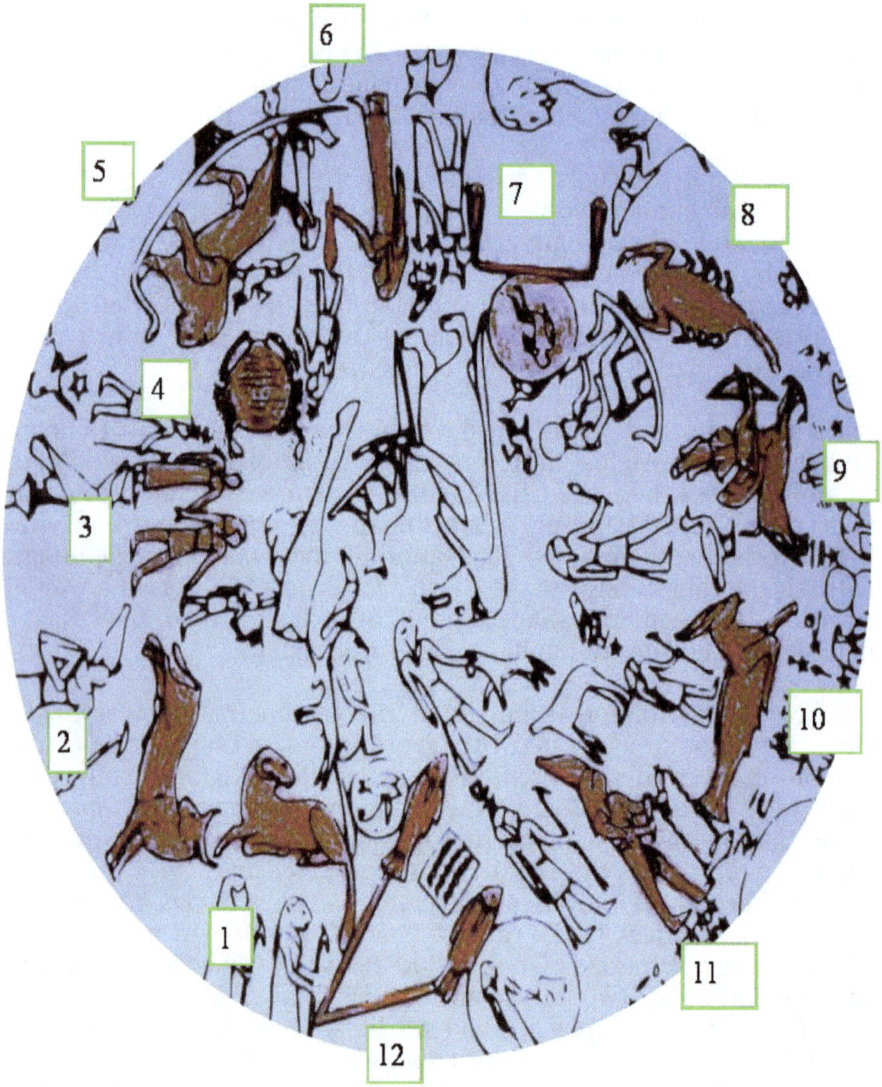

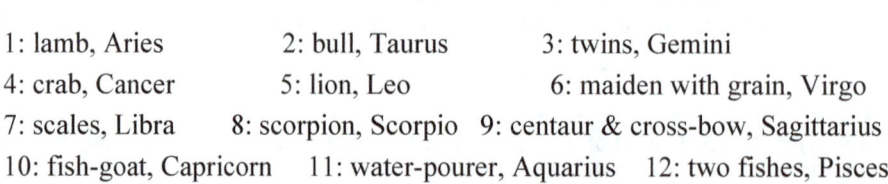

The constellations and their later Latin names.		
1: lamb, Aries	2: bull, Taurus	3: twins, Gemini
4: crab, Cancer	5: lion, Leo	6: maiden with grain, Virgo
7: scales, Libra	8: scorpion, Scorpio	9: centaur & cross-bow, Sagittarius
10: fish-goat, Capricorn	11: water-pourer, Aquarius	12: two fishes, Pisces

The SUN in the Zodiac Signs
The core meaning and significance of each zodiac sign.

NB: the dates of the zodiac signs given here are only a guide ! There are no perpetually correct dates for when the sun enters and leaves a zodiac sign ! This is because there are variations in the calendar, such as the Leap Year, and also the role of time zones and the international dateline, which have to be factored in. There are indeed correct dates, but these are correct only for one year.

ARIES   21st March - 19th April

Aries is a fire sign with the planet Mars ruling it. The traditional symbol for Aries represents the head of a ram, with its two horns. This symbol was in use in the Babylonian culture, about 1000 BC, and perhaps somewhat earlier. Before it became 'the ram', it was called the 'agrarian worker' (no artwork for this sign from this older era has survived). Physiologically in people, Aries forces influence our forehead and the head in general.

Psychologically, the chief characteristic of the Aries person, and this means their sense of self (or ego), is experiencing ideas which give an inducement to action. In Rudolf Steiner's teachings, the frontal lobe of the brain, the Aries region, is the organ used for individual thinking or individualized ideas. But here is another really important aspect to the Aries symbol of a ram; in ancient times, its head is shown as turned towards its back. Rudolf Steiner taught that this alludes to the Aries person gazing at, or into, their own soul; to the cosmic reality that exists, veiled, in the human soul.

With Mars as the ruler, these people are often fiery; in particular they will take offence at someone who hinders their initiative. They want to be active, on the basis of an idea. But the carrying out of ideas usually demands seeing and assessing the world around one. So Aries people are also quick to 'size up' their sensory impressions; and then they are ready to get something happening.

Since the Inherent Zodiac has nothing to do with the seasons, the zodiac signs have no connection to the seasonal cycle. Hence Aries, as a power that influences human psychology, is not connected to springtime or to the beginning of the year. Aries people are capable and competitive, eager to encounter challenges. In one of the four new series of symbols for the zodiac signs developed by Rudolf Steiner, the Aries faculty of 'seeing ideas', as it were, is shown as metamorphosing in the future into a capacity to see clairvoyantly.

TAURUS   22nd April - 20th May

Taurus is an earth sign with Venus as its ruler. The traditional symbol for Taurus represents the head of a bull. This symbol was also in use in the ancient Babylonian culture. With ancient peoples Taurus is one of the four most prominently noted constellations, (along with Aquarius, Leo and Scorpio). So depictions of Taurus as a bull are not only found in Babylonian artworks of about 1,000 BC, but from millennia before that, (but not in a zodiac series). In the Babylonian culture, it was called the Bull of Heaven. Physiologically in people, this sign governs the shoulders, neck and throat.

The chief characteristic physically of the Taurus person is a more solid build around the neck and shoulders. Many Taureans also have a good singing voice. Psychologically, the positive qualities of the Taurean mean that they are stable, predictable, calm, and seek a familiar environment, disliking sudden change.

The negative qualities lead to a plodding, non-adventurous and stubborn mind-set. If a Taurean does become angered, through constant annoyance, they can become eventually angry – very angry. With Venus forces implicit in them, Taureans can also be very sensual. Taureans are earthy in various ways; they have a liking of fine foods and coziness. Vocationally, their work is often connected to the soil, such as farming and gardening, and in the crafts, pottery is prominent.

GEMINI 20th May - 21st June

Gemini is an air sign, with Mercury as its ruler. The traditional symbol for Gemini is two people, similar in appearance. This symbol goes back to Babylonian times, where it was called the Great Twins. Physiologically, just as the star constellation of Gemini is depicted as twins, so too Gemini governs the two shoulders, arms and hands, and the lungs as well. A prominent quality with Gemini people is being dexterous and agile.

With Mercury ruling this sign, these people usually also have a quick mind and often a good sense of humour. Gemini people are sanguine, that is, their mind is drawn to changing topics, to new ideas, to new tasks and also to new life situations. Gemini people seek variety, and avoid predictable routines. Vocationally Gemini people can make successful teachers, salespersons, and work in jobs that involve travelling. They are also gifted at assessing a situation, responding quickly and ably.

CANCER 21st June - 22nd July

Cancer is a water sign, and its ruler is the Moon. The traditional symbol for Cancer is a crab. This symbol goes back to Babylonian times. Physiologically, Cancer governs the chest cage, which provides a hard protective cover to protect the internal organs of the chest. The chest cage has a slight similarity to the shell of a crab. But why does this zodiac sign share a name with the terrible disease, cancer? It is said that this is because Hippocrates, the famous Greek doctor, noticed a similarity of shape between some malignant tumours that formed a hardened shape on people's skin and the shape of crabs.

Rudolf Steiner pointed out that the origin of the Latin word 'cancer' means to enclose, (from the Latin word, *cancelli*). So the word 'cancer' refers to 'enclosing'. Crabs have the enclosing shell, whilst Cancerians have a way of enclosing themselves against emotional vulnerability. Whether from the awareness of this closing oneself off from the world, or from cancer observations by doctors, in the Hellenistic Age the same word was used for 'crab' as for cancerous growths. But Cancerians should take note that the old Babylonian name for their sign meant either a crab or a snapping turtle, and medieval depictions often show a lobster-like crustacean. One of Rudolf Steiner's zodiacal graphics for the sign of Cancer also shows a lobster rather than a crab. The point here being that any little sea-creature with a hardened shell is meant. A prominent soul quality of Cancerians is seeking to shelter their very vulnerable emotions behind a tough mask, or by withdrawing into their own inner shell.

Cancerians have the strongest emotional responses of the zodiac, and are therefore more easily traumatized by emotional setbacks. If Cancerians feel secure, they are probably the most nurturing and compassionate people of the zodiac. But they can easily feel unloved, because they register even a slight emotional coolness from someone as a strong sign of being rejected. Then, similar to the behaviour of a crab under threat, they withdraw into a shell. Cancerians are also very sensitive to noise, and it is interesting to note that sounds travel better in water than in the air.

Life as a Cancerian brings the major life-lessons of emotional vulnerability, and of empathy with others. It is not surprising to learn that Cancer is a water sign, considering the ease with which water responds to external influences, such as the changing wind. But even so, Cancerians can become highly successful entrepreneurs and business people, keeping their emotional vulnerability hidden. They should not rush into a new career or opportunity, with the restlessness of the sea. It is advisable for them to wait and see if their interest in the project remains with them for a while, as their emotional nature creates some volatility.

LEO 23rd July - August 22nd

Leo is a fire sign and its ruler is the Sun. The traditional symbol for Leo is a lion; this goes back to Babylonian times. As it is one of the four cardinal signs, its symbol exists in artwork predating the Babylonians, some dated back to 4,000 BC. Physiologically, Leo governs the heart, and Leo people have a warm-hearted inclusiveness, which helps make them socially successful. The role of the sun in the solar system is echoed in the psychology of Leo people. If we can see the planets, it is because the light of the sun is shining on them. Similarly, a Leo person is drawn to giving practical help to other people, so that in becoming capable and successful in their tasks, they 'light up' as it were.

This interest in helping others is a way for Leos to manifest their warm-hearted quality, but it is also how the Leo can manifest the innate wish to manage a project, or be in charge of others. The Leo person also has subtle psychological similarities to the lion, which is an animal species linked to Leo forces. The lion tends to hide itself if wounded, emerging only after it has regained its healthy, majestic state. Leos also have to resist a domineering tendency. A Leo person is very aware of their public image and is highly irritated if they appear less than admirable to other people.

VIRGO 22nd August - Sept. 23rd

Virgo is an earth sign, and its ruler is Mercury. The well-known symbol for Virgo is a maiden, or a feminine goddess, who is usually holding a sheaf of grain. In Babylonian times, Virgo was called 'the furrow' and was represented by the goddess Shala holding a sheaf of grain. In our physiology, Virgo governs the stomach. The constellation of Virgo itself has names which reflect a common trait in Virgoans, namely a quality of an inner purity which can manifest as a disinterest in sensuality as well as a focus on hygiene and orderliness. Virgo means in Latin, 'pure maiden', in India it is known as 'Kanya', which means virgin. In Chinese the name for this sign is 'She Sung Nu' which means 'purified maiden'. Negatively, the Virgoan has to watch out for being prudish, pedantic and obsessively orderly. The ruler of Virgo is Mercury, and Virgoans have a pragmatic, precise logical mind-set. But there is a hidden side to the use of a maiden as its symbol.

Because of the presence of the sheaf of grain, it is often concluded that Virgo is about the earth's fertility, especially since Virgo is an earth sign, and is prominent in the springtime of the northern hemisphere. But brief references from Rudolf Steiner give another perspective, namely that this classical symbol, which appears to represent the fertility of nature, is really about the achievement in the human soul of new spiritual life, out of a condition which otherwise could go into a desiccated state. The earthly soul, if not spiritualized, becomes inwardly dry. (Just as old grains will eventually dry out). So the essence of the Virgoan quality, at its best, is to feel the urge towards integrity and goodness, which is spiritually renewing for the person.

Rudolf Steiner drew new images for the zodiac signs, and the one for Virgo shows his interpretation. It depicts a feminine figure who has a sun-like radiance, or a dove, in the heart area. This symbol in anthroposophy represents spirituality, especially as in one form of this symbol, the figure is aware of a radiant cosmos around about her. Being an earth sign the Virgoan is consequently a grounded, practical person, not given to flights of fancy.

LIBRA 24th Sept. - Oct. 23rd

Libra is an air sign, its ruler is Venus. The symbol for Libra is a set of scales (also called balances), this name goes back to ancient Babylonian times.[15] Physiologically, Libra governs the hips, which are associated with our capacity for balance. The reason for this symbol, the only non-creature in the zodiac, has always been a riddle. Rudolf Steiner explained that the zodiac symbols, for Libra and through to Pisces, arose from the insights of ancient initiate-astrologers into the evolution of humanity in remote ages, occurring over millions of years.

Long ago there was an era when, for a considerable time, Libra became an active influence in humanity's evolving. At this time a balance had existed in the cosmos between the zodiac forces. Six were then successfully operative in the upper part of the body,

---

15 It is not the ancient Egyptian symbol of the setting sun; this rumour is in error, as a different symbol, not really similar at all, was used for that in ancient Egypt.

refining the body. Whilst six were operative in the lower half of the human body and had yet to achieve any refinement of the body.

The distinctive feature of Librans is the struggle to affirm their ego or sense of self. For the Librans there is an on-going challenge to find the balance between manifesting their own intentions and wishes, and incorrectly surrendering to the intentions of others. Often Librans work vocationally with one other person, and they also yearn for a reliable life-partner. This is because the interaction that they have with a significant other person helps them to feel their own self. But this dynamic is usually mixed with a reluctance to express their own self. So in social interaction, they can strive for a balance that undermines their own best interests.

This means, they try to avoid confrontation. Therefore indecisiveness is often a primary feature of the Librans, when different opinions are voiced. They also have an artistic capacity, or at least a keen appreciation of beauty. They are also intuitive, and yet they can trust the wrong person, but greatly resent this fact if it is pointed out to them. And since Venus forces have a very strong and positive reception in this sign, Librans are often artistic people. The urge for beauty and for a loving partner is strengthened by the inherent influence of Venus.

SCORPIO   23rd Oct. - Nov. 21st

Scorpio is a water sign and traditionally its ruler is Mars, but Pluto is also regarded as a ruler in Scorpio. The sign of Scorpio is the only sign to have two symbols. Scorpio physiologically governs the reproductive organs. One of its two symbols is the scorpion; this name occurs in ancient Babylonian data. This is understood today to allude to personal degeneracy, and the 'soul-death' it produces.

The other symbol is the eagle, which represents the opposite: the regeneration of the soul, which transforms the lower desires and urges, to enable the person to ascend up to the heights of higher insights and creativity. The origin of the idea that there is a second symbol for Scorpio, an eagle, is hard to determine, and usually left unclear in astrological books

But we can conclude that it came into usage in early medieval times from unknown persons, who were aware of esoteric wisdom associated with the Old Testament times. In the Babylonian culture leading priests had created the fabled sphinx, a creature with human head, lion claws, eagle wings and a bull torso.

Then the Hebrew seer, Ezekiel, in the 6th century BC, who was living in Babylonia, wrote about his vision of a spirit being with the faces of a human, lion, eagle and bull. And later the Christian seer who wrote the Book of Revelation also presents these four elements. Since three of these are also symbols of Aquarius, Leo and Taurus, it follows that the fourth of them, the eagle, does represent Scorpio, but a higher aspect of it.[16] Awareness of this mystery led to astrologers keeping this perception alive, although in practice, Scorpio is almost always symbolized by a scorpion.

Rudolf Steiner's teachings concerning the past history of the Earth provides a new perspective into the complex dynamics of the Scorpio person, and why it has two symbols. Millions of years ago, humanity changed from primitive mono-sexed creatures into the two sexes of today. This process enabled eventually the development of a personal individualized intelligence, and also personal desires. The scorpion represents the desires (in their lower aspect) and the eagle represents thinking (in its higher spiritual aspect).[17] The after-effect of this momentous change in humanity's evolving is reflected in the psychology of Scorpio people.

Scorpio people have a more intense inner awareness of life's experiences, and hence intense yearnings and desires. As a result, they may appear secretive to others, but this is only because they feel that other people cannot experience what they are experiencing with sufficient earnestness and intensity. Scorpios are liable to jealousy in relationships and can be very sharp-tongued if they wish. Generally they have an inner calmness and strength, quietly moving ahead, shrewdly working their way around obstacles, without any fuss. Their inner life can be the source of renewal of self and society.

SAGITTARIUS 22nd Nov. - Dec. 21st

Sagittarius is a fire sign and its ruler is Jupiter. The symbol of Sagittarius is a centaur who is also an archer; this symbol goes back to Babylonian times.[18] Rudolf Steiner's research indicates that this symbol, like the symbols of other zodiac signs, refers to what Babylonian initiates knew about the role of the zodiac in the

---

16 Rudolf Steiner affirmed that these four signs are the most powerful, each being the major influence in one of the four major evolutionary phases of humanity's existence.
17 Rudolf Steiner designed an image for Scorpio which showed an eagle.
18 The earlier culture, the Sumerians, may possibly have called it by a different name, which is actually not decipherable. (Univ. Penn. project: Ancient Mesopotamian Gods & Goddesses)

evolution of humanity. In a distant age, when the primordial, turbulent earth was still presenting a strong challenge to human beings to come into life on Earth, Sagittarian energies were predominant.

The human being had to exert considerable force to penetrate this foreign environment. Hence the arrow of the archer, and also the repugnant centaur shape, representing the strong but primitive soul-qualities in the human being of that era. As an after-echo of this challenge, Sagittarians today are drawn to challenges which demand a lot of them, and which are always giving new possibilities for initiative.

Sagittarians can be fiery at times, but they are also honest, generous and helpful. Sagittarius governs the upper legs, and Sagittarians like sports' activities and bush-walking. With Jupiter as a major influence for Sagittarians, their mind can expand to encompass higher, spiritual ideas.

Physiologically the expansiveness of Jupiter, coupled with the Sagittarian tendency to go beyond any boundaries, can cause a large-frame body. But with negatives in the chart, especially to Jupiter, this can lead to being over-weight. Sagittarians are also prone to such frankness that they find it very difficult to be diplomatic.

The most significant negative factor with Sagittarians comes from their un-grounded wish to be free to enjoy trusting in the world and in people. But this leaves them open to be deceived and badly let down. However, this is a state of affairs which is so full of heavy, restrictive problems and burdens – something that the Sagittarian always resents – that they endeavour to never admit being deceived. Another feature of the Sagittarian is that of being drawn to grand or challenging ideas and how these could be realized in a project. These dynamics also result in enjoyment of travel; a typical feature of the outgoing Sagittarian.

Capricorn   22nd Dec. - Jan. 20th

Capricorn is an earth sign, and its ruler is Saturn. The symbol of this sign is not actually a mountain goat, it is an entirely mythical creature, a goat-fish.[19] It was already depicted like this prior to Babylonian times, back in the earlier Sumerian culture, about 2100 BC. This symbol represents the dynamic that was present in an ancient age, prior to the earlier remote Sagittarian era, when humanity was attempting to form and inhabit a body suitable for the still fluidic, turbulent planet.

The effort required to do this was considerable. This struggle echoes-on in the remarkable persistence and capacity for endurance of the Capricorn person. This capacity to survive harsh conditions is aided by an affinity to the planet Saturn, which is at its strongest in Capricorn. Capricorn is an earth sign and physiologically governs the knees.

The Capricorn person, if evolved, can use their powers for the greater good, and can have a potent sense of a 'mission' in life which they must fulfil. Hence any failures or deficiencies that they manifest will be particularly annoying to them; they are unwilling to admit defeat, and hence keep on trying to succeed.

They can go through very harsh times of poverty and lack of recognition, before they finally decide to stand up for themselves and leap ahead, instead of blindly resolutely butting ahead. But the un-evolved Capricorn can callously use people for their own selfish goals, and have little capacity for empathy.

The evolved Capricorn does have emotions, but often does not like to let this be known. However, people born in this sign can have a delightful, if unexpected, wry sense of humour. The Capricorn is always living in the future, but with an eye on how it is conditioned by the past, hence they often neglect to really live in the present moment.

---

19 However it is likely that goats are a Capricorn animal species; they can exhibit for example, the unusual unexpected humour typical of Capricorn people.

AQUARIUS 20th Jan. - March 19th

Aquarius is an air sign and it traditional ruler is Saturn, but Uranos is also regarded as a ruler here.[20] Aquarius governs the ankles. The symbol of Aquarius represents waves; it goes back to the Babylonian times. But Rudolf Steiner also taught that this symbol is not limited to a watery dynamic. It also alludes to the subtle life-forces that underlie the physical world, so it refers to the ethereal or etheric level of the universe. (In ancient mystical works, water can symbolize either the soul or life-forces.) This is probably why the ancient Babylonians called this sign the "Great One", meaning their god Ea whose presence they discerned in the ethereal-astral universe.. So the 'water-pourer' image which they devised is really this deity, but pouring forth ethereal energies.

However in addition, according to Rudolf Steiner, this symbol was devised to represent an ancient epoch before that of the Scorpio, Sagittarian and Capricorn eras. In this era the Earth was less substantial than in those ages. It was a watery, airy planet with powerful ethereal energies weaving through it, and humanity, in a very primitive ethereal, aquatic world, had to struggle with a constantly metamorphosing, restless watery environment.[21] The forerunner to what we now have as ankles in that ancient time were instrumental in the helping primordial humanity move directionally in their watery world.

An after-echo of this interactive time with the airy-fluidic environment in the evolution of humanity, has become a prominent psychological features of Aquarians. They are very drawn to dialogue with others; and in the interaction on the mental level that this brings, they find a deep satisfaction. But also as an after-echo of the powerfully ethereal environment, evolved Aquarians can also have a distinctive capacity for insights or intuitive flashes, which show that they are sensitive to ideas, moving through the ether. This capacity is enhanced by the influence of the planet Uranos, which has an affinity to people born in this sign.

So the Aquarian person has a strong focus on ideas, especially new ideas; and on discussing these ideas with others. With the presence of the underlying influence of Uranos, their ideas are often very original. Through the communication with others, on the level of

---

20 Normally spelt 'Uranus', I use the correct transliteration from the Greek, not the Latinized ending 'us', as it is a Greek word, ending in 'os' (pronounced 'yew-raan-os').
21 In the new art of movement called eurythmy, developed by Rudolf Steiner, the gesture for Aquarius is the only gesture which is always in motion.

ideas, Aquarian people experience their own truth; in other words, they gain a clearer sense of themselves.

Aquarians are often described as somewhat cool and able to leave a relationship without emotional trauma. But an Aquarian person can be quite emotional, and have very sensitive feelings, especially if they have Pisces or Cancer fairly prominent in the chart. (For example, Pisces rising or Cancer governing the 4th house, or the moon in Cancer.)

PISCES 19th Feb. - Mar. 21st

Pisces is a water sign, and its traditional ruler is Jupiter; but Neptune is also now regarded as a ruler. The symbol of Pisces is that of the two fish alongside each other; however it was not quite like this in ancient Babylonian times. Although the precise details of how the ancient Babylonians pictured Pisces are still unclear, the symbol included one fish and a long crooked river-like segment, which replicates the shape of the constellation of the Fishes. At one end of this river shape there was probably a second fish, but there is a possibility that might have been a swallow, and not a second fish. However an early Egyptian zodiac does show **two** fish and the long crooked river-like shape; so this is probably how it was pictured also in the Babylonian era.

But, later on, zodiacs in the Hellenistic Age, including ones from Egypt, show the symbol which we know today, of two fish side by side. Since Pisces is a water sign, the use of two fish appears to simply indicate this, but since physiologically Pisces governs the feet, the two fish may also be an indicator of our feet.[22] Rudolf Steiner taught that the two fishes of Pisces are meant to allude to the two feet. (Steiner taught that the sole of the foot is approximately the form of the most primordial state of humanity's body, in an epoch before that of the Aquarian era.)

The Piscean person can see or feel the over-view of the entire situation, and also visualize an ideal situation that they would like to manifest. In a similar way, the sole of each foot has zones wherein the whole of the body is reflected; an overview of the body is offered

---

22 It is interesting that there is a fish species called *sole,* and when bunions form of our feet they are called 'fish-eyes'. This usage of words seems to indicate a veiled awareness of a common Piscean link between our feet and fish.

in the feet. So an illness in the kidneys, for example, can cause an otherwise inexplicable pain in a specific part of the sole of the foot.

With Pisceans, the sense of ego is usually not strong, hence the Piscean has a social vulnerability. They are very prone to being bullied or dominated, because there is an inner feeling of being obliged to sacrifice themselves for the common good, or for someone close to them. This also opens them up to the danger of being manipulated. A negative dynamic of Pisces is that alcohol or drug abuse can have a potent effect on them, as their ego-sense is easily weakened through these substances. The Piscean is very sociable and empathetic and can generously pass on their insights to help others. Their dedication to an ideal can cause them to work away quietly but capably to bring about a better world.

We shall now consider the influence of the moon in each zodiac sign. The moon's position in a zodiac sign confers qualities associated with that sign on the personality. But these manifest in the temperament or background predisposition, not in the fully conscious 'ego' or sense of self.

The MOON in the Signs

ARIES
This position of the moon creates the predisposition to be an upfront type of person, with an urge for power, and for success in the career (often there is a preference to be self-employed). For a woman, this results in an assertive nature, which can lead her to choosing a gentle, non-assertive man. The Aries forces here create a choleric (fiery) tendency, but someone who is calm in a crisis, yet who also has a rash tendency. The father usually has an intense connection to this person, and he may cause a diminished confidence in facing life.

TAURUS
This position of the moon creates robust health, and a very earth-connected predisposition. The person is possessive of the partner, and their awareness of sensory impressions is strong. There is a liking of parenthood, but they often have a lack of communication with one of their own parents. A Taurean moon usually means an aversion to the sight of blood, and a moodiness tendency, and a dislike of changes happening in life. This person is usually attached to things, has a good memory, and needs emotional security.

GEMINI
This position of the moon leads to a sanguine temperament, although the temperament is also determined by the relative number of planets in fire, air, water or earth signs. This person's sanguine tendency can be strong, leading to a dislike in regard to duties and commitment. This leads to two typical outcomes: overworking to avoid relationships, and also a dislike of helping the long-term ill. This person tends to stay young for a long time, and can be quite witty (or if negative, sarcastic); they can also be scattered, yet shrewd.

CANCER
When the moon is here, the person is very emotionally sensitive. The Cancerian likes to start up an initiative, but is happy to let others

continue it on. They are very loyal and caring to the family. Their partner must provide emotional security, but this Cancerian-type person may take on a parenting role in relationships. In negative dynamics, this person may brood and sulk, and have an emotional blackmail tendency, as well as being a worrier. Their sense of hearing is very acute, so loud noises are intolerable. In relationships they are slow to commit because of a fear of rejection. They are generally cautious regarding new people. There is a deep bond to mother, and they themselves are usually maternal in their way of relating to others.

LEO

The person with the moon in Leo must appear very upright; if they are caught out in some way, this person can become aggressive. If they are offended, they respond with a dignified silence. As with the solar Leo, their appearance is important (looking in the mirror is second-nature to them). They can be stubborn, but selfless for a loved one, who must show appreciation to the lunar Leo person. This person seeks excitement, is a good organizer with leadership capacity, they can quickly appraise other people. They are honest, often lack a sense of curiosity, and negatively can be self-centred.

VIRGO

The moon in Virgo means this person never quite finishes a task, or gets the right situation in life or the home, because they are always wanting perfection, or perfect orderliness. If this is not possible, they retreat into fidgeting, pointless tasks. In relationships, they are often unsure if the partner is the right one. Relationships can be difficult as this person can make him/herself too useful to partner; and may in fact deliberately get excessively busy to avoid these difficulties. But as with the solar Virgo, they feel the need to restrain their sensual desires, and to maintain a good standard of hygiene in the home.

They may also intuitively seek to achieve a clearly defined purity and integrity. In a negative dynamic, Virgoans have to be on guard against meddling, criticising, and a too detailed self-analysis. Many lunar Virgos are the early morning type, with an interest in flowers and gardening. The logical mind is strong, they seek verification of facts and are very logical, making good accountants, and yet possibly do have a psychic tendency. Vocationally, likely areas are in healing, health, accountancy and teaching. They do want to share life experiences with others. They form prejudices easily.

LIBRA

When the moon is in Libra, the person seeks glamour and artistic environs. Music appeals, as does comfortable travel. A flirtatious element is always there in regard to relationships, but an inherent yearning for a family wins the day. The lunar Libran is sometimes gifted with machinery, and enjoys fast cars. They are excited by the moment, in effect by trial and error discoveries, as their sense impressions are strong.

SCORPIO

With the moon in Scorpio, there are strong recuperative powers and capacity to assess others very quickly and to use those insights. Often there are two sides to this person; a yearning for excitement, and yet remaining content in a secure constant life and work. There can be choleric outbursts, which release bottled up emotions.

This person can sense lonely types who want to lean on them; they are also jealous and possessive of their partner. They are gifted at design work, and possibly have an interest in alternative healing activity. The lunar Scorpio is wilful, and yet has a pleasing, attractive personality. They can have intense sensuality, and like solar Scorpios, have an intense inner feelings and yearnings. Some lunar Scorpios like to dominate and must learn to forgive.

SAGITTARIUS

In this position of the moon, one is not so good at touching or caressing – or the exact reverse. There is an inherent seeking of freedom and independence, so they must be free of criticism. There is a predisposition to contradictory duality, such as being in debt, yet hating the idea of indebtedness. Or they can want something very much then, after getting it, losing interest in it.

This person is a good teacher, adventurous and insightful, but can be very choleric, and sports oriented. They may appear lazy, because life glides along well for them, but underneath, much hard work is done. Sometimes the lunar Sagittarian has a connection to a mentally ill person. They also have difficulty finding a partner who does not partly annoy and also partly please them. Like the solar Sagittarian they are often socially naïve and awkward. The sense impressions are very acute, and there can be a one-track mind.

CAPRICORN

With the moon in Capricorn, the emotions may be repressed; yet the emotions are strong. But the un-evolved Capricorn will have little emotive rapport with others. The lunar Capricorn is inwardly shy and vulnerable, but practical, sensible and resilient to illness. There is a depth of soul and tenacity; they are self-disciplined and hard working. Negatively, there can be a tendency to scheming, to being too sensitive to criticism. They can be insecure regarding their own worth. They can be fanatical, and enemies then form against them easily. There is a possibility of being melancholic.

They carry authority well, have a good sense of humour; the temper is controlled, but potent when aroused. They dislike new people and time in hospital, but otherwise easily fit in with new places. They want recognition, are cautious and often very considerate.

AQUARIUS

When the moon is in Aquarius, the person is cool, detached, but pleasant, and very capable of weighing up others. They can also be somewhat calculating or detached in regard to the emotions; so they can leave a situation without any regrets. The same quality is found with solar Aquarians. But one has to note that evolved Aquarians are, or can be, deeply emotional, sensitive souls, especially if their Venus is in trine or sextile to Neptune.

Negatively there can be a selective memory, and they can manipulate others. Lunar Aquarians have a bright mind, and a multicultural gift in regard to communicating and ideas; and often prefer unconventionality in their friends. Cooking or handyman activity is often a hobby. They must be free inside the relationship; and the temper can be a problem when young, but it mellows.

PISCES

With the moon in Pisces, there is a natural tendency to surrender to the wishes of others, and to be overly sensitive to criticism. There is a fear of ridicule and of antagonism. Romance creates anxiety, because one is aware of an intense need for love, yet restricted by an insecurity about oneself; hence adolescence can be terrible, for the lunar Piscean is very romantic. There is a natural capacity for creative visualization, and to see the over-all picture, the grand vision behind an idealistic project.

These people are very considerate, and may become a listening post for too many people. Their home is a haven for themselves and others. They are rather blind regarding other people's defects. But they are very loyal, creative, resilient and capable in a crisis. They perceive what people are really like; and despise injustice. Negatively, they hold a grudge for long time, are easily upset, and can have a lonely childhood. They can veil their inner nature for years, even from the spouse.

A psychic tendency is very common, and they are good parents because they understand the playfulness of children; and they usually like dancing. They can moan about their partner, but in an affectionate way. The evolved lunar Piscean is interested in the meaning of life, because their spiritual orientation and psychic ability creates a natural awareness of spirit worlds.

****

Chapter Three   New perspectives on the planets

Beyond myths: the spiritual influences from the seven classical planets, on the various facets of human consciousness

When Rudolf Steiner's extensive teaching on the planets is incorporated into the long-established astrological knowledge about them, our understanding of the planets is really deepened. It was only in the 1970's that the idea of referring to Greek myths in connection with the planets became popular. But these myths are only of limited use. In the writings of the greatest Hellenistic astrologers, who formed the basis of astrology, such as Vettius Valens and Claudius Ptolemy, the myths were not used. Let's see how the planets are connected to us, in Rudolf Steiner's teachings. But first we shall start with a brief contemplation of the symbols (or 'sigils') used for the planets, and the artistic images for them.

THE PLANETARY SYMBOLS
These commonly used symbols are actually of unknown origin; they are shown in illustration Seven. They first appear in Byzantine manuscripts about astrology written in medieval times. New symbols were designed for Uranos, Neptune and Pluto. But in the 18th century a Roman astrological artefact was found; it is a planisphere in the form of a ceramic plate depicting the heavens, known as 'Blanchini's Planisphere'. It dates from the second century AD, and it is of great interest to us, because has the earliest known pictorial depiction of the planets, see illustration Eight.

It shows simple drawings of each planetary god, but with an additional feature for each of them. The order of planets on this ancient plate follows the days of the week, but starts with Saturday, not Sunday. The names that we have today for the days of the week are derived from the names of the planets, a fact which this old planisphere affirms.

7: The symbols for the 7 classical planets, derived from pre-medieval Byzantine documents

☽ | MOON (Monday)

♀ | VENUS (Friday)

☿ | MERCURY (Wednesday)

☉ | SUN (Sunday)

♂ | MARS (Tuesday)

♃ | JUPITER (Thursday)

♄ | SATURN (Saturday)

Modern symbols for the 3 main outer planets

♅ | URANOS

♆ | NEPTUNE

♇ | PLUTO   ⚳ | An alternative symbol for Pluto

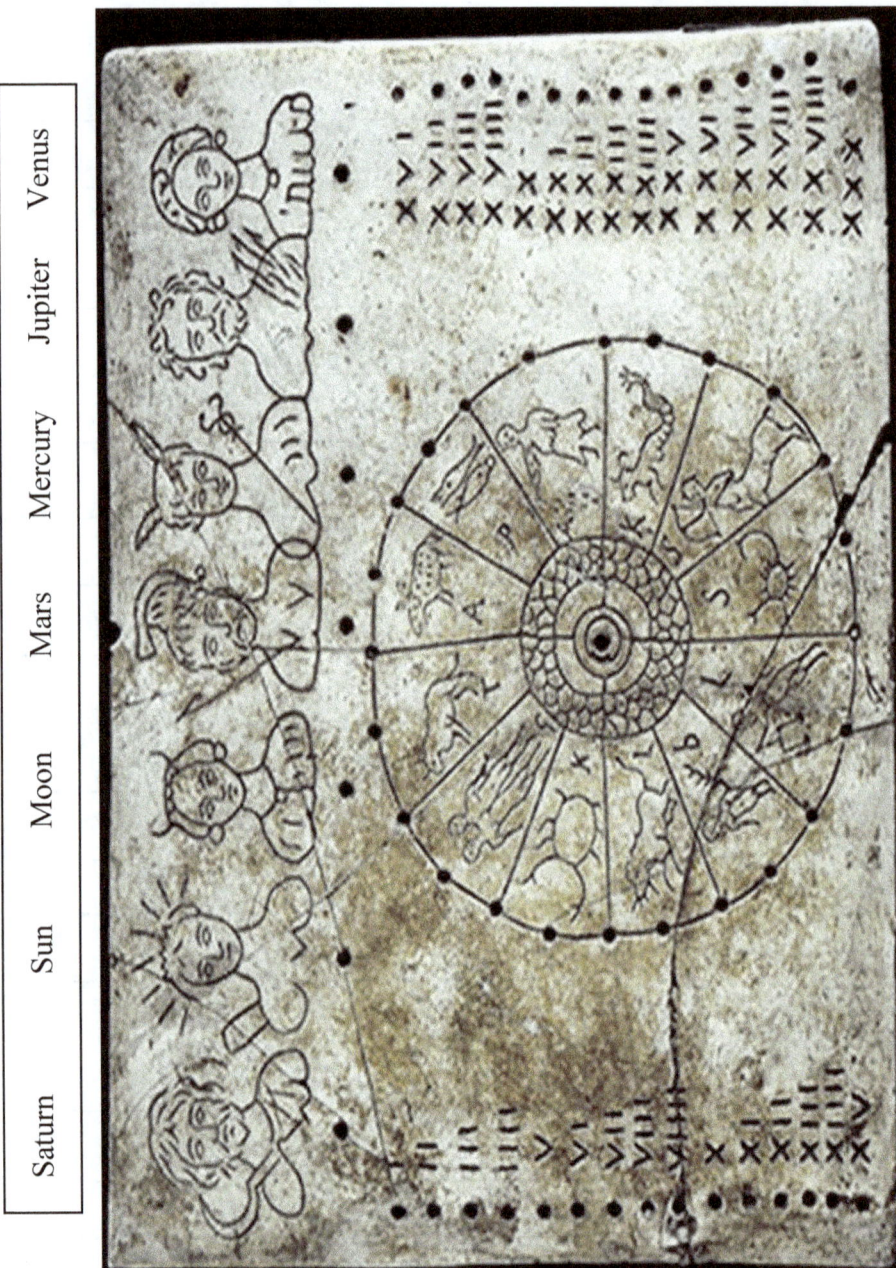

8: The Blanchini Planisphere;
A Roman ceramic plate from the 2nd century AD. On the top are the earliest symbolic depictions of the seven classical planets.

SATURN
The graphics follow the days of the week sequence, and hence start with Saturn, who is shown as a deity who carries a sickle. This is because the Romans equated Saturn with the Greek god Cronos, an agricultural deity, who was linked to seed-sowing. But eventually the crop that is sown has to be harvested; and hence Saturn in classical astrology has an association with death, but in the positive sense of a harvest of life-experiences. The wisdom behind the sickle, I conclude, has two deeper meanings. One is about a harvest of life-experiences from the life as it draws to a close.

In the 'Seven Ages of Man' view of life, as found in Shakespeare, the Saturn phase comes last. So again Saturn has a link to the end of life and hence again to death. This same sequencing is also part of Rudolf Steiner's teachings. But a second reason for the association with death is that Saturn manifests our (mainly subconscious) sensing of what our destiny demands of us. The insights involved here derive from the spiritual worlds, which is the realm of the after-life.

The symbol used now, deriving from medieval times, shows a cross above a curved line; this line may be a sickle or the letter "S". There are many theories as to what this indicates, but no actual texts from earlier times exist which explain it.

SUN
The sun deity is shown on the old Roman plate as having rays going out from his head. This is a straightforward symbol of the sun's rays. The abstract symbol used since medieval times, is that of a circle with a point in it. There are many theories today about what this means, but no original texts exist that explain it. However, it is possible that the Byzantine creator of the symbol was thinking of how the sun encompasses all of the Earth (and indeed, with its rays, all of the solar system). Yet this sigil is also a symbol of how, as a spiritual reality, the sun provides the central element of the human soul, namely our ego-sense. So the point and the surrounding circle form a unity.

MOON
In the old Roman ceramic plate, the moon is shown as a goddess (or feminine figure) who has two horns, or crescents, arising from her head. This is quite different to the crescent moon symbol, created in

medieval times, and still used today. As Rudolf Steiner points out, the moon governs the Earth's life-forces (or its 'etheric energies'), hence it governs the fertility and reproduction cycles of all living things. The two horns shown in the Blanchini planisphere may refer to a cow, owing to the understanding in ancient times that bovines are linked to the moon's powers, whether the potency of bulls or the milk-producing capacity of cows. In ancient cultures there were consequently such figures as the Egyptian moon goddess, Hathor the cow, and old Babylonian parallels (Geme-sin, the moon goddess's cow).

MARS
In the Blanchini planisphere, Mars is depicted holding a spear. So he represents a warrior, and also initiative, desire, aggression, and courage. The symbol which we use today, deriving from medieval Byzantine times, incorporates the spear of Mars the warrior, used as from the Hellenistic Age. An ancient Greek statue of Mars exists, from about 500 BC, which depicts the god of Mars holding a spear. A similar depiction was made already in 1,100BC in ancient Babylonian times.

MERCURY
Mercury is shown in Blanchini's planisphere as a deity holding the well-known Caduceus or Staff of Mercury. It seems very likely that the top part of this symbolic form became incorporated into the symbol used today for Mercury. It alludes to the rapid and complex motions of Mercury, which, being so near to the sun, is the fastest moving of the planets. This feature of speed and nimbleness are also appropriate for the speed with which thoughts can race through the ether, from mind to mind, and also for how rapidly thoughts can metamorphose.

JUPITER
The deity representing this planet in the old planisphere is holding what appears to me to be lightning flashes. Some writers have called it a sceptre, which is Jupiter's symbol in ancient Grecian art. But a sceptre is different; it is a straight rod which has a simple rounded end, and represents justice and authority. However in the old planisphere, there are several jagged forms, like lightning, next to Jupiter. Since Jupiter was thought of as manifesting within lightning

bolts, this is very likely what the drawing shows. Jupiter is associated with authority because the especial quality of this god is wisdom, and the vocation associated with him is the law, especially judges. And law courts have authority and are meant to exercise wisdom. What the symbol for Jupiter depicts is unknown, although many theories have been put forward.

VENUS
In the second century Blanchini planisphere, Venus is depicted with indicators of beauty; a necklace and possibly ear-rings. As we shall see, Venus influences are directly linked to the artistic capacity and things of beauty. The symbol for Venus very probably represents a mirror. Mirrors in antiquity were made from polished copper (or bronze), which is a metal associated with Venus.

The Sevenfold Human Being
The reason for studying the nature of the planets is to enable horoscope interpretations to give accurate and very relevant practical insights into the psychology of a person. Rudolf Steiner emphasizes the long-known truth that the planets' influences together literally constitute our soul. So to understand what a planet actually signifies in the horoscope, as regard a person, is crucial.

To understand this we need to know that the human being consists of seven or more elements. This is called the sevenfold human being in Rudolf Steiner's teachings. We will now briefly look at these. For a more detailed view see my book, the Rudolf Steiner Handbook.

ONE: the life-forces   the MOON
In addition to the physical body, there also exists what Steiner calls the 'etheric body'. This is a definable, gently glowing energy organism that permeates every cell of the body. These etheric energies are more subtle than those of the electro-magnetic spectrum. These energies have approximately the shape of our physical body, but they extend slightly beyond the body, only a half-inch or so, except at some points, such as the finger-tips, from where it rays out a short distance. The astrologer has to know about this in

order to interpret the horoscope fully, because it actually plays a vital role in a person's psychology.

The etheric body or our life-forces (or one could also say, our Ch'i energies) is the force behind our temperament, our pre-dispositional tendencies or habitual attitudes. So the kind of moods we have, and our general habitual mindset and its feelings are derived from this part of our human nature. The **moon** is the planet associated with our life-forces. Just as the sun's rays draw down into the soul influences from the zodiac, so too does the moon. Whatever zodiac sign it is placed in becomes activated in our moods or predisposition. And whatever planets or other elements of the horoscope are affecting the moon, will have an effect on the person's predisposition.

So the moon is responsible for the tone of our life-forces or etheric energies, and therefore it has an influence on our moods. Moods are not the same as emotions, they are a less changeable, semi-conscious function of the soul in the background, determining subtly how we approach life.

TWO: the logical mind   MERCURY

We have three main strands to the mind or soul: firstly our thinking or logic, secondly our feelings or emotions, and thirdly our will or intentionality. In Steiner's terms our logical intelligence is called the intellectual-soul. Steiner confirms what has long been known to astrologers, that Mercury forces, raying into the aura, determine the nature of our logical mind or intelligence.

We need to note here also that each planet has a positive and a negative side to it, and hence can bring about influences of different kinds. Further, each planet can also bring about a very high spiritual quality, if the person is an evolved soul. Mercury's influence in the horoscope determines the individual nature of our mental processes. In Chapter Four the planetary Aspects are explained, and then the way that a planet's energies influence a person is presented in detail.

THREE: the emotional capacities   VENUS

We have our emotional capacities, too. Venus energies, raying into the soul as we descend down to re-birth, determine the range and quality of these emotions. (In Steiner's terms, the emotions are called the 'sentient-soul' and, and on a higher level, the 'Spiritual-self'. Both of these are Venus-influenced.) The emotions (or sentient-soul) in normal human terms, our are feelings of kindness, indignation, love, yearning, etc, etc. This also includes our capacity for artistic appreciation and talents. But in less ethical human dynamics, this includes lust, spite, hate, revenge, etc.

Venus, as with all the planets, has a good and an evil aspect to it. Furthermore, it also has very high spiritual energies, which manifest in an evolved soul; these manifest as deep compassion, selfless kindness, and purity of heart. It is from Venus that such high spirituality, in the original deeper sense, actually derives, and creates what Rudolf Steiner calls the Spiritual-self. (However other planets also contribute to spirituality, especially Jupiter.)

The qualities of the planet Venus traditionally have been described in astrology since the Hellenistic era by identifying vocations and human qualities that are expressive of energies from this planet. Traditionally, in terms of human qualities, Venus is associated with the feelings, which can also be called the emotions, and in particular with romance, love and artistic appreciation or artistic capacity. Traditionally, in terms of vocations, Venus is associated with painters, musicians, singers, poets, costume-designers, jewellery makers, beauticians, and confectioners.

All of the above is confirmed as accurate by centuries of astrological experience, and by Steiner's indications. The qualities that Venus confers on the human soul such as compassion and kindness, are really a form of empathy or sympathy with others. In regard to deep, and beautiful artistic works, there is an inner empathy with high spiritual realms.

FOUR: the sense of self (or ego)   the SUN
We also have of course, our sense of self, or 'ego'; that is, the sense of "I am". The Sun is the celestial body that creates this, so it represents the ego or self wherever it is placed in the horoscope. It is from the sun that the majority of the aura or soul derives; and of course this gives us our personality or every-day sense of self. (The ancient Egyptians called human beings 'children of the sun' for this reason.) One notes also that as the sun sets, we prepare to lose our 'ego-sense' by going into sleep, and as the sun rises, it calls us back to ourselves. So the 24-hour rhythm of the sun is also a kind of ego-rhythm.

The term 'ego' or self as used in this book, refers to our every-day self, our personality. The self manifests in our decisions and general outlook, but it also manifests in our responses to the world around us, when we have the impulse to do something on the basis of assessing our surroundings.

FIVE: the intensity of our soul   MARS

We also have a degree of vehemence, or intensity with which we feel an emotion, or a thought or our will. Mars forces active in us are responsible, Steiner taught, for the degree of vehemence inherent in our soul. In other words, Mars determines how intensely a person feels their feelings, or thinks their ideas or acts on their will-impulses (including base urges).

This is acknowledged in cultural terms in a more limited way as the libido or driving force. Negative Mars energies in the emotions produce aggression on the one hand and lust on the other. But Mars forces at their finest, operative in the will, produce the capacity for selfless action, without any 'martial' aggressive tendencies.

Rudolf Steiner indicates that the actual quality of the planets can be subject to change; he taught that Mars energies themselves are undergoing a transformation, becoming more refined. I have had clients of high integrity with strong Mars forces of a type which would normally indicate some abrasiveness. However these people are peace-makers, but with powerful initiative and social-forming intentions.

SIX: wisdom   JUPITER

There are occasions when we consciously strive for a higher idea or intuition. This is given to us by the planet Jupiter, and includes the works of the higher intelligence, such as deep poetry, profoundly nuanced literary works, and spiritual wisdom itself. This dynamic is reflected in the old, traditional defining of Jupiter vocations; clergymen, students of religious-spiritual subjects, judges, advisors, and statesmen.

There are also subconscious intuitive flashes, but these have to do with Saturn, see below. So influences from the planet Jupiter, at their finest, contribute **wisdom** to the soul, which is an element of the Spiritual-self. As a preliminary to developing the Spiritual-self, Jupiter brings about the sixth part of human nature, the consciously intuitive mind, or what Steiner calls the spiritual-soul. He taught that during sleep our soul comes into contact with the planetary spheres, and the energies of the Jupiter sphere confer wisdom upon us. So people who go into sleep with a deeper question consciously in their soul, can find the answer is present in their mind, the next morning. This is expressed in an old German proverb, "The morning is wiser than the evening."

However, at a more normal level, Jupiter confers good common sense and an expansive intelligence, which is open to larger ideas; it also confers a jovial mindset. On the higher level, Jupiter confers the capacity for insights which lead to wisdom or literary greatness or social reforming initiatives. Negative Jupiter influences are quite weak and not of a serious nature, they are mainly a lack of discipline or lack of orderliness.

SEVEN: the subconscious will   SATURN

The planet Saturn governs our subconscious will or the underlying intentions of our soul. Most of our deeper will or intentions are subconscious; whereas the ones we are very aware of, tend to be actually desires and intellectual intentions, rather than 'will' as such. As I wrote in the Rudolf Steiner Handbook,

> Most of our will is subconscious, only a small part is consciously functioning in us. Do we really know why we are doing our jobs, or even in many cases, married to whom we are married, or living in this country?
>
> And ultimately, do we know why we were born in these times? It is often from our intuition that we made these decisions ! Our will or volition, being in essence an intuitive capacity, normally functions behind our conscious mind, and so it is not accessible to our ego or self.

So Saturn has much to do with those subtle moments when we are searching for the right course of action. This involves being impelled to sense consciously, or more often semi-consciously, what our karma requires of us. (But if Saturn has negative influences, then the person struggles to intuit their life purpose.) Hence Saturn also has a sombre, stern quality, because there are spiritual forces operative in us, in our subconscious from Saturn. These attempt to ensure that we do meet our negative karma, and in other ways, fulfil our life's 'mission'.

The outer planets

The traditional astrological system does not include any planets beyond Saturn; hence Uranos, Neptune and Pluto are not referred to in ancient Hellenistic astrology. It may well be the case that the ancient priests knew of these planets, especially Uranos, which can be seen with the naked eye under ideal circumstances. The deeper reason for these outer planets not being included is that the major strands which together create the personality or soul, come from energies raying out from the classical planets. The outer planets contribute influences, which usually remain in the subconscious. These planets can contribute very positive influences, although this is not so common.

Although this book endeavours to present a deeper understanding astrologically of the classical solar system, it does include the three outer planets. But it cannot extend to a consideration of other celestial bodies, especially the asteroids and the so-called trans-Neptunian minor planets; these are still being researched by astrologers. Here we are attempting to deepen and clarify the forces at active in the human soul from the classical planets, based on Steiner's direct acquaintance with these forces, and the author's decades-long astrological work with clients. To attempt this involves integrating the enormous heritage of Rudolf Steiner (about 400 volumes) into astrological knowledge; this is already a substantial task. So the influence of the asteroids and the trans-Neptunian minor planets is not part of this project.

But Rudolf Steiner did comment on the spiritual energies in Uranos and Neptune, and over a century has elapsed since astrologers began to work with the effect of Uranos and Neptune. So it is possible to briefly include their influences in this book. The influence of Pluto is also considered briefly, although it was discovered only after Steiner's life. This is because nearly a century has elapsed since it was discovered and this has allowed substantial astrological research to be carried out.

With regard to Uranos, Rudolf Steiner taught that the spiritual entities who exist there are regressive. Long ago, they opted out of the progressive evolving that the classical planets in the solar system are involved in. He also taught that these outer planets are somewhat alien to our solar system, having separated themselves off in remote Ages, but eventually coming back into the outer part of the solar system. Steiner also taught that the names given to Uranos and Neptune when they discovered are not an indicator of their nature and influence (and the same could be said for Pluto).[vi] However, the name for Uranos in Greek means the 'firmament of heaven' far beyond the planetary sphere, and this is where distant Uranos seems to be.[vii]

Uranian forces consequently tend to create a chaotic situation, either outwardly, or in one's soul-life. They raise the dilemma for the person of what is true freedom and what is an immature, unrealistic freedom. But in an evolved soul Uranos can bring about a glimmer of psychic awareness or originality of mind. Neptune energies are likewise described by Steiner as being in effect either regressive, or being active where the person is highly intuitive. It is not surprising that astrological research has established that in their negative mode, Neptune energies create tendencies towards self-deceived states of mind, an atavistic psychic ability or even criminality.[viii]

But in their finest mode there is a polarity reversal so to speak, with the influences from both these planets and they can then bestow a high spiritual awareness, even including clairvoyance. This indicates that the energies from these planets are of a particularly primal, unpleasant type, but that above them is a higher matrix, which is usually not active in people. Pluto's forces intensify or empower whatever part of the soul it may be influencing, whether our thinking, emotions or will. But negative Pluto energies, streaming in from an even more remote area of the solar system than Neptune, bring about empowerment without regard for ethics; in other words, domination tendencies.

REVIEWING the link of the planets to the sevenfold human being
  (terms in italics are the Steiner's terms)

MOON: life-forces or the 'body' of *etheric energies.*
= the predisposition, moods, habitual attitudes

VENUS: the **emotions** and also the *Spiritual-self*
= desires, yearnings, romantic-love, artistic abilities & spirituality

MERCURY: **thinking**
= intelligence, cleverness: the *intellectual-soul*

SUN: *the ego* or our actual sense-of-self
= initiatives, decisions, attitudes

MARS: the ***vehemence of the inner-life***
= the intensity of desires/feelings, thoughts, will

JUPITER: **intuitive insights**, logical thinking, expansiveness
= joviality, deep poetry, wisdom: *Spiritual-soul*

SATURN: *subconscious Will*
= sensing of our life-purpose/karma, our spiritual matrix

  * * * * * * * * * * *

URANOS: = Freedom yearning, originality/eccentric traits and influences from spiritual realms (psychic tendencies)

NEPTUNE: = Primeval influences from spiritual realms (wholesome or malignant, a clairvoyant tendency)

PLUTO: = Empowers whatever it affects

(The emotional nature is known as the *sentient-soul* in Steiner's works.)

CHAPTER Four   Aspects, the main elements of the horoscope

What are Aspects

The angles that form between the various planets at the time of birth are called 'aspects' and these aspects are responsible for core elements of our personality. So a really clear grasp of the 'Aspects' is essential. As strange as it may sound, the angles between any two planetary influences which stream in towards the place of birth (which is represented by the centre of the horoscope) greatly determine one's personality. The sharp angles activate the challenging, or negative, qualities in a person. Of these, the main ones are, Opposition (180°), Square (90°) and Inconjunct (150°, also called a Quincunx). In contrast, the 'rounded' or less sharp angles, the trine (120°) and sextile (60°) activate the positive qualities.

The Conjunction occurs when two planets are together in the sky, that is, up to 6° apart; if the two planets are further apart than this, there is no discernible effect. The Conjunction is in a category of its own, as it activates both negative and positive qualities. As we noted in Chapter One, the 'negative' or challenging aspects cause a problematical personality trait to be really tangible - and it is by making effort to overcome these that the person progresses. These negative qualities are weakened as the person experiences them during his or her life, and then either consciously or unconsciously strives to overcome them. There are other minor angles which are only weak in their effect. But two of these, the Semi-square and the Semi-sextile, do have a discernible, if slight, impact. Their presence causes an influence which is half the power of the Square and of the Sextile.

We also noted earlier that if the day or hour of birth is delayed or speeded up, this does induce personality traits which are somewhat incorrect to the personality who is descending to re-birth. They form a kind of over-lay to the actual personality. It is also the case, indeed a very major fact, that in any horoscope the personality traits activated by one aspect may be the opposite of those activated by another aspect.

This contradiction does not mean that the basis of horoscope interpretation is faulty; it simply shows that we human beings have varying qualities in our soul, including direct opposites. For example we can be at times quite laid-back, but at other times we can be very determined to bring intense energy to a project. We can have lots of self-confidence with regard to a given challenge, but acute lack of self-confidence in other areas of life.

New insights into the Aspects
The special feature of this chapter is that entirely new and important insights from this author are made available. These are the result of this author's work over decades with Rudolf Steiner's teachings on the subject of planetary influences and the human soul, and the interaction between these.

Every astrologer builds upon the work done by earlier generations over many centuries. Some of the qualities indicated by the planetary aspects presented here are commonly known and derive from many earlier astrologers; this starts with the Hellenistic researchers, Claudius Ptolemy, Vettius Valens and Marcus Manilius. In particular I wish to acknowledge the work, in regard to Planetary Aspects, in historical sequence, of the 19th century astrologers 'Sepharial' and Alan Leo, and modern researchers such as Llewellyn George, Alan Oken, J.McEvers & M. March, Robert Hand, Robert Pelletier, and Jean Avery. (See the Appendix for a list of books by these authors which I highly recommend.)

Each aspect has a title
Another very important new contribution to understanding the 'Aspects' in this work is that every one of 363 aspects in the horoscope has been given a brief, but very important, title. This title tells the practitioner the essence of that aspect. So when working with a client, the counsellor will be able to see at glance what that aspect means, psychologically.

Understanding of the planetary aspects started with Babylonian astrologers, or perhaps in even earlier cultures in Mesopotamia. During the mid-to-late 20th century a large body of knowledge had been created with regard to these aspects. Many brilliant minds applied this old knowledge to their clients and deepened it in the light of modern psychological studies.

Note:
"Negative": where this word appears at the end of a description of an aspect, this means that, if other factors in a person's chart include challenging influences from either of the two planets involved, then the negative personality qualities belonging to this aspect will manifest.

About the temperaments:
As we saw earlier, the zodiac signs are divided into four types; fire (Aries, Leo, Sagittarius), air (Aquarius, Gemini, Libra), water (Cancer,

Scorpio, Pisces), and earth (Virgo, Capricorn, Taurus). These types are responsible in part of what we can call the 'four temperaments'. These four words also refer to what was once called the four 'elements'; of fiery-ness, airy-ness, fluidity and earthiness. These elements in turn derive from subtle energies (etheric energies). These energies do imprint their mark on the personality. The position of a planet in a zodiac sign bestows the quality of that sign's 'element' on the soul. The more planets are in, say, watery signs, then more the person will have a 'phlegmatic' temperament (see below for what this means).

And in addition, some of the planets also have qualities that are similar to a zodiacal element. Therefore planetary aspects can also add a specific temperament; for example, some aspects to Mars can cause a fiery quality in the person. So we need to briefly note here the four temperaments.

The Four Temperaments
Choleric: this temperament gives to people a strong over-all libido that is, an intense driving force. Their wishes merge into 'will', that is, into action. They are very capable people, and know what they want, like and dislike ! They can be easily angered, but they are usually also very generous.

Sanguine: These are the sensitive, optimistic, changeable people, easily drawn into engaging with sense stimuli (they are like birds in this respect) and like to move from one mental process to another, too quickly passing over ideas, too strongly influenced by ideation (that is, their mental images).

Phlegmatic: These are the patient, good-natured, awkward, listless, people who tend to be lethargic, seldom have anger, but when they do, fury arises. Like a large lake or pond, they are generally quite placid, but if sufficiently stirred, can become tempestuous.

Melancholic: These are the people who have a simmering dissatisfaction with life, and who are often despondent, withdrawn and resigned to enduring "the trials of life". They are introspective, and sardonic. Often there is a long-suffering attitude, because this, they tell themselves, is how the world (or God) wants him or her to be.

The sun-sign and rising sign 'element' (whether fire, air water, earth) strongly determines the temperament, but another core factor is the position of the planets, as we noted earlier.

The Midheaven point
The 'aspects' or mutual angles are not only formed between planets, but also between a planet and two other features in the horoscope which are not planets. These are the Midheaven Point and the Ascendant. The Midheaven point is also the start of the tenth House; so the Midheaven point determines the zodiac sign of the tenth House, which governs the dynamics of the person's social reality. That is, one's marital and vocational situation (whether employed or self-employed, married, single, etc). So the Midheaven point determines one's social dynamics (marital and vocational).

The Ascendant
Note: The ego or sense of self is determined mainly by the sun sign, that is, that zodiac sign where the sun is situated at the birth time. However, in addition to this, the zodiac sign located at the Ascendant point at the birth time creates what is called the Rising Sign. The zodiac sign here, the rising sign, is almost as strong a factor in forming the ego-sense as the sun sign itself. The Ascendant point is on the eastern horizon, where the sun rises and is the start of the first house. It is like a reflection of or an affirmation-point of the ego.

In addition, if there is an aspect existing between a planet and the lunar nodes, this too is important. We will discuss these later in the book.

Other technical terms:
The Nadir or imum coeli (IC) = the bottom point of the chart, hence the beginning of House 4. So it is opposite the Midheaven point or Zenith (which is the beginning of House 10).[23]

---

[23] The Vertex is an intersection point pointed out in the 1930-40's. It is the theoretical point formed where the Ecliptic meets the line that divides the celestial sphere from back to front.

9: The symbols used for the main Aspects & features

Conjunction	☌	(up to 6^0 apart)
Trine	△	(120^0)
Sextile	✶	(60^0)
Square	□	(90^0)
Opposition	☍	(180^0)
Inconjunct (quincunx)	⊼	(150^0)

Minor Aspects, which exert a weak influence:

semi-sextile	⊻
semi-square	∠

North lunar node	☊
South lunar node	☋
Part of Fortune	⊗
Retrograde	℞

THE ASPECTS BETWEEN THE PLANETS

SUN TO MOON

Conjunction: the predisposition enhances the ego-sense
This aspect can bring about a harmony between the habitual predisposition and the ego, but more often it causes a subjective attitude to life. There is vitality and zest for life, and one can go fully into experiences; this person is a catalyst, helping things to occur. But with the predisposition strongly present in the ego-sense, there is a need to be more aware of one's impact on others. This aspect also means that the sun sign and the moon sign are in the same sign, so the self-sense (or ego) and the temperament resonate to the same zodiac force.

Trine: harmony between the life-energies and the ego
This aspect indicates self-confidence because the goals formed by the self are affirmed by the person's predisposition (or, one could say, absorbed by one's life-energies). This subtle, but potent, factor is not necessarily consciously recognized by the person however. In essence, it means that the habits and unconscious background moods receive, rather than impede, one's goals. It gives inner stability, a balanced temperament. Once a decision is made, this person proceeds confidently, so there is an easy approach to life.

Negative: If other factors in the chart indicate negative qualities, then laziness can be a characteristic.

Sextile: harmony of ego and predisposition creates social skills
This is similar to the trine, but here there is also a natural co-operation between ego and one's social environs, especially other people. This person is sociable, inwardly independent, and stable.

SUN TO THE MOON continued

Square: the life-energies impede the ego
This aspect in the horoscope causes the ego to be subdued and inhibited. This in turn manifests as an inner conflict between what one wants and the way to achieve anything.[24] This often results in many false career pathways. The presence of this aspect indicates that in the distant past[25] the ego-sense was not strong and thus the general soul-qualities (the desires, thoughts, etc) were allowed to dominate over the ego. Decades of living like this in the distant past, does make a predisposition for a subdued ego-sense in this life. Our predisposition is linked to our life-energies (or etheric energies), and these are directly influenced by the moon.

The integration of what karma requires with the present reality is difficult for this person; hence there is conflict between the past and the future, into which this person is trying to live. There can be resentment that one needs to make considerable adjustments in order to get one's goals.

Opposition: the ego is opposed by the predisposition
Obstacles in life come from an inner disjunction, but the person projects this out, and thinks that hindrances come from others. There is a conflict between the moods and the ego, that is, between conscious resolutions and subconscious attitudes or feelings. With no real rapport between self and the predisposition (or life-forces) this person becomes very aware of others and concludes that they and the environs are in effect, an obstacle to their own goals. This attitude causes other people to feel negative towards this person.

This inner, self-created, isolated state unconsciously leads to a deep longing for a true partner, i.e., a person with whom a real rapport is possible. This person has the karmic struggle of being objective about the world they live in. This is achievable only by learning to perceive what others think or feel about something.

---

[24] Robert Hand notes that here the chosen partner is often the embodiment of what one is unaware of in oneself.
[25] The 'distant past' is understood to be a previous earthly life.

SUN TO THE MOON   continued

Inconjunct: the life-energies are not responsive to the sense of self
This aspect means in effect that the life-forces (etheric body) are not aligned to the ego, so habits arise which unconsciously contradict personal attitudes; this means that decisions are difficult to make. The moods (or pre-dispositional qualities) are not aligned to the conscious personality. This person feels too much connected to the past, and wants to hold onto the past, i.e., to that which represents security, such as old friends.

Unconsciously sensing this problem, the person in seeking a relationship, makes concessions which are too substantial. So she or he may link up to unsatisfactory people and even have a tendency to be servile. But this aspect does often mean that the person is really compassionate, although perhaps too concerned about the pain suffered by others.

SUN   TO   MERCURY

Conjunction: the ego manifests well in the intellect
Here there is keen mental activity, and one is a talker, a good communicator, and quick-witted. Usually this means that one is a natural teacher or lecturer.

Negative: Indicates a poor listener in a conversation, someone who could be selfish in communicating without realizing it. One relates all things to one's own self.

(Mercury stays close to the sun, so there is only the Conjunction possible between the Sun and this planet.)

****

SUN   TO   VENUS

Conjunction: the emotions colour the ego-sense
Since Venus governs the feelings or emotions, this person desires harmony, and usually has a sensual tendency.[26] This person needs to be liked by people, and likes recognition. Usually congenial, sociable, cheerful, affectionate, feminine, charming, artistically aware; others normally find this person to be quite likeable.

(Venus stays quite close to the sun, so there are only the Conjunction, the Semi-square and Semi-sextile possible between the Sun and this planet.)

****

---

[26] The emotions in general are called the "sentient soul" in Steiner's works.

SUN   TO   MARS

Conjunct: the driving force colours the ego
This leads to a forceful, competitive, strong-willed, athletic person, who has good vitality. There is also courage and leadership qualities, and an inclination to sports and to experiencing thrills.

Negative: could be stubborn, uncompromising, and unable to take criticism.

Trine: the driving force responds to the ego
This aspect brings leadership ability and self-confidence. This person needs to experience challenges and responsibility, so that they learn how to use their strengthened ego-sense. There is a need to acquire self-discipline.

Sextile: the driving force provides the ego with ethical urges
Here one has good vitality, can gather the energy needed with respect to a goal, and can also be assertive. In a fine chart there is through this aspect, a will to carry out ethical deeds and there is also a natural self-confidence.

Square: the driving force dominates the ego
This aspect results in a person who can have sudden anger that flares up, and also rashness, and they can often be too self-assertive and restless; the choleric person. This person can be subject to anger from others, seemingly without provocation. This is actually due to the person's own subconscious anger sending out fiery signals (within their aura). It is difficult for this person to see the need for concessions. There is no patience with another's ideas for this person when they are confident of being right. This person may work especially hard, but they will expect this to be recognized.

SUN TO MARS continued

Opposition: the driving force contradicts the ego

This aspect creates contradictory emotive responses, as the ego is unable to integrate the driving force of Mars; so this person can be subject to an urge to action that is not really properly guided or planned. This person must learn to acknowledge and give space to other people's initiative and needs. Parental actions during childhood can be very significant in adulthood for this person. This aspect often makes for rashness, and stirs up opposition in others. The person's relating is limited to self-focussed desires, and so they can feel antipathy and liking for the same person.

This aspect is one cause of the choleric temperament. External factors continually bring challenges which he or she has to overcome in order to achieve; so inner resentment or anger may well be present. In a woman this aspect can cause a masculine quality, or a domineering tendency. This imbalance needs to be resolved in order to relate to any male person properly. Competitive or aggressive tendencies are common.

Inconjunct: the driving force impedes the ego

With this aspect, similar to the Opposition, the ego does not master the driving force, so the desires can be fired up for an activity that impedes what this person would really want to do, if he or she could express their the actual intentions clearly. So this person gets into very difficult cul-de-sacs in life. It can also cause rashness, derived from an attempt to properly manifest an initiative from oneself.

SUN   TO   JUPITER

Conjunction: the ego has an expansive attitude
This aspect activates optimism, buoyancy, and a generous disposition. Foreign travel can appeal and the mind can be capable of more complex ideas. In a fine chart, there is an interest in spiritual-philosophical wisdom. The body also can have an expansive quality. In a good chart, the self is spiritually strong and quietly helpful. This person appears to be lucky to the observer, but this feature is the result of an inner jovial attitude that invokes success.

<u>Negative</u>: the person could be conceited, or extravagant or overweight, especially if Mars or Saturn is negative to Jupiter.

Trine: the self experiences an expansive life
This is a very positive dynamic, often called "the cosmic blessing". There can be many pleasant journeys which are spiritually enriching, and there is a yearning for knowledge, as well as material ease, (unless other aspects work against this). Since Jupiter at its highest confers an intuitive thinking capacity, there can be an interest in spiritual wisdom. This aspect leads to a jovial person, a good luck person. Life brings bountifulness to the person, because the attitude is one of plenty. This person may encounter karmically a wise person who guides them, or they may even work towards personal development to invoke their own spiritual wisdom.

Sextile: the self has an expansive mind, even wisdom
This person can act at the right time and, similar to the trine, be interested in higher ideas, and possibly have an intuitive thinking capacity. This person is outgoing and usually is a good debater with a clear well-focussed mindset, and have lots of ideas. As with the trine, since Jupiter at its highest confers an intuitive thinking capacity, the person has an inherent interest in attaining, or actually already has, spiritual wisdom.

SUN TO JUPITER continued

Square: the self is often unwisely expansive
This aspect produces a tendency to over-work, and makes one over-excitable. There is often a poor judgment of life-situations and in regard to actions. This person can spend years working to maintain a relationship which has a faulty basis. This person can go overboard in their actions, and also have a tendency to exaggerate. Taking on too much, and being over-confident are common traits here. There can be a superficial interest in pleasurable pursuits or new ideas.

Negative: a dishonest tendency and a love of display can be present.

Opposition: the self is unwise and ungrounded
This aspect brings about a conceited, extravagant, 'penny wise, pound foolish' attitude. This person is too expansive with regard to promises, but is often quite talented, and fond of travel. But discretion is needed, and there can be a resentment of authority. This person can be so idealistic, positive and enthusiastic that there is little that can modify the ungrounded optimism.

It is important that this person really considers the opinions and advice of others, who can offer a properly grounded outlook on what one is planning to do. Insisting on having an ill-considered freedom inside a relationship is common with this aspect, or this dynamic can occur in reverse; one's own valid freedom may be blocked by another person.

Inconjunct: the self is hindered by a lack of wisdom
There is a lack of self-confidence, and one can over-react to criticism. Medically this aspect can indicate a liver weakness, so alcohol is not advisable. (One client was actually hospitalized after drinking wine really moderately.) This person can wait for the world to provide, and also over-extend himself or herself in a hurry to plunge into big plans. There is poor insight into life's priorities.

SUN TO SATURN

Conjunct: the self is burdened by an exacting urge for order
This aspect indicates a solemn person, with either a powerful force for achievement, or, depending on how Saturn is aspected to other planets, a personality who feels that they won't ever achieve success in life. The person is serious, mature beyond their years and can show self-restraint. In some cases the person can be a disciplinarian, and their life often brings lessons in discipline. The father is usually stern or neglectful or absent. There can be a loner tendency, a strong sense of pride, and an unhappy childhood due to parenting issues.

Trine: the self senses its karmic duties and ethical values
This person is self-confident, and can achieve goals more easily than others, because their intuitive sense of their own life-purpose (or karma) means that they can accept responsibility. This happy union of conscious ego-sense and subconscious intentions allows them to take hold of opportunities as they arise. In romance, the partner must be 'saturnine' in the best sense, namely sincere and self-disciplined. This aspect can signify good health. In a good chart there are high ethical standards, and a strict behaviour code. This person likes to learn in a structured setting.

Sextile: the self defers to karmic duties and orderliness
With this aspect, the ego's impulses harmonize with the life-lessons, that is, with the karma that unfolds in life. Consequently this person inwardly accepts life's duties and obligations. Often older people are helpful, and there is common sense and self-confidence, but the person is also reserved. This person dislikes disorder, and instead seeks to achieve his or her goals in a prudent way. This aspect creates a reliable person, so this person can be a valued employee.

SUN TO SATURN continued

Opposition: the self has to struggle against restrictions

This aspect brings many obstacles and limitations but, like all challenging aspects, it offers the positive outcome of improving the person's inadequacy in the area concerned. This person must learn to work within these strictures, and learn to accept and endure. So this aspect is an inhibiting influence, producing a person who has a serious nature, but too self-critical. Aware of their inner struggles, self-confidence can be low and thus they are too sensitive to criticism. Since Saturn is a karma-dispensing or regulating influence, the person can encounter difficult people who reflect back to them what they once did to others, in a past life.

Square: impediments between the self and the subconscious will

This aspect means that their ego or self-consciousness impedes their own karmic requirements, so this person does not seem to grasp what life wants to offer or teach them. So this is another Saturnine karma-learning influence, where everything is achieved the hard way. Often hard work is needed to achieve anything, so rigidity and pessimism are possible outcomes of this. If the inner blockage is too strong, there is antipathy to authority figures and this person is too strict on himself or herself.

Karmic awareness is the problem, in the sense of a need to develop a subtle discernment of what is appropriate for one's life and what life-lessons are telling one. But, considered more deeply, this karmic awareness is lacking either because it has not been developed in the distant past, or because this person seeks to strengthen even further precisely that quality, by having this blockage.

Inconjunct: the self struggles to act from its true will

This aspect means that this person is subtly aware of a blockage to actually living out their real, their deeper, intentions for this life. This causes a lack of self-esteem. Clients often indicate their

SUN TO SATURN   continued

Inconjunct: continued
frustration caused by a feeling that the outer world conspires against them. This can mean that this person allows other people to dominate them. There is tension through striving to be accepted; some people with this aspect go into self-pity. The mental attitude which is projected out by this person is all-important, if others are to be supportive of their ideas. (Robert Hand notes that the person must learn the difference between self-discipline and self-repression.)

SUN TO URANOS

Conjunct: the self is burdened with urges for freedom
This aspect creates an impulsive person, with many flashes of insight, but also an intense need for freedom. Herein lies the key dilemma for this person: what is freedom? When is it unrealistic, and when is it a valid urge? This person is often quite sanguine, that is, enjoys changing situations and new ideas. But it can also create an arrogant and stubborn quality. In the case of a woman, this aspect gives an excessive masculinity (especially if the south node is in Leo). Unusual activity in electrical devices can be triggered by this person.

Trine: freedom and originality entice the self
This aspect creates the strongly sanguine type, drawn to thrill-seeking activity. They have a personal magnetism, many ideas, and are generally enthusiastic. This is someone who breaks out of any mould, or is sanguine in another way. The person needs to be productive otherwise a restless energy may create a nervous disorder. In a positive mode, it makes the person a motivator for others.

Sextile: the self embraces freedom and originality
This aspect creates an inventive, progressive personality with originality and an intuitive mind. This person prefers a new procedure rather than staying on with usual one; these traits are part of being 'sanguine'. There possibly might be a healing capacity, and often an interest in social reform.

Square: lack of freedom haunts the self
This aspect indicates that the ego or self is not empowered over the three dynamics of the soul; namely thinking, emotions and will. This creates, in response, the rash and impulsive personality, who rebels against authority, and who can stir up hostility or defensive behaviour from others. The person likes power, and can express the frustration through being a practical joker, or excessive witty comments. There is in this person a hidden feeling of being

SUN TO URANOS continued

Square: continued
threatened by others, which derives from a semi-conscious awareness of their own inner disempowerment. A previous Aquarian life (south lunar node in Aquarius) can often occur in such a horoscope.

Opposition: regressive Uranian forces blind the self
This aspect indicates a negative influence on the self; the person does not sense intuitively in many situations what others would normally sense. This leads towards involvement with adverse groups or projects, and even with dangerous activity. The self struggles to have a better discernment. The self is sensitive and independent, and can be highly-strung, finding it hard to relax. This person must learn to consider other peoples' viewpoints. There may possibly be some erratic behaviour which can alienate one from others. One needs to be careful about taking risks and seeking excitement. Mental health issues can arise.

Inconjunct: lack of inner freedom frustrates the self
This aspect creates the rebel who is impatient about rules, wanting to do their own thing. A rebellious tendency can rise up out of the blue, and the person may also be imposed upon by others who suggest that only he or she can do some task. This person can yield to this, and this eventually brings the risk of becoming embittered.

SUN TO NEPTUNE

Conjunct: the self is affected by spiritual energies

Neptune influences create a susceptibility in the self to take in both the life-energies and the soul (auric) energies of others. This influence creates an aura of mystery around the person, who will have a potential for spiritual visions, and be a 'dreamer of dreams' or even have a clairvoyant potential. The person will also be very earnest, yet often they are sentimental, romantic and too sensitive regarding aggression. There is a strong artistic tendency.

Negative: If Neptune is weak, there will be an overly strong day-dreaming tendency, which leads to an illusory view of the world. Also, there can be a lack of self-confidence, and a tendency to be untruthful in order to please. Medically this aspect can cause an allergy tendency. Addictions to drugs of various kinds are also possible.

Trine: the self has a potential for spiritual awareness

This aspect produces an interest in spiritual themes. The person is aware generally of non-physical realities, but whether he or she consciously focuses on these or not depends on their over-all nature. The person will be artistic, with a strong and rich imagination, and a day-dreaming tendency, and is very sensitive to other people's feelings.

Sextile: the self is receptive to spiritual inspiration

This aspect produces the imaginative person who is an idealist, subject to fantasy and very sensitive. The person is socially adaptable, but may not be forthright enough; they can also be quite shy. The self (or self-sense) is receptive to spiritual insights.

Opposition: the ego is deceived by unrealistic, otherworldly influences

This aspect creates the ungrounded idealist who pictures the world as better than the reality; and he or she will over-idealize other people, and will also be too sensitive. The person can easily be

SUN TO NEPTUNE   continued

Opposition, continued
discouraged, and can have a tendency to manipulate, rather than directly deal with people, or even to be obsessive. In the ego there is confusion, which indicates that the self is not very receptive to the deeper, subconscious intentions which underlie every person's existence (i.e., the veiled karma-directing one receives from realms of spirit). Yet, this aspect also usually indicates a psychic capacity.

The person can misunderstand authority and feel singled-out for bad treatment, thus becoming inherently defiant; and can have a paranoia tendency about any opposition they encounter. Also this person fears challenges, and struggles with self-doubt; a good therapy here is a vocation that requires some independent decision-making. In romance, the person has suspicions of being trapped. There is often a tendency to lies, especially in regard to confrontational situations.

Square: the ego is weakened by the domination of non-integrated impulses or by spirit forces
This aspect causes an inferiority complex and a strong tendency to occult or spirit interests, but also a tendency to be unclear about one's motivation or the implications involved in a decision, and hence the possibility of getting into difficult situations. This person can also become misdirected in life generally, including choice of vocation. The person very easily senses the auric qualities of others (or of places), and hence experiences an emotion without knowing its origin, and this causes indecisiveness.

Lack of good parenting here can easily contribute to lack of self-confidence; the person will be sensitive, avoid confrontation and have some indecisiveness, even lethargy. A more negative side of this aspect is a deceptive trait (the hallmark of negative Neptune) which veils a dark side to the personality, who nevertheless projects a positive attitude and good intentions. This problem is softened by a well-aspected Saturn. Medically it can indicate a tendency to infections and allergies. If aspects to Neptune from other planets are negative, there can be seriously distorted psychic experiences. (Isabel Hickey comments that there may be karmic debts to be repaid with regard to the house position of Neptune.)

SUN TO NEPTUNE continued

Inconjunct: a psychic sensitivity suppresses the ego
This aspect leads to a very sensitive person, who feels the quality of the environs and of people, but finds it difficult to express or articulate what they perceive. There is a strong tendency to lack self-confidence and if this is so, the person will give in to other people's demands, and people will at times attempt to impose their will on such a person. If Pisces is prominent in the chart, being dominated by others then becomes a serious problem. Yet this aspect can result in a positive quality of selflessness.

SUN TO PLUTO

Conjunct: the self is dominated by the urge for control of others
This aspect tends to make for an extreme, intense, strong-willed person who finds compromises hard to accept, and group teamwork difficult. The person has an urge to be dominant. But this kind of will-force can be alluring to some people.

Trine: the ego seeks to have initiative
The person makes an impact on others, is courageous and likes change, and is a born leader (unless other aspects modify this). The person yearns to understand others, but can be extreme regarding their actions. They often seek to bring about environmental changes, and are intuitive. This person can be good at finances.

Sextile: the ego can powerfully manifest initiatives
This aspect brings about the strong willed type, with an intensity of will, but the will here has integrity and consequently is not dominating. They can work very hard and have a will intensity which impresses others. They are very capable at communication. Vocationally, this aspect suggests a skill at handling other peoples' resources, and there is also an interest in social ideals. This aspect confers an inner psychological strength, and with some people a psychic ability.

Opposition: the self has a destructive urge for empowerment
This aspect produces the frustrated, very wilful person, the choleric personality, even destructively so. The person arouses opposition or antagonism in other people. Relationships are difficult as this person is drawn towards conflict. There can be extreme anger. This person tends towards extremes, and in the workplace could be a workaholic.

SUN TO PLUTO continued

Square: the ego fights against a feeling of disempowerment

Here the choleric temperament appears strongly; the person is in conflict with others in authority and conflicts arise unconsciously. Rudolf Steiner reveals that the choleric temperament manifests the after-effect of potent, long-term troubles or restrictions in a past life. Others misunderstand this person's intentions, and so there is often opposition from colleagues. This person can be violently angry when upset, and seems to have an inherent, wilful resentment. The person can very controlled, but can become wildly angry. From childhood on, they need justice and fairness, and they respond well if their initiative is affirmed. This person must overcome obstinacy in their own soul-life, which sometimes is reflected back to them from others.

Inconjunct: the self is frustrated by disempowerment

This aspect creates an extreme tendency in feelings and attitudes. So there can be a serious stubbornness as well as resistance to any pressure to conform. This indicates a past-life situation which now leads to a fear of being controlled, or of becoming disempowered. The father's role during school years is important with regard to self-confidence. Sometimes this aspect also creates a guilt factor (again, this derives from a past life) which drives the person on to be over-helpful to others and to get other peoples' approval.

THE SUN TO THE ASCENDANT

Conjunct: the primary ego sense is intensified by the secondary ego-sense
This leads to a strong-willed, intense person who seeks power, and who must learn to compromise. There is a charisma to the personality. This person can't understand apathy or weakness in others. There is often an extremist tendency.

Trine: the secondary ego-sense affirms the primary ego-sense
This aspect brings about a strong self-confidence. This indicates someone who likes the limelight and who is honest, breezy and sanguine. This person dislikes activity if it's not enjoyable.

Sextile: the ego is socially harmonized by the secondary ego-sense
This leads to a sociable, outgoing person who finds it easy to communicate and express themselves, and the personality is projected with finesse. This person is articulate, so people listen when they speak. Usually a warm person, with a youthful outlook, who dislikes solitary activity. They are not dominating, just enlivening and a good conversationalist, sanguine, with a sense of humour, and frankness.

Square: the ego feels blocked from the secondary ego-sense
With this aspect, there is difficulty in co-operative activity. Progress is only attained through friction with other peoples' goals; this dynamic may cause a withdrawal into the self.

THE SUN TO THE ASCENDANT continued

Opposition: the primary ego-sense is weakened by the secondary ego-sense
This aspect causes a need to have other people around, to reinforce their sense of self. This person will either clearly compete with others, or co-operate. This person can attract powerful egos that dominate. This person seeks approval and compliments from others.

Inconjunct: the primary ego-sense is hindered by the secondary ego-sense
This person is a very hard worker and often works to excess and yearns for recognition. But because the sun (the ego-sense) is at odds with the rising sign (a reflection of the ego-sense), there is an inner contradiction in this soul. With this kind of inner disharmony, this person can be misunderstood by others, who are themselves (subconsciously) confused by this person's internal conflict.

THE SUN TO MIDHEAVEN

Conjunct: the ego identifies with its social dynamics
With the sense of self being united to the Midheaven point, which governs the dynamics of a person's social reality, personal success is important here. One's impact on others is important, and one is very independent. The father's influence is always pivotal for this child's sense of self, as the Midheaven point, which determines the way we encounter the world outside, has a strong connection to the ego-sense, as does the father.

Trine: the ego seeks to affirm its social dynamics
With this aspect, the self (or ego) is in alignment with the Midheaven point, where the self has a major interface with its social and vocational context. So this the person is an achiever, with strong ideals, which are usually linked into the social dynamics of career or marriage.

Sextile: the ego feels affirmed by its social dynamics
With this aspect, the self (or ego) is supported by the effect of the Midheaven Point, where the self has a major point of interaction with the world. This creates an achiever who is able to compromise, yet who is also quite independent in his or her actions and decisions.

Square: the ego seeks opposition to its own social needs
With this, the ego or sense of self is out of alignment with the the point where the self has a major interface with the world around. So this aspect indicates a person with inner conflict; someone who is self-assertive, but may attract dominating associates and have conflict with their father. The father himself will be an angry person, (clients report that if their biological father is absent, the adoptive father or step-father is angry or dominating).

THE SUN TO MIDHEAVEN   continued

Opposition: the self is insulated against social dynamics
With this aspect, the self (or ego) is not in alignment with the Midheaven point, where the self has a major interface with the world. This aspect causes the person to determine their own path through life, with less regard for their social dynamics, i.e., the role of other people in their life. (Because this aspect locates the sun in house four, there is a focus also on the core feelings and the home being an harmonious place.)

Inconjunct: the self struggles to sense its social reality
With this aspect, the person finds it difficult to decide which career to take up, and often has an impatient and impulsive tendency.

THE MOON TO MERCURY

Conjunct: the temperament predisposes the intelligence to being sympathetic
With this aspect the moods have a strong influence on the thought-life. It indicates a person whose intelligence is sympathetic to other peoples' ideas, but it often brings about a vacillating mindset.

Trine: the temperament predisposes the intelligence to be discerning
This aspect makes the person extraverted, sensitive and a good listener who has noticeable empathy with groups of people. Hence this person is a good speaker at, or on behalf of, groups of people. There is a quick evaluation of sense impressions, and this person becomes a storehouse of information, and has an excellent memory.

Sextile: the temperament predisposes the intelligence to social interaction
With this aspect, the person is a good communicator whose temperament and thoughts are nicely balanced; and who absorbs knowledge well. This person is a good conversationalist, sensitive to others' feelings, and is able to communicate to or interact with groups very well. This person is tactful, and likes people who are sociable and intelligent.

Square: the life-forces make the intellect rigid
With this, the thoughts and moods (or predisposition) intermingle in a negative way. Hence if this person is upset, what they say goes against them. The thinking is too rigid and orderly; minor details are too focused on; (a little child was annoyed at a small strip of cloth in an odd place on a shirt). Intellectually, little matters get greatly exaggerated, so a different opinion is regarded as a hostile act. This person is very sentimental about those close to them, but they feel insecure in the presence of strangers. It can be very advisable for this person to obtain legal advice before signing documents.

THE MOON TO MERCURY continued

Opposition: the life-forces impede the intelligence
This aspect brings about some distortion between the temperament (or mood), and thinking, hence this person can react to personal and social situations in a confused way. They can sometimes be quite cold and at other times, very emotional. This can mean that people with this aspect can offend others without knowing why. They are also easily irritated, and can argue with small provocation.

Inconjunct: the life-forces stifle the intelligence
Here the moods impede thinking, so there is difficulty in expressing oneself, because the life-energies cannot absorb and reflect the underlying intention of the intellect. This person can feel guilty about these inner conflicts, and can experience anxiety from this. This person reacts badly to criticism, for unconsciously he or she is seeking approval.

THE MOON TO VENUS

Conjunct: an inherent inclination to emotional warmth
This aspect confers gracefulness, charm, sensuality and artistic qualities. It indicates a compassionate, sociable, affectionate person, who likes comfort and elegant decor items. This person enjoys gardening and care of animals, but is not fond of 'grubby' activity or manual work. The mother is of considerable significance to this person (whether in a positive or a negative role), more so than the father.

Negative: if Mars is afflicted, then eroticism is likely.

Trine: a predisposition to loving kindness and beauty
This is a very positive aspect. The person is gentle and harmonious, with finely developed emotions and sensory perception. This person can perceive the subtle soul-beauty in good people. It can be said that, with this person, even in anger there is goodness present. There is also an artistic sensitivity and a natural liking of children. To perceptive people, this person's real, inner nature is attractive. Vocationally, public relations work is indicated.

Sextile: a predisposition to be warm hearted
With this aspect, one likes to have fun with friends and is sensitive to beauty. One is not emotionally reserved, but warm and caring, and there can be a tendency to laziness. This person is charming and is usually a very congenial partner or friend, and he or she is protective of a relationship, is a sociable person and has a creative leisure capacity. (Often found when the south lunar node is in Taurus).

Square: the emotional capacity is restricted
This aspect indicates a strong need for affection ! Hence one is indiscriminate about the choice of friends, and seeks their approval and warmth for personal status. Often there is a problem with

THE MOON TO VENUS continued

Square, continued
vanity. This person may fear forming close personal relationships because of the responsibilities involved; hence they are very subject to manipulation and can attract the wrong type. They are often overly solicitous or over-bearing; this can cause them to be over-protective or possessive of a partner. These problems appear to be the karmic result of unlovingness. A negative connection to the mother is possible. (Often found when the past life, indicated by the south lunar node, is in Cancer or Capricorn or Virgo.)

Opposition: the emotional capacity is predisposed to blockages
With this, one has a subconscious feeling of not being loved, because the temperament (the outcome of the life-forces) is non-receptive to the emotions. Hence the person can choose the company of other people un-freely, linking up to unsuitable people. There is often a social awkwardness; this person can accept invitations to activities which are not actually suitable to them. Also there can be the loss of the mother, either physically or inwardly. (Note: this is an example of a personality trait, induced by an aspect, which directly worsens the predicament – but thereby pressures the person to deal with the issue.)

Inconjunct: an inherent tendency for emotional isolation
There is an enhanced need to be loved, and there is in childhood especially a need for maternal love. Sweets are craved when this affection is not present. This person may become self-indulgent and have a low self-confidence. Sensing that their emotional capacity is poor, this person can respond in very awkward ways to others socially. Until the capacity for emotional interaction is improved, in romance, this person feels that they always have to prove their love. Curiously, it is also the case that money lending is not advisable, as the money loaned may not be returned.

THE MOON TO MARS

Conjunct: the predisposition is vehemently restless
This aspect activates the choleric temperament quite strongly. The predisposition, or the inherent mood, is fired up by Mars energies. However the person can suppress their anger, if for example their sun-sign or rising sign is a gentle sign, like Libra. But this leads to illness or a nervous condition or even to mental health problems. The person inherently infers insults from others, and wants close relationships, but is often unable to relate clearly to others.

Trine: the personal drive and inherent attitudes harmonize strongly
With this aspect there is courage, vitality, good recuperative powers and high levels of energy. Opportunities are sensed, there is initiative for a challenge, the need to express the drive forces (or libido), and he or she will defend themselves in social interaction. The person is active, quite often in a competitive way, but not necessarily combative (unless Mars has negative aspects to other planets).

Sextile: the personal drive affirms the inherent mood
This indicates that one can make the best of a situation through an inner sense of confidence and courage. Opportunities are readily seen, and there is a lot of initiative. There is an inherent sense of one's rights, one likes to be a leader, has a lot of energy, but tends to take negative comments and situations very personally.

Square: the personal drive is fiery and ego-centric
This person has an inherent choleric tendency, so the emotions can get out of hand, and they then act without thinking. Other negative traits are selfishness, being shrew-like, and an alcoholic tendency. An inflexible attitude is common. If male, there is an inherently poor understanding of women, and one's friends are often also choleric. Finding ways to deal with their pent-up anger is a valuable skill.

THE MOON TO MARS continued

Opposition: the personal drive is enflamed by the temperament

This aspect also activates the choleric personality, so this person is competitive and sees challenges to himself or herself from others and from their actions. Personal relationships are subject to crises because of this inherent choleric, overbearing quality. Such people resent criticism, and are frequently given to anger. Medically they can be prone to digestive upsets caused by resentment and general stress, (one client defined it as 'abdominal migraine').

Inconjunct: the inherent attitudes enflame an insecure personal drive

This aspect creates the so-called choleric or fiery temperament. There is emotional involvement with ideas, and the urge to be aggressive if these are slighted. The relationship to the mother is very important for a positive relationship to other women. This person misjudges other people, and with their core drive or 'libido' blocked from activating their life-energies, they doesn't resist when manipulated by others.

THE MOON TO JUPITER

Conjunct: a predisposition to jovial expansiveness
With this aspect, one is popular, cheery, generous, fun loving, and yet also has a sincere concern about others, and will show a sensitivity to the environment. The influence of the mother is especially important. Vocationally, this aspect suggests that social work may be a good career path.

Trine: a predisposition to wisdom and optimism
This aspect activates many positive qualities, including a predisposition to assimilate higher knowledge and to seek personal growth. Also people (especially women) naturally assist this person's path through life. Travel can bring fortunate outcomes, and if this is undertaken in the quest towards personal growth, good results often occur. The personality is out-going, enthusiastic, self-confident, emotionally secure, generous and has a natural optimism. The mother's role is important. Civic duties are a possible area of work.

Sextile: a predisposition to social expansiveness
This aspect indicates a cheerful, sensitive, positive and generous person. The mother and the home are important factors in life. The mind is quite active and this person will be gifted at public relations work, because he or she will have an inherent capacity through their expanded life-forces (or expanded 'etheric body'), to sense other peoples' dynamics. This person learns a lot from every experience, and has a good memory and is warm and sincere.

Square: a predisposition to block sensible insights
This aspect indicates that one is emotionally immature, often reacting unwisely, drawing the wrong conclusions. One can also be fickle, and financially irresponsible. Liver weakness is likely, so alcohol should be avoided. This person might work with the intellectually or emotionally challenged, as this can help them understand the nature of their own inner restrictions.

THE MOON TO JUPITER continued

Opposition: an inherent predisposition to self-undermining attitudes

Here the life-forces are not responsive to the clarity of thinking that Jupiter could bring about, so a subtly confused mindset is the result. The person is then susceptible to strong, domineering types and opposition from other people. There can be troubles and disappointments in life through having a misplaced trust in someone. Any assets, including money, that they make available to others may be misused, due to a naïve blindness to the nature of their acquaintances. Vocationally, social work is indicated.

Inconjunct: predisposed to make superficial conclusions

Similar to the Opposition, the life-forces are not responsive to the clarity of thinking that Jupiter could bring about, so shallow thinking is the result. This aspect indicates a sociable, optimistic person who is however subject to a number of challenges. This person can be self-indulgent or selfish, unless a good relationship to the mother existed during childhood. If the maternal influence is not good, there is a tendency to over-eat. This person finds it difficult to think with clarity or insightfully, when assessing others or sizing up a situation. In terms of tasks and projects, they can 'bite off more than one can chew'. Here a creative hobby is really useful.

THE MOON TO SATURN

Conjunct: the predisposition refrains from empathetic warmth
This aspect signifies that emotional support is required from the mother, and if this is not given, an inferiority complex can arise. The person is ill at ease with any emotional qualities in their predisposition or habitual inclinations, and is very self-controlled.

Trine: a predisposition to duty and ethics
Here highly ethical Saturn influences from the subconscious are absorbed by the life-energies (the 'etheric body'). This indicates a responsible, practical person with a sense of duty who makes a good teacher. This person gains an interest in idea or object once its practical qualities for helping people are seen. There is also an inherent business sense, and a capacity for insights about the possibilities in daily life for personal growth or gain. This person is conservative, respects tradition, and as a young person is ahead of their age. As an adult, she or he has high standards and common sense.

Negative: shy, introverted and too conservative, and consequently can miss out on interesting experiences because of this.

Sextile: A predisposition to be grounded and reserved
With this aspect, the moods are kept private; the person is reserved, and finds it difficult to accept affection. They remain calm in difficult times, and keep busy and have integrity. This is the common sense, practical person, who likes to see results and communicates data well. As with the trine, this person seems older and wiser than their years because of the saturnine feature in the temperament. This leads to a preference for conservatism, for being prudent and respecting tradition. In romance, this person is attracted to someone who has positive Saturn qualities, such as being decisive and competent about goals in life.

THE MOON TO SATURN   continued

Square: a predisposition to isolation and restriction
Alan Leo calls the keynote of this aspect, "the Lonely". Here there is a tendency to brooding and a general inability to express oneself. There is a feeling that things around oneself prevent one from being expressive; and this leads to a cold, depressive mood. One can feel lonely even in childhood, and this lonely or isolated feeling intensifies in adulthood if during childhood one's mother is not supportive, or if one commonly misunderstood the mother. A factor isolating this person from others is that the risk of being rejected is too potent. The person can be crafty and calculating and if male, he can be too feminine, and compensates for this by being tyrannical.

Opposition: a predisposition to sternness
This aspect causes the sternness and coldness of negative Saturn influences to inhibit the natural tendency of the life-forces to interact with the energies in the surroundings. (This is the so-called melancholic type.) There is also shyness and feeling both unloved and remote, unless the childhood was very positive in this regard. (Clients often report dreams about a little child crying.) This aspect usually causes the person to repress their feelings, including their need for a relationship.

The mother's role is very important in this person's emotional and mental health. There is an underlying sense of not being free. A man can attract an unloving mate. However this aspect gives depth of understanding of people, a strong sense of duty and the capacity to relate to older people. There can be a tendency to bitterness, and medically, digestive upsets are possible. (Hickey notes that the child can lose a parent, especially if the 4th house is governed by Capricorn or Cancer.)

Inconjunct: a predisposition incapable of empathetic warmth
This aspect leads to an acute shyness, and a guilty undercurrent in emotional connection to others; this dynamic impels this person to

THE MOON TO SATURN   continued

Inconjunct, continued
demonstrate that they really do care about the other person. An inferiority complex is common here, and in romance, this person could seek to be servile. Their emotional needs are in conflict with the reality of how best to survive in the modern world. If the Moon has other negative aspects or is predominant in the chart generally, perhaps through Cancer as the rising sign or sun sign, there is a fear of not having enough love, especially from the mother. But if Saturn is the stronger influence, this person distrusts their own emotions and becomes cold. Any partner is some years older than the person themselves. (R. Hand notes that this can cause the attitude that one has no roots, and no one cares about you.)

THE MOON TO URANOS

Conjunct: a predisposition to chaotic impulses
Here the somewhat psychic or sensitive influence of Uranos is active in the person's life-forces, and this creates a number of unusual results. These include a good rapport with other ethnicities, but erratic impulses which may lead to difficult situations. It also creates a dislike of the mundane and of routines, and leads to forming partnerships with unusual persons. It also causes malfunctions of electronic devices. (One client reported that electrical or electronic devices could suddenly start working in their presence.)

These people can be independent or even obstinate, emotionally charged, and sometimes find challenges and unconventionality exciting. These people can be rash and impulsive, but they are very self-expressive and strive to analyse life objectively.

Trine: a predisposition for personal freedom
This person needs their freedom, including also in their relationships. They don't seem to identify any one particular house or city as their home. With Uranian energies enhancing the power of the life-forces, this person can sense the wider environment, and can easily relate to unusual people, is inquisitive, and be a good public speaker.

Sextile: a predisposition to emphasize personal freedom
With this aspect, emotional freedom is needed. This person must be free to express his or her own feelings. This is the unconventional person, with an iconoclastic tendency as well as interests in esoteric themes and possibly a psychic capacity.

Square: a predisposition for a destructive freedom
Here the temperament is rendered chaotic by negative Uranian influences that create a yearning for so-called 'freedom'. This leads to being stubborn, and to being 'temperamental', that is, to sudden

THE MOON TO URANOS

Square, continued
and unpredictable moods and wishes. There is a deafness to one's own inner voice. This person is excitable, looks for excitement and also for change, and does not want to be restricted, and therefore does not want to be dependent on others. Their family home may have been upsetting and this can cause them to avoid a settled married life, because their childhood home life was too unsettled. As one client commented, 'the suitcase is packed and ready for a sudden departure'.

Opposition: a predisposition for chaotic circumstances
There is an inner contrariness here. There is a craving for excitement. This person misjudges their associates and attracts the wrong type of associate. There is a lot of nervous energy, and if a woman, there is often conflict with other women. This person's non-integrated, non-critiqued urge for 'freedom' makes him or her seek an eccentric or bohemian kind of friend (to obtain a vicarious freedom feeling from that person).

Inconjunct: a predisposition to constrict oneself
This aspect indicates the sensitive, indrawn person who hides their real feelings to accommodate others. This person feels the need to serve, and possibly could develop a martyr complex. Some people with this aspect may marry in order to play out the martyr role; and in romance they are subject to illusions, seeing the other person as very special, and then inevitably feeling let down. They are often subject to sudden outbursts of moods. Their relationship to their mother is difficult. (Often the south lunar node is in Pisces with this aspect.)

THE MOON TO NEPTUNE

Conjunct: a predisposition to fantasy and empathy

This aspect makes the person too empathetic and also sanguine. In Steiner's terms, one would say that 'etheric energies' stream out beyond the skin more than is usual, going beyond the boundary of the person. So people with this aspect are very sensitive, as the out-raying energies absorb other peoples' emotional energies. Therefore any negative energies of others will impact on this person, causing negative moods.

This person is a day-dreamer, prone to illusions about life, especially in romance, There are ungrounded ideals and often a psychic tendency. Vocationally, helping less fortunate people is advisable. The body is often not robust. In a fine chart, this aspect leads to an interest in spiritual themes, and dedication to high ideals.

Negative: there can be secret enemies who bring difficulties; and there can be a tendency to lying.

Trine: a predisposition to creative fantasy

Here there is a very strong capacity for fantasy, and this needs to be given expression for emotional health, so it is important that craft or art is undertaken. This person is very sensitive to other peoples' feelings, and feels them as their own. Vocationally, young people respond well to this person. (The south lunar node is often in Libra when this aspect occurs in the chart.)

Sextile: a predisposition for fantasy and predictive dreams

This aspect indicates a very strong fantasy or imagination. There is empathy with other peoples' situations. This person is poor at maths, experiences prophetic dreams, and has a psychic ability, but as this ability is veiled, clients with this capacity are often not aware of it !

THE MOON TO NEPTUNE   continued

Square: a predisposition for defeatist, illusory fantasies

With this aspect, the person's life-forces ray out too freely, and absorb other peoples' emotional energies. So the person is too sensitive to the emotions and thoughts of other people. This person may not feel sure about his or her own feelings towards others, or how others feel about them. Their sensitivity causes them to be too easily hurt by harsh words. Subconscious feelings of inferiority and insecurity are common with this aspect; this is a day-dreamer with a strong fantasy life. This aspect does, however, bestow compassion for the suffering of others. This person can be deluded about the world; and odd persons enter their life. There is a predisposition to being naïve about the opposite sex. They can be deceived into trusting the wrong person. (Note: if the south lunar node is in Cancer, then this aspect is common, and this also occurs if the similar, but weaker, Semi-square is there.)

Opposition: a predisposition to deceptive fantasies

This is a creative, talented, and sensitive person, but someone who finds it hard to separate truth from untruth, and reality from illusion. This creates problems in personal relations, as there is a great possibility of misunderstandings happening between oneself and others. This person is very aware of other people's problems, yet will be utilized by others, unless they are alert. (The south lunar node can be in Aquarius when this aspect occurs, but if this occurs in a fine horoscope, then this aspect is not so negative.)

Inconjunct: a predisposition to a self-undermining sensitivity

This aspect indicates a tendency to self-sabotage. This person is very sensitive to the perceived feelings of others, which causes problems. They become timid, withdraw into their own fantasy life and can develop a martyr tendency, as this person might seek out situations where they are tormented. It is said that for this person, if things are going well, they can even seek out trouble. But there is enjoyment of social work. The body is not strong, and in romance this person is too idealistic. (The south lunar node is quite often in Pisces when this aspect occurs.)

THE MOON TO PLUTO

Conjunct: the predisposition dominates in the soul
Pluto intensifies the temperament, causing very deeply felt moods, and a generally intense temperament to dominate the personality. One needs a good connection to one's mother in childhood to moderate this. There are often mood swings, and often this person feels guilty or bad about something which is hard to define.

Trine: the qualities of the predisposition are intensified
This aspect indicates that the person is really interested in personal growth. They have an interest in knowing why they have certain moods. There is a tendency to act out intense moods. It takes an effort to concentrate, so study is disliked. Depending on the over-all chart, this person can exhibit extreme behaviour and be rash and foolhardy; even display cunning and be manipulative, liking to shape other peoples' lives. But there is a talent for psychology.

Sextile: empowered life-forces make one empathetic
This aspect causes the life-forces (or 'etheric body') ray out more than is usual, hence this person becomes too exposed to other peoples' energies. This causes the person to feel empathy for other people, and for their challenges. Hence there is a good understanding of human nature and often a compassionate nature. This person can be subject to day-dreams, and is fond of fantasy stories. Vocationally: working with young people is indicated and there is also a good business sense.

Square: moods of self-focus and dominance prevail
This aspect indicates deeply felt moods, and difficulty in letting go of the past, as well as apprehension about the future, and withdrawing from it. This person can be a loner, but if they are in a relationship, they are predisposed to force themselves on their partner. They are also demanding, and like to enjoy relationships

THE MOON TO PLUTO   continued

Square, continued
without accepting the duties involved. Their vocation may involve working with people in unfortunate circumstances. Their attitudes are subject to being dominated by their moods. They can be jealous of a close relationship.

Opposition: moods dominate the personality
This aspect usually brings very intense moods, and often this person's mother was very demanding and gave insufficient freedom. This person is demanding of their partner, and argues over domestic issues.

Inconjunct: a predisposition to be dominated by dark, obscure moods
With this aspect, intense moods occur and the person can feel the impulse to carry out a deed without knowing why; a condition which derives from the previous life. This person may feel jealous or possessive of others; but this condition may be worsened by childhood insecurities. They often suffer from 'dark thoughts' and may feel obliged to submit to others to obtain their affection; hence there is a possibility of being manipulated. (This aspect is often present when the south node is in Scorpio).

THE MOON TO ASCENDANT

Conjunct: the predisposition is egoistically self-centred
With this aspect, this person is emotionally demanding on anyone they help, insisting on a great amount of attention. This person is also very defensive, and critical of any interested people as well as possessive or jealous about their friends, yet wanting also to withdraw from relationships. This person's moods are obvious to others, and yet they find it difficult to discuss their feelings and moods with other people.

Trine: the predisposition seeks to support the secondary ego-sense
With this aspect, the person's temperament is in rapport with their self (its secondary point of manifesting). So this person's initiative is inherently affirmed by their temperament; making them easy-going, creative and resourceful. This same dynamic also means that this person has a natural empathy with others; so he or she likes being social, likes belonging to a group of friends. The moon is linked to the mother in a horoscope, and so here the mother's influence is very important; it affects how this person forms relationships as an adult.

Sextile: the predisposition supports the social dynamics of the self
Here there is a tendency to what could be called a group-soul dynamic, that is, this person wants to be involved in a group, in every situation. But this person is too emotional in interactions with other people, although community interaction and civic interest are strong, often leading to charity work. There are high standards in both the work and personal life.

THE MOON TO ASCENDANT   continued

Square: the life-forces are not supportive of the secondary self-sense
This aspect causes the self to have changeable moods socially, affecting social interaction, and creating tension in relationships. With this aspect a person retreats from conflict, as well as being a sentimentalist. There is a subjective rather than objective attitude to events and people in life. Their life is assessed through the temperament rather than through a clear, alert mind. With the predisposition not supportive of the ego-sense, this person tends to be powerless with regard to dominating persons, who can mould such a person into a reflection of their intentions. (R. Hand notes that this person feels that to show their real feelings to a person close to them is to damage the relationship.)

Opposition: unresponsive life-forces weaken the sense of self
With this aspect, the temperament is blocked from resonating with the Ascendant which is a kind of secondary ego-sense (or 'ego-reflection' point), and hence this person seeks emotional support from others, becoming too interwoven with friends. This person seeks excessively for an inner link to others. The mother's influence is very important; this person may seek a mothering partner if their mother was a failure.

Inconjunct: the life-forces are not supportive of the self
With this aspect, similar to the Opposition, the temperament is blocked from resonating with the Ascendant, the secondary ego-sense. So, this person tends to suppress their own personality if faced with any external demands. It is also possible that this person attracts people who become a problem.

THE MOON TO MIDHEAVEN

Conjunct: the predisposition is strengthened by the secondary ego-sense
With this aspect the moods and general temperament are empowered within this person's sense of whom they are. Hence this person's predisposition readily takes up any initiatives, helping this person to be a success in life. The way the mother parents this person, will have a strong effect on into their adulthood.

Trine: a predisposition to be fond of one's social context
With this aspect this person is inherently attached to, and kindly disposed towards, the things and people of their life in general. This benefits the person in their social and vocational interaction.

Sextile: the predisposition is supportive of one's social reality
This aspect brings the life-forces into empathy with the social environs, so this person is sensitive to the society they live in. It also means that there is probably a talent as a counsellor or psychologist. This benefits the person in their social and vocational interaction.

Square: the predisposition does not sense the social dynamics
With this aspect, the moods are not in alignment with the Midheaven point, where the self has a major interface with the world. With this aspect, one experiences conflict between one's own moods and the expectations of society. Or this person's mood is to proceed in a particular path, even though the self knows that another way is better. This aspect hinders the person in their social and vocational interaction.

MOON TO MIDHEAVEN   continued

Opposition: predisposed to ignore the social reality
With this aspect, the temperament or life-forces are not aligned at all to the Midheaven point, where the sense-of-self has an important presence, so this person's social reality is subject to very unhelpful dynamics, such as jealousy, or being too possessive of significant others and, disinterested in helpful friends. In general this person is unable to sense what would be the best path to take socially. This aspect strongly hinders this person in their social and vocational interaction.

Inconjunct: inherently predisposed to be confused about one's own social dynamics
With the life-forces not aligned to the Midheaven point, where the sense-of-self has an important presence, this person can find their moods and habitual predisposition often cause problems, undermining them socially (i.e., with choice of partner and friends) and in terms of their workplace relations. This aspect hinders this person in both their social and vocational interaction.

MERCURY TO VENUS

Conjunct: the intellect and the emotions are intertwined
This aspect gives a graceful, charming self-expression, together with a light-hearted, tactful and gentle way of being. There is a gift at writing, and also in working with finances. Since the intellect and the emotions are in harmony, this person expresses their feelings openly and sincerely. This creates a person who is oriented towards people and being of service, and who often has artistic talents as well. These gifts can be combined successfully in business activities.

Trine: the emotions support the intellect
This aspect creates the articulate speaker, someone who is direct, self-assured, and with firm opinions. Vocational indications here include working with young children, or as a craftsperson.

Sextile: the emotions bring gentleness to the intellect
Here the person is diplomatic, charming, liking beauty and harmony in the environs. They are also sociable, disliking aggression, and gifted at self-expression.

(Mercury is never in Opposition, Square or Inconjunct to Venus; although it can be in a Semi-square to Venus, which produces mild disharmony between the emotions and the logical mind. This can cause for example, a hesitancy to speak meaningfully about personal or emotive issues.)

MERCURY TO MARS

Conjunct: the intellect is fiery and assertive
In communicating, this person is somewhat martial, acting immediately on a decision. The intellect is mechanically inclined, but strong. This person talks their way to success, and has determination, courage, and can think for themselves. They feel a need to speak up for themselves, even if this is rash at times; so this person argues when compromise would be wiser.

Negative: sarcastic, an aggressive, sharp tongue, and getting into arguments. One decides on a viewpoint and holds to it, feeling threatened if proven wrong. This person puts their viewpoint forward too strongly.

Trine: the intellect is confident and martial
A self-assured person, who usually requires that others accommodate themselves to their ideas. A determined, good debater, but there is a slightly harsh nuance.

Sextile: thinking and speech are powerful and martial
With this aspect, one thinks for oneself, and has a powerful interest in grasping and acquiring knowledge. There is a very active mind, which enjoys debating. This person has independent attitudes (also as a child), and their own choice is defended vehemently. But this person is a good listener as well as a good speaker. Vocationally, this aspect favours journalism and politics.

Square: thinking and speech are ego-centric and martial
This aspect creates the incessant talker, with lots of mental energy for tasks, but possibly insufficient will to carry them through. The person is strongly opinionated, argumentative, and a poor listener. Usually fault-finding, with no tact, and prone to boasting. This

MERCURY TO MARS continued

Square, continued
person must learn to give others their rights; they may also suffer from muscle spasms, and act rashly.

Negative: cruelty, especially mental cruelty, the more so if there are negative Scorpio factors. This person is sarcastic, often bad-tempered, and can be dishonest or exaggerating.

Opposition: the intellect is unclear and aggressive
This aspect is a primary factor in creating the choleric person. That is, someone who is combative, argumentative, always ready to defend their situation and wishes, and who often has strong ambitions. This person says the wrong thing at the wrong time, and can have rash thinking. Their ideas often illogical if they have to debate anything when angry. They can be fault-seeking, but they do like mental challenges. This aspect often occurs in charts where the south node is in Sagittarius.

Inconjunct: the intellect is confused and ego-centric
This person holds very subjective opinions, always defending their own ideas. They may be well informed, but cannot assess their data objectively, as the capacity for discernment is not well developed. A lack of self-esteem is often found in these people.

MERCURY TO JUPITER

Conjunct: the intellect is open to new ideas
This aspect indicates substantial travel is likely, and this person has wide interests, but the mind is not exacting, nor gifted at detailed, analytical thinking. There is a gift in the communicating of one's ideas. But if Jupiter is well-aspected, then this person has a natural capacity for an acute grasp of higher truths.

Trine: the intellect is inclined to wider horizons
With this aspect, this person is generous, tolerant, optimistic and interested in many things. The more universal the subject, the more they are interested. There are good planning skills, and an enjoyment of travelling. As with the conjunction, if Jupiter is well-aspected, then this person has a natural capacity for a good grasp of higher truths.

Sextile: the intellect is expansive and forward-looking
This aspect indicates a mentally alert person with an active mind and a thirst for knowledge, and a capacity to accumulate information. But there is the wish to apply this knowledge to life. There is also a debating skill, and the mind is good at getting an overview, but there is a tendency to neglect the details. This person is gifted at communication (both verbal and written). Vocationally this aspect indicates a gift in teaching.

Square: unwise and phlegmatic thinking
This aspect indicates poor judgment, and a need to guard against unwise decisions. The person is phlegmatic (that is good-natured and easy-going, but dislikes lots of mental disciplined activity) and is a procrastinator. This is someone who is forgetful, and who bites off more than they can chew, but they can be generous.

Negative: One avoids accepting responsibility, can distort facts, and is subject to sloppy thinking. Medically, liver problems can arise.

MERCURY TO JUPITER continued

Opposition: the intellect is ego-centric and has little depth

This aspect invokes the 'know it all', someone who has lots of data, but little insight, and can be too talkative, and must learn to really hear what other are saying. Opinions are strong, but often inaccurate, because of undisciplined thinking. In effect, many mental pictures are made, but there is little capacity to see the deeper meaning behind them. But there can be a yearning to travel, in order to expand the understanding of the world by exploring the beliefs of others.

Inconjunct: the intellect is undisciplined and pedantic

This person is ambitious, but has unclear thinking, and often rather sloppy in appearance. There is a tendency to preach about morality, but also to be hypocritical. There is some frustration in expressing one's own creative potential. In romance there is often a feeling of low self-confidence.

MERCURY   TO   SATURN

Conjunct: the intellect is prudent and methodical
With this aspect, this person's intellect is saturnine; that is, careful, prudent, and not in a hurry, but in a fine chart the intellect can be quite subtle. There is a tendency to be a loner, and the temperament is somewhat melancholic. One resists changes, and has the same religious beliefs as the parents. In romance this person seeks someone who reflects the best qualities of Saturn, that is maturity, honesty, sincerity, and over-all, a responsible person.

Negative: If Saturn is ill-aspected, then one is suspicious, and shows a lack of empathy, even a depressive quality.

Trine: the intellect is strong and conscientious
This aspect creates an intelligent, clear thinking, organized person, who finds or creates opportunities. This person is disciplined, efficient, a hard worker who has integrity. This is not a day-dreamer type, but someone who can be quite insightful and disciplined in their thinking.

Sextile: the intellect is cautious and disciplined
This aspect brings a practical, disciplined, responsible attitude, with marked common sense, and this person is mature for one's age. This person is capable of achieving goals through careful planning, and through an enhanced sense of existing opportunities. Usually this is an intelligent person, with good self-control.

Square: the intellect is rigid
With this aspect, the intellect is disciplined and thorough; but there is a poor memory, and a depressive tendency which shows as negative thinking, as a narrow outlook, and in habitual thought-patterns. This person often does not hear what others say, and also has a tendency to worry.

MERCURY TO SATURN   continued

Opposition: the intellect is ego-centric and non-intuitive

Here the person considers that they are often misunderstood; but in fact they themselves have an impediment to the expression of their thoughts, or to the understanding of other people. This in turn causes negative interpretation of others' words. The thinking is conservative and there is little capacity for empathy. This person may bend the truth and get into scheming.

Inconjunct: the intellect is subject to the Shadow

This aspect allows the unwholesome energies of the lower self (called the shadow) to access the mind. This condition indicates a person whose intelligence is disconnected from the subtle guidance of Saturn influences in the subconscious will that discretely leads us through our life. This disconnected state leads to hidden, internal stresses and fears, which lead to strange behaviour (such as blinking or rubbing the eyes). Often there is a tendency to melancholia, to rigid thinking and also to feeling suspicious of others' motives.

MERCURY TO URANOS

Conjunct: the intellect is acute and sanguine
When the Mercury energies are permeated by rays from Uranos, the intellect can immediately find a solution to complex situations. This person is mentally bright, articulate, curious, sanguine, and in a fine chart, a touch of genius is possible. They may also be opinionated. The mental processes are seldom inactive, but may be too inconsistent (sanguine) to be productive. This person can open new doors through their innovative ideas, which are sometimes radical. A strong sense of humour is possible.

Trine: the intellect is receptive and psychic
Here the positive energies of Uranos are activated within the intelligence. This makes the intellect open-minded, creative and even intuitive. In a fine chart, future positive Uranian forces are active already; this means that esoteric spiritual topics are of interest. In addition this person may well seek knowledge for advancement of humanity. Vocationally, this person can be a teacher.

Sextile: the intellect is acute and has originality
With this aspect, there is a progressive thinker with originality of expression and consequently inventors often have this in their horoscope. The mind is very quick, (above average intelligence). There is a talent in writing and speaking, but this person is probably not inclined to deeper kinds of thoughts.

Square: the intellect is unclear and erratic
With this aspect, negative, atavistic energies from this strange planet influence the intelligence, creating an erratic mentality, which is impulsive and eccentric, but can still be intuitive. So this person can have odd thoughts, and in their speech can use unexpected phrases. The problem here is for this person to really say what is truly in the context of the dialogue they are having with someone.

MERCURY TO URANOS continued

Opposition: the mind is erratic and rebellious
With this aspect the person becomes active with others in a nervously sanguine way. They can also select the wrong kind of associates to be with. The intellect can be quite sharp, but since it's subject to the 'freedom' urge of Uranos, it is rebellious about accepting current ideas or authoritative beliefs. There is an inherent resistance to conforming to modern ideas.

Inconjunct: the intellect is erratic and sanguine
Similar to the Opposition, this aspect indicates that the person is mentally sanguine, and can get excessively excited. Their mind focuses intensely, but their attention span is limited.

MERCURY TO NEPTUNE

Conjunct: the intellect is enmeshed in fantasy
With all aspects involving Mercury and Neptune, the intelligence is affected by spiritual influences crossing over 'the threshold', that is, raying in from spiritual realms and influencing the mind. So with a conjunction, thinking is very imaginative; the person can be subject to delusions. The fantasy life is strong, and there is an artistic sensitivity.

<u>Negative</u>: A state of psychic confusion exists regarding the soul-life of other people, their mental images come inside one's own mind. There can be tendency towards lying.

Trine: the intellect is intuitive
This person is an idealist, with a creative and strong imagination, as spiritual thought-forms or 'intuitions' weave around their mind. There is usually also a psychic ability and empathy with the ideas of other people.

Sextile: the intellect inclines towards fantasy
With this aspect, there is a rich imagination, and this person can almost 'see' ideas. A psychic capacity exists. There is an escapist tendency in speech, adding extra details to make the topic more exciting to the listener.

Square: the intellect is the servant of fantasy
Here, fantasy impedes thinking. This person can be a drama queen, catastrophizing and exaggerating simple setbacks. There is a rich fantasy capacity, and the mind is very sensitive. This person can be drawn to vocations where some mental health issues exist; this kind of work can bring clarity about one's own problems. In romance, ungrounded ideas about a partner will cause problems.

MERCURY TO NEPTUNE   continued

Opposition: the intellect is deceived by fantasies
With this aspect, the imagination is too vivid, so this person is a daydreamer, sensitive and absent minded, with a fear of competition, and of facing challenges. A lack of self-confidence is common, and this person can be deceived by others.

<u>Negative</u>: Lies, fuzzy thinking, and being too unrealistic are possible problems, and these can cause a cynical outlook on life.

Inconjunct: the intellect is affected by fantasies
The person's rational thinking processes are muddled by fantasies, and such a person can be a day-dreamer to the point of being problematic. These traits result in a low self-confidence, but if effort is made through soul exercises for self-assertiveness and for facing the real world, these could be lessened.

<u>Negative</u>: If other aspects to Neptune or Uranos are negative, a tendency to feel suspicious about other people can become paranoia.

MERCURY TO PLUTO

Conjunct: the analytical mind is accentuated
Here the empowering quality of Pluto strengthens the force of the intellect. So this person is very curious, and can possess investigative skills. The person is stubborn with regard to their own ideas. Vocationally, this person could be gifted as a psychologist.

Trine: the thinking is deepened
This aspect allows Pluto to empower Mercury's intellectual energies in a good way. In a fine chart, this leads to a deep interest in, and fascination for, thoughts about the purpose of life, and the nature of the world. This person likes to study people, probably has good financial management skills, and can see the potential in people.

Sextile: the intelligence is enhanced in several ways
With this aspect, the person's mental processes are sanguine, as well as strongly analytical, and often psychic. A distinctive ethical quality can manifest in the way the intellect is used. This can result in an ability to find solutions to civic or social issues.

Square: the intelligence dominates by speech
With this aspect, speech is resented by others because they feel imposed upon by it. The speech is harsh, and often rudely upfront. But this kind of dynamic can reverse, and come upon the person from outside; then people are encountered who force their opinion on this person.

Negative: An obsession to shape other people's lives can occur.

Opposition: the intelligence asserts itself too strongly
With this aspect, there is conflict about ideas, because this person assets what they think in an aggressive way. Consequently, people

MERCURY TO PLUTO continued

Opposition, continued
don't like to be involved in dialogue with this person. But the dynamic can reverse, and this person can encounter people who, if their Mars or Pluto energies are strong, draw this person into angry exchanges of opinions.

Negative: Obsessive tendencies about an idea, and being arrogant when one's ideas are questioned, as it seems that oneself is being questioned.

Inconjunct: the intelligence is devious
With this aspect, thinking is complex and tricky. This person is a mystery-solver, and maintains secrecy about their projects. In frustrated response to these powerful, but suppressed energies pervading the intelligence, a martyrdom tendency exists, which manifests in undertaking burdensome tasks.

Negative: If other negative aspects exist to Neptune or Mercury, delusional states are possible.

MERCURY TO ASCENDANT

Conjunct: the mind is enlivened, expansive
This person enjoys an exchange of ideas, as the intelligence is sanguine, and this person is a good speaker. Extensive travelling is also possible. Over-all there is tendency to being too self-centred.

Trine: the ego's reflection enhances the intellect
With this aspect, the intelligence is stimulated both in logical and creative modes. One enjoys handcrafts, and is good at writing.

Sextile: the mind seeks lively social interaction
With this aspect there is a social butterfly tendency, and a need to keep busy. The analytical skills are strong, and there is good self-expression. Often there are craft skills.

Square: the thinking is ego-centric
This aspect produces an active thought life, but one which is too opinionated. This person expresses their thoughts with too much intensity, and is misunderstood when expressing ideas. A gossiping tendency is common.

Opposition: the thinking is lively but superficial
With this aspect the person needs mental stimulation, especially through debating, and likes to compete mentally with others, yet as the intelligence is not harmonized with this reflection point of the ego, the mind is not actually deeply engaged in thought. So this person may not be seriously concerned about an idea which is under lively discussion. There is a dislike of emotional people.

Inconjunct: the thinking is not aligned to the ego's reflection
This aspect brings impeded communicating. People do not hear what you really wish to say, or vice versa. But this person enjoys learning challenging skills.

MERCURY TO MIDHEAVEN

Conjunct: the thinking is socially oriented and future focused
With this aspect there is a sharp intellect, so one is a good communicator, but the intellect is sanguine and thus may be emotionally shallow or restricted. This person is intent on improving their future, being aware of their social situation; so they continually re-evaluate future plans. There are strong powers of communication, making this person an effective speaker.

Sextile: the thinking is strongly intuitive
Here the thought life is quite intuitive, and this person plans for the future. Vocationally, there is a definite capacity for psychology.

Trine: the thinking is focused on one's social profile
With this aspect, the person considers the future carefully, even as a child, and plans well for it. This person is self-disciplined, but the parents do influence their ideas on into adulthood.

Square: there is insufficient self-sense in the thinking
With this aspect, the thinking is not in alignment with the Midheaven point, where the self has a major interface with the world. The result here is the person experiences confusion within their thinking. Although they consider the future a lot, this lack of integration of their self with the intellect, causes a very sanguine mindset, and so unguarded speech can lead to enemies. (It is common to have Sagittarius in the south lunar node with this aspect.)

Opposition: the thinking is self-focussed and not in alignment with one's social dynamics
With this aspect too, thinking is not in alignment with the Midheaven point, where the self has a major interface with the world. With this

MERCURY TO MIDHEAVEN continued

Opposition continued
aspect, this person's own viewpoint is regarded as absolute, and the mind is inflexible. Because this position places Mercury in house four, the world-view of this person is often based on family or parental ideas, and not their own thinking, and childhood ideas stay on in adulthood.

Inconjunct: the thinking is disconnected from the self
With this aspect too, thinking is not in alignment with the Midheaven point, where the self has a major interface with the world. This brings unclear thinking, as this person's own self is not easily able to express ideas. This makes the person confused about what is taught by others, and what one thinks. Additionally, as an adult, one makes indiscrete or odd remarks that let the inner tension come to expression. (R. Hand notes that it is also common for this person as a youngster, to be unable to accept his or her own ideas, if they conflict with those of authorities, such as teachers.)

VENUS TO MARS

Conjunct: the driving force strengthens the emotions
This aspect indicates the sensualist, with a strong sex drive, (especially if Mars is in Scorpio) with strong emotions, unless other higher influences counter this. A demanding person with strong needs in regards to their emotions. The other-gender parent is important; if that person was negative, then this person could draw a similarly unsuitable partner to oneself. The intensity of the desires lead to a volatile situations in relationships.

Trine: the driving force ennobles the emotions
With this aspect, the person is warm, affectionate, sociable, and attractive, as well as creative at entertaining, and good with children. This person brings out the best in people, with their diplomatic and charming qualities. With an artistically gifted person, this aspect indicates substantial interest in the arts.

Sextile: the driving force enlivens the emotions
This creates the congenial, lively, vivacious, and sexually intense person, but a person who can remain in charge of their desires. This influence indicates an artistic talent and also someone who has lots of friends, and who purchases decor items. Vocationally, public relations work would be a good choice.

Square: the driving force strengthens antipathy & desire
With this aspect, the desires are strong, so this person partners at a young age. But there is a mixture of antipathy and physical attraction in relationships. The attractions to partners derive from basic body desires, and little of the higher qualities of the mind play a role in a relationship.

VENUS TO MARS continued

Opposition: the driving force enflames feelings and desire
This aspect produces intense emotions and strong desires. It also produces the choleric personality, and hence relationships are often stormy, alternating between like and dislike. This person is often emotionally immature.

Inconjunct: the driving force intensifies self-centred feelings
This aspect, similar to the Opposition, causes excessively self-focused desires and feelings, and constantly going between liking and dislike, as well as a strong sensuality.

VENUS TO JUPITER

Conjunct: the feelings are attracted to beauty and wisdom
The intuitive insightfulness of Jupiter resonates with a finely developed sentiency from Venus, creating an ability to see beauty in all sorts of subtle ways. This means that life for this person is generally harmonious. This aspect indicates a lucky person, one who attracts wealth and opportunities, and who is optimistic and co-operative. There is an interest in meaningful values, not trivial ideas.

Trine: a discerning heart
This aspect brings inner poise, optimism, social graces, a diplomatic mindset, and it can cause financial success. Here Jupiter's wisdom can manifest particularly strongly in a finely developed sentiency from Venus. The person abhors vulgarity, has high ethical standards, is warm and affectionate. This aspect also bestows the capacity to perceive beauty, in terms of fine artistic tastes. But in a fine chart, it also bestows in the heart the capacity for discerning the inner beauty existing in other people. Vocationally it can bring success in public relations.

Sextile: the emotions are expansive
This creates ease of expression, and someone who is popular, who praises others, is warm-hearted, and who likes a comfortable life. This person is honest, and can attract material goods.

Negative: This person can be extravagant, and in need of self-discipline (this is worsened by negative Jupiter aspects.)

Square: a restless heart lacking depth
This indicates a lack of wisdom in the feelings. This brings extravagance, an ostentatious lifestyle and a tendency to arrogance, and to live beyond one's means. This person is very sanguine, flitting from one experience the next. This person likes company, and lacks self-discipline. (Clients' report that credit card debts are a problem for them.)

VENUS TO JUPITER continued

Opposition: the emotional focus point is one's self
This aspect indicates extravagance, vanity, ostentatiousness, but a sociable person, who is willing to share. This person needs self-discipline, and social approval of their deeds. In romance, there is often a lack of a real commitment, as their own self-love is a dominant trait, inhibiting love of others.

Inconjunct: passive emotions impede the self
With this aspect, one is passive, with little ambition, and a need for warmth from others. This person can unwittingly attract people who order them around, and this person tends to submit to such people. A lack of self-confidence is therefore quite common.

VENUS TO SATURN

Conjunct: solemn admonitions inhibit the feelings
With this aspect, one is over-cautious, inhibited, and can suffer from the selfishness of others, or be miserly oneself. But it does give one a capacity to offer a long lasting, loyal partnership. One is reserved, yet affectionate, but not on the surface. This person, sensing the divide between their consciousness and their feelings, may feel impelled to make concessions to others, to succeed in finding a partner.

Trine: sincere spiritual insights ennoble the emotions
With this aspect, Saturn's lofty but solemn 'spirit-intuitiveness' which brings awareness of one's karma, is echoed in the person's feelings. There is an inherent respect for older people and a high level of social tolerance, and he or she will seek a mature partner for themselves. This person can also receive loving help from their partner or, later in life achieve business success.

The affections are reserved, but this person can be very loyal and self-disciplined. In romance, there is some hesitation, which arises from their own emotional restrictions. In a fine chart, this person is attracted to those on a spiritual path. This person is a good judge of people. The early years of life are hard, but the later years are easier. Vocationally, working with children and youth or in a craft activity is indicated.

Sextile: intuitive admonitions make the emotions serious
There is a serious attitude to friends, and one is very earnest, hence not outwardly warm. This person considers duty as important as love in a relationship. There is a dislike of coarse behaviour and considerable capacity to assess the personality of other people.

VENUS TO SATURN continued

Square: karmically inhibited emotions oppress the life

With this aspect there comes a significant life-lesson, that of learning to share. For these people refrain from giving the emotional support in a relationship when it is needed. Or this dynamic reverses, and significant other people withhold the emotion which this person needs. As an intuitive awareness of one's own emotions is lacking, there is a feeling of being isolated from other people. So naturally, loneliness can be the result of these characteristics, especially if Saturn is located in, or rules, the 4th house.

<u>Negative</u>: If Saturn has further negative aspects, there can be a tendency to greed, and inner coldness.

Opposition: emotional inhibitions weigh down the soul

With this aspect, there is a lack of self-esteem, so personal relationships may be disappointing, as choices are made from a low standard. However the career life could be quite successful, as the sense of duty is strong. This person has to learn patience and compassion, and often very hard work is undertaken which brings little gain. A feeling of loneliness persists; even pessimism and melancholia. In romance, a coldness tendency is present.

Inconjunct: inhibited emotions isolate the heart

As with the Square, here the person needs warmth, but it eludes them, as their own feelings are very restricted. Often there is a feeling that duty comes before love; and this person may attract an unloving partner. This is a disciplined, but cold person.

VENUS TO URANOS

Conjunction: very sanguine emotions with an urge for freedom

With this aspect, an inappropriate urge for freedom manifests in the emotions, especially in romance and relationships. The person is attractive and sensual, but very changeable (has mood swings), and is not easily deeply committed to a partner. Consequently relationships are formed impulsively and don't last long.

Trine: a freedom urge manifests in the emotions

This person enjoys life, is affable, unconventional, has a sense of harmony, and is quite intuitive, but friends must leave this person free ! There is a need for unusual partners, which is a strong sign of an inner need for freedom, but the kind of freedom yearned for, may be false or not critiqued; it is at any rate, suppressed. An eccentric friend becomes a way that this person can feel the freedom that they are yearning for. Vocationally, this indicates the teaching profession is advisable.

Sextile: a strong freedom urge in the emotions

With this aspect, the person is spontaneous and likes unusual friends, but dislikes any jealousy from them. This person also likes much freedom in a relationship. The dilemma for this person is: what is true freedom and how do I get this in a relationship?

Square: a hidden freedom urge distorts desires and romance

Unrealized Uranian influences plague the emotive life. This person is attracted to unusual Bohemian characters who feel strongly the need to be "free". Hence subconsciously this person attracts unstable partners who are sure to suddenly leave them. This person must learn to make commitments to a relationship, and as with the sextile, the challenge is to understand what is true freedom and how to get this in a relationship. This aspect is also an indicator of lesbian tendencies.

<u>Negative</u>: sexual perversions and other mental disturbances can occur.

VENUS TO URANOS continued

Opposition: a hidden freedom urge dominates relationships

This aspect causes the person to be emotionally unclear in personal relationships, yet there are often strong desires. As with virtually all aspects to Uranos and Venus, in romance this person attracts a partner who is unstable, who will suddenly depart. This stressful pattern is due to a subconscious feeling in this person of being deeply restricted by any relationship. There is a dislike of authority figures, but this person can be charming and witty. This person must learn to develop a more mature view of freedom within a committed relationship, otherwise they can detach themselves from others, if this is expedient.

Inconjunct: a suppressed freedom urge dominates the emotions

With this aspect, again in relationships the person feels trapped in a close relationship, unless the partner is eccentric. They can neglect their own desires to help others, but this can be a 'martyr complex', for a guilty feeling arises if they don't respond to others fully. The person is very intelligent, but gets involved in situations that cause anxiety. They are also usually impulsive and excitable.

VENUS TO NEPTUNE

Conjunct: in the heart lives a gentle idealism
With this aspect, the person is a gentle dreamer, an idealist who idealizes a partner, with a strong love of beauty and artistic, feminine tendencies. There is usually a musical talent. Normally this means that the emotions are changeable. In a fine chart, this aspect gives an interest in spirituality.

Trine: a high spirituality and a feeling for beauty
With this special aspect (one of the highest that a horoscope can have), Neptune's higher, future, spiritual potential becomes activated now, and invokes into this soul the capacity for energies from Venus which create the Spiritual-self. Such a person has a mystical or spiritual awareness, and responds to high ideals, but also needs to express themselves creatively, e.g. in a craft or in the arts. In other words, the person is talented in regard to music and painting, is idealistic and is naturally a loving person.

This person is also romantic, dreamy, and attractive to the opposite sex, as well as generous, sensitive, not aggressive and usually psychic. In romance, this person chooses a partner who is idealistic. There is a wish to serve Love, in the sense of being a person of goodwill to all. But if there are un-grounded tendencies elsewhere in the horoscope, then this aspect would invoke similarly un-grounded idealistic yearnings.

Sextile: in the heart lives compassion and a sense for beauty
This aspect bestows higher emotive capacities, such as compassion, and artistic gifts, and a yearning for a creative life. So vocationally, it indicates humanitarian or artistic work. In romance, as with the trine, these people are drawn to idealists and refined people. These people are very sensitive, and seek an ideal loving relationship. They have a strong feeling for romance, and an active imagination.

VENUS TO NEPTUNE continued

Square: self-centred, burdensome romantic delusions
This aspect also invokes self-deception in romance. There is a compulsive entering into relationships, blindfolded, which leads to disaster. This person has to learn to transmute a self-centred ungrounded desire into a more selfless love; into a yearning for the Spiritual-self. Often personal relationships bring disappointment, this leads easily into a fantasy world. This person needs to note that 'if someone wants to be a martyr, a tormentor will be invoked'; in other words, a very demanding partner is invoked.

Opposition: self-centred romantic delusions
This aspect invokes being ungrounded in romance, and thus being subject to deception in romance, (such as secret affairs). There is a projecting of subjective, idealized images onto people, resulting in disappointments. This person may not feel confident in personal relationships, and may takes up other peoples' burdens in their relationships. This person has to learn to transmute a self-centred, ungrounded desire into a more selfless Love, into a yearning for the Spiritual-self. As with the Square, they may marry unwisely because of ungrounded attitudes to others, and can endure a lot of loneliness.

Inconjunct: self-debasing romantic delusions
Here there is an idealistic attitude in regard to love, and also the 'martyr' syndrome, which creates a self-sacrificing delusion about love, leading to the feeling that one must deny one's own needs and sacrifice, in order to be loved. This person can feel that they are only good enough for the remnants of society. This person is very sensitive, and needs artistic environs. (If Pisces is a major influence in the chart, then this person can easily invoke a tormenter into their life.)

VENUS TO PLUTO

Conjunct: desire is enhanced and very ego-centric
This indicates that sexuality is strong, and that this person is possessive. If there is an ill-aspect to Uranos, then perverted lusts occur. This person may attract harmful partners.

Trine: all emotions are strong and tend to dominance
With this aspect, one is very warm, and loving and very concerned for a close friend. This person identifies with their partner closely, but may have an ongoing 'conflictual' relationship.

Sextile: affection is strong and assertive
With this aspect there are very strong affections, and this person is a loyal friend; but there will be very intense dynamics in a relationship.

Square: ego-centric emotions which seek aggressive interaction
This aspect invokes a warm person, but one who places excessive demands on the partner. Relationships are not easy, as there is a veiled drive for conflicts to occur in relationships. Inappropriate relationships are invoked, and these are traumatic to this person. There is a strong sexuality, and a pressing need to learn to be loving.

Opposition: emotions seek to dominate, and invoke aggressive interaction
This brings power dynamics amongst friends; each seeks to dominate the other. Or this person can suppress their power-seeking urges and then the reverse occurs, so demanding or difficult people are attracted. There can be a tendency towards an actively aggressive dynamic between oneself and the partner, often caused by intense

VENUS TO PLUTO continued

Opposition, continued
jealousy. The source of the conflicts is hidden in the sub-conscious area of the emotions. Some exposure over years to creating, or just experiencing, noble and uplifting beautiful works of art is helpful here.

Inconjunct: the self is undermined by aggressive emotional confusion
With this aspect, difficult dominating persons who are hard to get away from are invoked into one's life, or this person is manipulated by a deceptive partner. In a relationship this person is too demanding of their partner, even aggressive to them.

VENUS TO ASCENDANT

Conjunct: the self is emotionally insecure
With this aspect, the person is very charming, and a peace-maker, possibly artistic, but since this aspect this does not bring out the higher Venus energies, the emotions are not ennobled, so this person may be insincere and sometimes use flattery.

Trine: the self is emotionally sensitive
With this aspect the Venus energies are enhanced, and this person is sociable, artistically gifted, gentle, but also pleasure loving, and has a tendency to timidity.

Sextile: the self is emotionally vulnerable
With this aspect, similar to the trine, this person is quite sociable, avoids negative themes or dynamics, and likes being comfortable.

Square: the emotions seek security in the familiar
With this aspect there is a blockage between the self, that is, the Ascendant, which is its reflection or secondary presence, and the emotions. The result is that the person is very attached to the childhood home; a source of security. As a child they can want to go back home when on holidays (a client felt this even though only 2 years of age), and are devastated when the family home is sold. This is regretted even if it happens when this person has become a mature adult. This aspect creates a sociable nature, but keeps the person from establishing their own independent life. There is a tendency to laziness and to flattery.

VENUS TO ASCENDANT continued

Opposition: the self is emotionally ego-centric
With this aspect there is a blockage between the self (its reflection or secondary presence is the Ascendant) and the emotions. But here the effect is that this person seeks to be sociable, sensing that other people are a means of finding inner support. This person may use other people or situations to achieve a goal. So this person's emotions are especially self-centred. But if there are other factors that urge the person towards a meaningful social interaction, this dynamic might be moderated, and this person may consciously seek to achieve personal growth through interaction with others.

Inconjunct: the emotions are obscured to the self
This aspect brings a blockage between the self (its reflection or secondary presence is the Ascendant) and the emotions. But this causes the person to feel insecure in relationships, so he or she feels that they must be servile to get any affection. A further complication is that there is feeling that one should not be too frank about how one is actually feeling.

VENUS TO MIDHEAVEN

Conjunct: emotionally confident in one's social role
When Venus is close to the Midheaven point, the person is attractive and has much warmth and the ability to attract the right type, and is often artistic.

Trine: artistic and sensitive to one's social role
With this aspect, the person is attracted to beauty, is capable of appreciating artistic works, and is also probably drawn to working in the arts. This aspect indicates a warm, affectionate and probably physically attractive person, who is sociable and non-aggressive.

Sextile: sensitive with tactful social dynamics
With this, the person is sociable, agreeable, but makes compromises to avoid conflict. Vocationally it indicates a career involving art, beauty, counselling or entertainment.

Square: one feels socially insecure
This person may be affectionate, but as the feelings are not in alignment with the Midheaven point, where the self has a major social interface, this person feels better if someone else is guiding them through life. This misalignment creates a subtle feeling of insecurity, which can lead to the use of flattery and charm with people, rather than a direct, open way of relating.

Opposition: social interaction brings a feeling of security
Again with this aspect, the feelings are not in alignment with the Midheaven point, the result here is the need for close, harmonious relationships to significant others. But as this position puts Venus in house four, it also usually leads naturally to a closeness to family members.

VENUS TO MIDHEAVEN   continued

Inconjunct: the self feels emotionally vulnerable
Again with this aspect, the feelings are not in alignment with the Midheaven point, the result here is a need for affection and general emotional support from the partner and friends. If this is lacking this person will tend to retreat into a shell.

MARS TO JUPITER

Conjunct: the driving force is expansive
This conjunction creates a tendency to be excessive in sensuality, and to feel overly important. However in a fine chart, there is advanced processing of sensory stimuli. This person is frank and generous, and a buoyant type, athletic and someone who can sense inwardly the right time to act. This person can get others to carry out their intentions. Vocationally, a military career is possible.

<u>Negative</u>: this indicates rashness, poor judgment and an inclination to gambling.

Trine: the driving force is blessed with wisdom
This aspect allows intuitive insights (wisdom) from Jupiter energies to be taken up by the driving force. This person has ethical principles, and can actually do what they will to do, for their mind can apply their driving force and their resources in a well-integrated way. An optimistic, frank person who lives an untrammelled, untroubled life-style. A person who is successful without annoying others. This aspect also brings about what we call 'a good luck' into the person's life.

Sextile: the driving force has integrity
The sextile allows intuitive insights from Jupiter energies to be taken up by the driving force. This aspect allows a broader outlook (even intuitive ideas) to be taken up, creating an optimistic nature, with a practical interest in higher knowledge. This is someone who is sincere and straightforward in action, and who has a strong sense of justice and responsibility. An element of good luck occurs, especially with regard to the house position of Mars and Jupiter.

MARS TO JUPITER continued

Square: the driving force is brash and militant
With this aspect, the driving energies are subject to unwise, undisciplined ideas, where the boundaries of what is socially appropriate are not discerned. These people are impatient, lacking in tact, but energetic.

Opposition: the driving force in the speech & thinking is undisciplined
With this aspect, the person is not only too talkative, they often push their ideas onto others. This person has strong opinions which are not insightful, nor very consistent, because the Mars energies here muddies the results of any broader, clearer attitudes. There is a know-it-all tendency.

Further negatives: this aspect can bring about a sleep-talking tendency, indicating the need for an enhanced ego-presence in the soul to moderate the Mars influences, (which are active in the throat-speech function).

Inconjunct: the driving force is unwisely focused
With this aspect, similar to the Opposition, the person's capacity to clearly register ideas, is not assimilated by the driving force. The result of this is that he or she is sanguine, takes risks, is often too critical of others and also appears to be accident-prone. This person may offer to help people in ways that don't lead to any real benefit.

MARS TO SATURN

Conjunct: the driving force feels confined, even threatened

This aspect results in the driving force being blinded to the subtle promptings about which decisions are aligned to one's life. This causes the person to be restless and unconventional, disliking pressure, and then, in a classical projection of their inner reality onto the world around them, feeling that any authority figure is against them.

More negative: rash, headstrong, a closed mind, and accidents can occur. They are eccentric, and can become very choleric if angered, especially if their own goals are thwarted.

Trine: the driving force is responsible, alert and ethical

This aspect results in the driving force being receptive to the subtle promptings about which decisions are, or are not, aligned to one's life and its purposes. This leads to a reserved, controlled, pragmatic, dutiful person who is perhaps too cautious, and who has a strong and disciplined ambition. He or she is good at fine detail, and the temper is controlled. In terms of vocation, there are good managerial skills. There is insight, prudence and skilful placement of personnel and assets.

Sextile: the driving force is prudent, but restricted

This person moves or works slowly, being careful about details; so they are not flighty, but pragmatic, very down to earth, with a strong sense of discipline. But they are choleric, however they generally hold their anger inside, and if so, need to ensure they have an outlet for this.

MARS TO SATURN continued

Square: the driving force is deaf to intuitive guidance
Here the deeper intentions in the person (karmically determined), from Saturn, are blocked by an unresponsive personal drive, and this results in a feeling that life seems hard and the world unloving. This person might also become unloving, especially if their father was not supportive. The many setbacks in their life could cause despair, bitterness and a lack of confidence; but other aspects in the horoscope may help them to overcome these obstacles, and become decisive in an insightful way.

Opposition: the driving force has a weak response to intuitive guidance
Here the (karmically determined) deeper intentions in the person from Saturn, are blocked, similar to the Square. There is often the feeling that people or circumstances are opposing one's goals, but this person holds their frustration and anger inside. This can later result in sarcasm or a bitter attitude to life. However, there is a good sense of discipline. Other aspects in the horoscope may help this person to overcome these obstacles, and become more intuitive as to which pathway to go down.

More negative: An inner hesitancy leads to difficulty in being in the moment, and thus making timely and appropriate decisions.

Inconjunct: the driving force resists intuitive guidance
This aspect indicates that, with the deeper intentions in the person (karmically determined) from Saturn being blocked, this person feels conflict between what they sense within, as their duty to society and the direction of their own driving force. This inner split leads to indecision, so irritability arises. Hence people who can bolster this person's self-esteem are needed, and experiences that result in an enhanced capacity to sense intuitively the right action to take are important.

MARS TO URANOS

Conjunct: the driving force is strong but rash
With this aspect, Mars energies strengthen the Uranian urge for self-expression, producing a rebellious type, who is rash, uninhibited, impulsive, and also forceful. Any restrictions that this person encounters will cause a strong surge of anger and further rebellion; if Mars has a number of negative aspects, then aggression is likely. The desires are very strong; and energy levels high.

Trine: the driving force defers to others
With this aspect, Uranian energies, which seek a free flowing, unrestricted unpredictable outlet, weaken this person's driving force. Therefore the usual capacity in any person to stand up for themselves, or to strongly push forward to achieve their life-goals, is undermined. The effect of this aspect is that the person is discouraged easily, and this psychological attitude is a state that medically causes a lack of physical energy. But with this non-aggressive quality there is often a selfless, humanitarian capacity.

Sextile: the driving force is psychically receptive
This aspect activates those Uranian influences that open a vague doorway to psychic-spiritual dimensions; this infuses the person's driving force with a psychic sensitivity. There is often a psychic tendency present when this is in the horoscope, and that is probably why this person detests insincerity.

This person has a sense for rhythm, and they are often good at dancing, and very creative in general. In a fine chart, this person may not have a conscious psychic capacity, but spiritual help and guidance is available to them flowing in across kind of threshold. Vocationally, a career in healing or medicine is indicated.

MARS TO URANOS   continued

Square: a frustrated driving force subject to rash impulses

Here the influence of Uranian energies that tend to make the soul susceptible to other, wider realities is subconsciously confusing the driving forces or intentions of the person. This leads to a person who is rash, accident-prone, often irritable, and who can be aggressive. This person experiences a strange urge to be free, but their urge to achieve this may be restrained by a concern about the implications of giving in to such urges. When working with machinery, this person may be accident-prone, or there may be malfunctions with electronic devices that they are using.

Opposition: a frustrated driving force invokes opposition

With this aspect, Uranian energies, which seek a free flowing, unrestricted, unpredictable outlet, undermine this person's driving force. The result is an inherently frustrated person who can be headstrong, self-willed, and competitive. This is the reflection of the struggle to be "the captain of their soul, the master of their fate". But as we have often noted, these dynamics sometimes come into the person's life from outside. Then this person has to deal with a frustrated eccentric or aggressive associate.

Inconjunct: frustrated by a confused driving force

This aspect is similar to the Opposition; Uranian energies restrict this person's driving force. This creates an angry, frustrated mindset. So the person is rash, impatient and choleric, they are driven along by a driving force which is not fully integrated.

MARS TO NEPTUNE

Conjunct: the driving force is confused but idealistic
Here influences from beyond the threshold have an effect on the driving force, causing confusion about one's goals, so the person is easily discouraged, through not having enough assertiveness. But this person feels the urge to serve the world, and also has an inclination to spiritual ideas.

Negative: defeatist, self-deluded, and obsessive. In romance there is the possibility of deceit.

Trine: the driving force is either weak or idealistic
With this aspect, in a fine chart, higher ideals can be pulsing within the core drive of this person and these can be put into life. But otherwise, this person's assertiveness is weakened, and they become easily discouraged; so confrontations are avoided. There is often a lack of energy due to these conditions. But in a fine chart, this person has the will for humanitarian activity.

Sextile: the driving force is spiritually ennobled
This aspect signifies the practical idealist, whose personal drive absorbs and brings into action their higher self's impulses. For here spiritual realms can bring about a high, spiritualizing influence in the driving force. Some kind of spiritual protection exists around a person with this aspect. (One client changed lanes on busy highway, for no reason, just prior to an accident occurring in the previous lane.) In particular, there is protection against deception and fraud. This person is humanitarian, and also has a sense of rhythm. In romance, one can find positive qualities in the partner, and there is an interest in being socially active.

MARS TO NEPTUNE continued

Square: the driving force is obscured by unwholesome influences

With this aspect, negative influences from beyond a kind of threshold have an effect on the driving force, obscuring the driving force. This leads to confusion, so strange impulses often manifest in the core driving energies, There is some danger from involvement in unwholesome psychic or occult adventures, and the sexual drive needs refining. This person can feel discouraged or unworthy, and can be an escapist. Underhanded, deceitful actions are common, and generally not being upfront with others is likely.

More negative: in a poor chart, if Neptune or Mars have further negative aspects, then mental instability, in particular, psychoses can arise, and stealthy criminal acts can occur, perhaps even a self-destructive tendency.

Opposition: the driving force is distorted and weakened

With this aspect, pernicious psychic-spiritual influences (from beyond a kind of threshold in human consciousness), have an effect on the driving force, distorting its functionality. There will be a life-lesson for this person in regard to deception; the houses of these planets show the areas where acute discernment is needed, to avoid being deceived.

This person can be subject to opposition from others. Dubious, negative people have a detrimental effect. This person must avoid narcotic drugs, as these have a potently negative impact, allowing unpleasant spiritual influences to become dominant. There is an unclear motivation in regard to what one undertakes with others.

MARS TO NEPTUNE   continued

Inconjunct: a weakened driving force impedes social interaction

Here the driving force is undermined, preventing one from being self-assertive. This person feels too tired to try to meet a challenge, thus becoming defeatist or escapist. Wrong social dynamics are invoked, such as becoming associated with inappropriate people, and not seeing one's actual significance to others, who can then take advantage of this. Medically, this aspect indicates that the immune system is weak.

MARS TO PLUTO

Conjunct: the libido & driving force are too empowered

Mars is the source of the vehemence with which we do anything, (which we have been calling the 'driving force') and Pluto empowers whatever it affects. So all these Mars-Pluto aspects will intensify a person's driving force. Here the Conjunction bestows lots of energy, courage, and a strong competitiveness, but also a disregard for the rules and regulations of society. It also causes strong desires and a strong personal will. There is a determination to attain one's goals, and intolerance for any restrictions. Women with this aspect need a very good connection to their father, otherwise this can result in an aversion to men.

<u>Negative</u>: This person could use sexuality to achieve their goals, and be too forceful in general terms, making others feel threatened.

Sextile: the driving force is empowered

Here Pluto energies empower the Mars driving forces in a pleasant way. So this person is very upfront, with strong desires and high energy levels. This person is hard-working and becomes very determined in projects once they are under-way, getting very involved in them.

Trine: the driving force is empowered but ennobled

Here Pluto energies empower the Mars driving forces, and direct them towards ethical intentions. This aspect allows the finer Mars energies to be empowered, so this results in a stronger social conscience manifesting in the intentions. It indicates an ambitious person, with strong desires and high self-confidence, but one who is good at co-operative work, and who offers their energy to help society because they feel an inner obligation to be of help in the world.

MARS TO PLUTO   continued

Square: the driving force is aggressively empowered
Here Pluto energies empower the Mars driving forces but in a way that impels them towards aggressive behaviour. This aspect results in a nature which is too self-centred and thus forceful; the person is aggressive with strong desires. This person wants to be in charge and works hard, but can attract aggression, even violence.

Opposition: the driving force is very aggressively empowered
Here Pluto energies empower the Mars driving forces but in a way that impels them towards intensely aggressive behaviour. This aspect is a major cause of the <u>choleric temperament</u>, creating difficulty in co-operating with others. This aspect results in strong desires, and a feeling of being discriminated against. Powerful enemies can arise, leading to formidable opposition, because this person is unintentionally setting off this antagonism through the presence in their own aura of militant anger. This is a very intense, determined person who can scare away possible colleagues and friends. The father relationship is very important here. The driving forces can get out of control. If other negative Mars aspects exist in the horoscope, this can lead to anti-social or criminal behaviour.

Inconjunct: a strong but repressed driving force invokes opposition
Here Pluto energies empower Mars' driving forces, but at the same time, thwarting their ability to manifest. This aspect leads to a strong determination to do what one desires, but also to experiencing strong opposing forces from other people. This is caused by the way this person sets out to do something. But this dynamic could manifest in reverse; one may become the victim of a dominating person oneself.

MARS TO ASCENDANT

Conjunct: the driving force defends the personal self
This aspect intensifies the driving force, but in a self-centred way. This creates a person with a strong determination to get their way and who is, daring, and very competitive (who may also be courageous). But they are however also, quarrelsome, choleric and sports oriented.

Trine: the driving force affirms the personal self
This interaction of the ego's reflection point (the Ascendant) and Mars, intensifies the driving force, in a somewhat self-centred way. This leads to a person with a strong determination to get their way, and their own beliefs are very important to them. There is enthusiasm, but more self-discipline is needed.

Sextile: the driving force enhances the personal self
This interaction of the ego's reflection point (the Ascendant) and Mars, intensifies the driving force, in a noble way. With this aspect, one is a very independent and self-reliant person with much self-confidence, yet able to work in a group. This person can express their own will, perhaps diplomatically, and knows how to utilize their strengths and weaknesses. This person seeks a definite purpose to their actions.

Square: the driving force makes the personal self defensive
This interaction of the ego's reflection point (the Ascendant) and Mars, constricts the driving force, in a frustrating way. So this person, classically projecting out onto society their own inner problem, feels that the world is opposing them, blocking their initiative and desires. So they feel that they can only get their own needs met by causing dislike and antagonism from others.

MARS   TO   ASCENDANT continued

Opposition: the driving force produces an aggressive personality
This interaction of the ego's reflection point (the Ascendant) and Mars suppresses the driving force, in a potently frustrating way. This aspect is a major cause of the <u>choleric temperament</u>. So this person is competitive, aggressive, and very defensive regarding other people, and will become aggressive if annoyed or blocked by someone. Or this dynamic can occur in reverse: he or she attracts aggressive people into their life, who then ensnare this person into aggressive interaction.

Inconjunct: the driving force makes the personality abrasive
This interaction of the ego's reflection point (the Ascendant) and Mars, restricts the driving force, in a frustrating way. So with this aspect, the person lives with an awareness that their capacity to do what they want to do, is being restricted, in a way that they cannot quite understand or overcome. This leads to an irritated, aggressive personality who guards his or her social space jealously,

MARS TO MIDHEAVEN

Conjunct: the driving force makes the personal self socially very assertive
The Midheaven point is where the self has a major social interface. In this aspect, the Mars energies, that create the driving force in the person, intensify his or her personality. This is a person who must do what they want, and who reacts strongly to any hindrances, and who plans a career already as a child. This person is usually athletic, and very career oriented.

Trine: the driving force makes the personal self socially more confident
With this aspect the sense of self in its social context, enhances the driving force in a socially acceptable way. So this person has a strong sense of self, and hence self-confidence and vitality. There is the pressing need to be independent, so this person dislikes relying on others for anything.

Sextile: the driving force makes the personal self more socially skilled
With this aspect, the sense of self in its social context, enhances the driving force in a socially positive way. The person's enhanced sense of themselves in this aspect is not ego-centric. This person can work well in a group situation, assuming that the initiative allows him or her to be true to their own nature and purposes. There is self-confidence, and the need to have a definite purpose in life.

Square: the driving force creates an abrasive, martial personality
With this aspect the sense of self within its social context, is not aligned to the driving force of their soul. The result is inner conflict and a socially detrimental attitude. This person's driving force tends to impede his or her own intentions. There is a tendency to be

MARS TO MIDHEAVEN continued

Square, continued
dominating and aggressive; this is partly due to a feeling of inner disempowerment and partly from the intensified ego-centric nature of their libido. This person resents people in authority.

Opposition: the driving force disrupts the personal self's social context
With this aspect, the core driving energies in the personality cause the sense of self, in its social context, to be seriously at odds with society. There is an ego-centric drive that is compulsive, leading to rash and choleric actions. This problem is moderated by any positive Mars aspects in the horoscope and by good parenting during childhood.

Inconjunct: the driving force leads to a self-assertive personality
Similar to the Opposition, with this aspect the core driving energies in the personality greatly hinder the capacity of the sense of self to relate to its own social context. So this person is too assertive, too rebellious, and needs an intense energy release as in sport.

JUPITER TO SATURN

Conjunction: clear thinking and intuition interact
This aspect occurs as a possible feature in a horoscope only every 21 years. It can bring a concern with social issues, and possibly a deep thinking capacity. But Jupiter is outgoing and optimistic, whereas Saturn instils caution and invokes karmic trials. The effect of this conjunction depends upon the over-all significance of these two planets in the chart. In a good chart, Jupiter's optimism and clarity of thinking can enhance Saturn's intuitive guidance. In a more difficult chart, these two dynamics cancel each other out to some extent, creating uncertainty, and inner stress. In a fine chart it greatly enhances an inner capacity to be guided in one's path through life (karma-sensing).

Trine: clear thinking & an intuitive sensing harmonize
With this aspect, clear thinking and an intuitive sense of one's life-path reinforce each other, leading to enhanced common sense, even wise insights, as well as patience and perseverance. Spiritual ideals and karmically pragmatic aspirations blend together. This person can be conscientious and hard-working, leading to a successful career life.

Sextile: insightful thinking and intuitive awareness are enhanced
This aspect brings out very fine qualities in both planets. The person will be enthusiastic and optimistic, but also gifted with an inner sense of the right steps to take in life (their karma). In a fine chart, there is high integrity, and interest in spiritual ideas, or at least in social issues. Generally, it leads to a very large general knowledge, a capacity for hard work, and good comprehension of data, and someone who is skilled in planning. Vocationally this indicates teaching skills, and a person who is patient and can work well alone.

JUPITER TO SATURN   continued

Opposition: Unwise thinking and blocked intuition undermine confidence

With this aspect Jupiter's clear thinking and Saturn's intuitive sense of one's life-path mutually block each other. So there is inner conflict and contradiction, and a lack of confidence. These lead to actions which don't yield worthwhile results and take the person into a path that is not helpful to their purpose in life. But in some cases, such challenging aspects prompt the person to seek out demanding situations, in which they can successfully develop a good common sense and some intuitive sensing of their path in life. (R. Hand notes that in romance, one can easily ignore a less than total commitment, but gets very hurt if one is then rejected.)

Square: Unwise thinking and blocked intuitions reduces confidence and conscientiousness

Similar to the Opposition, with this aspect Jupiter's clear thinking is muddled and so are Saturn's intuitive promptings. These promptings are embedded in an appreciation of the over-all social implications of one's decisions (i.e., will). If these promptings not heeded, then ethical dilemmas occur. There is also a lack of the famous Saturnine capacity for perseverance. Here the person has an inner confusion, and struggles to sense what their life context is. They can miss out on opportunities because their will (which is an intuitive faculty) is obscured on a deeper level. Another core Saturnine element, that of being dutiful and conscientious, is often weak.

Inconjunct: Blocked insights and intuitions reduce confidence and conscientiousness

This aspect seems to be similar to the Opposition, where Jupiter's clear thinking and Saturn's intuitive promptings about of one's life-path mutually block each other. Indecisiveness is common with this. (R. Pelletier notes that an inherent guilt feeling exists with this.)

JUPITER   TO   URANOS

Conjunct: the thinking is psychically sensitized
This aspect leads to a very strong imagination, and can also include a psychic tendency. In a fine chart there is an interest in mystical or esoteric ideas. These people are often idealistic and optimist.

Negative: this includes daydreaming, gambling and escapism.

Sextile: Thinking is enhanced by psychic sensitivity
This aspect creates acute powers of discernment. But in addition this person has the Jupiter wisdom that allows them to work properly with their intuitions. They are curious, optimistic and foresighted regarding the future and seek knowledge; they are also inventive. In a fine chart, can the mind can have almost an element of genius. These people have many ideas, and in a fine chart, self-knowledge is important. This aspect enables a person to see and utilize opportunities which others may not even see. There can be an unusual life with unexpected events. Vocationally, teaching is a strongly indicated.

Trine: Thinking is insightful and socially ethical
With this aspect, these people seek a fair deal for everyone, and want freedom in ideas and in codes of behaviour. They are sanguine regarding new places and new ideas. In a fine chart this person's thinking can rise to being wise and insightful, as fine Uranian energies create an intuitive capacity in the mind. This person is alert to opportunities because they can think outside the square, and are quite ethically inclined. (This aspect often occurs in combination with an Aquarian south lunar node.)

Square: the thinking is rebellious & socially disruptive
Here the potentially insightful thinking of Jupiter is replaced by immature and unwise attitudes, and through this, negative Uranian

JUPITER TO URANOS continued

Square, continued
energies are invoked. This leads to an unruly urge for so-called 'freedom'. This creates an obstinate tendency, so this person opposes social norms, to the extent of dogmatic opposition to the established order. There are unusual travel experiences, and poor social judgment about possible companions.

Opposition: the thinking is often socially isolating
Here the potential for insightful ideas from Jupiter is replaced by a self-centred mindset, and through this, negative Uranian energies are invoked. These enhance the ego-centric attitudes, leading to difficulties in social interaction, as there is a self-righteous or self-congratulating tendency with regard to proposals and ideas in general. The mind is open to new ideas, but not in a mature way.

Inconjunct: social attitudes are obscured by a ungrounded freedom urge
Similar to the Square, here the potential for insightful ideas from Jupiter are absent and instead this, negative Uranian energies are invoked. With this aspect, there is difficulty in integrating oneself socially. This is the social reformer whose ideas often lack insightfulness. They are the 'dreamer of dreams' for society, whose yearnings are distorted by their own sense of being unfree.

JUPITER TO NEPTUNE

Conjunct: Thinking can have a psychic quality
With this aspect, there is very often a clairvoyance, and possibly also some healing capacity; or at least, an awareness of the spiritual reality of the world. If the spiritual awareness is lacking, then there is an escapism tendency and a very strong fantasy life. But if there is an awareness of spiritual realities, there could be deceptive psychic experiences. This person is usually naïve in regard to other people, and experience considerable problems through being deceived. They can easily be tempted to 'bite off more than they can chew'.

<u>Negative</u> manifestations are gambling, and being subject to delusions about life.

Sextile: wise insights and psychic sensitivity
Here the Jupiter energies create the capacity for wisdom and this is integrated into the positive Neptunian influence that creates seership, or a strong inner spiritual awareness. This aspect indicates sensitivity to others' needs, being socially aware and having high ideals, yet not seeing the world through rose-coloured glasses.

<u>Negative</u>: If these planets were elsewhere badly aspected, then there can be an indulgence in fantasy, and personal relationships may be subject to illusions.

Trine: wisdom: intuitive assessment and reasoned judgment harmonize
Here the Jupiter energies at their highest level create the capacity for wisdom and this is integrated into a very positive Neptunian influence that creates seership, or at least a spiritual awareness. This very special aspect means that the person is spiritually aware, idealistic, unselfish, and humanitarian. In general, this indicates an evolved person, with interest in esoteric ideas. Obviously, in romance, a partner will be chosen on the basis of their interest in spirituality. A karmic blessing in the form of meeting a wise person, or encountering books that provide deeper spiritual wisdom is likely.

JUPITER TO NEPTUNE   continued

Square: the thinking is deceptive and ungrounded
With this aspect, the clear thinking of Jupiter is blocked and the mind is influenced by negative Neptunian energies which induce a self-deceiving fantasy state of mind. The person is an escapist; subject to unrealistic dreams and ideals and can be quite gullible. This person can also exaggerate, be too self-indulgent and yearn for the bizarre. The logical assessment capacity is obscured by a kind of neon-light glow, so these people are liable to be deceived or to deceive others.

Opposition: the thinking is ungrounded and suspicious
With this aspect, the clear thinking of Jupiter is distorted as the mind is influenced by negative Neptunian energies which distort the mental processes. With this aspect the mind is very clouded. There are subjective ideas and delusions concerning other people, and suspicion about other peoples' motives about oneself. This person is an idealist, but can be caught up in improbable schemes, and make promises which they can not keep. With regard to romance, there is the same unrealistic idealism, and they find being let down by a partner very hard to endure.

Inconjunct: the thinking is ungrounded and unclear
This aspect is similar to the Opposition; the clear thinking from Jupiter is distorted by negative Neptunian energies which distort the mental processes. So this aspect leads to the impractical thinker who must learn how to handle the real world, but who can become bitter and an escapist in the struggle.

JUPITER   TO   PLUTO

Conjunct: the mind's focus is on the world
Here, Pluto strengthens Jupiter's influence which enables clear thinking; the mindset then gets a wider and deeper focus. So with this aspect in the horoscope, there is a strong intention to achieve, and to help change the world for the better. In a fine chart, this could lead to a longing for spiritual experiences. In romance, this person admires a partner with strength of character, and who has social awareness.

Sextile: thinking is ethical and assists social change
Here, Pluto strengthens the capacity of Jupiter's energies, giving more clarity to thinking. This person strives to help any social group, and is a catalyst for change.

Trine: the thinking is ethical and has wisdom
Here, Pluto strengthens the capacity of Jupiter's energies to uplift thinking towards insightfulness, even wisdom. With this aspect, one sets high standards, has a good sense of morality and is a patient, sensible type of reformer.

Opposition: the thinking is self-focussed & socially disruptive
Here, Pluto blocks the capacity of Jupiter's energies to uplift thinking towards having insights, in regard to others, and to society in general. This can easily lead to fanaticism about ideas, especially ideas concerning social reform. People may then oppose any initiative this person pushes forward.

JUPITER TO PLUTO   continued

Square: the thinking seeks to dominate others
Here, Pluto blocks the capacity of Jupiter's energies to uplift thinking towards insightfulness, and makes oneself the centre of attention when it comes to having ideas. So this aspect creates a strong but self-centred will to succeed, and the urge to be able to influence people. Consequently opposition is experienced from anyone who feels unfree or pushed aside.

Inconjunct: the thinking seeks to dominate others
The Inconjunct is often similar in its effect to the Opposition, and here Pluto again blocks the capacity of Jupiter's energies to give thinking a capacity for insights, and makes one's own ideas central in any discussion.

JUPITER TO MIDHEAVEN

Conjunct: the thinking assists an ethical will
This person is ambitious, but in a humanitarian way, with global interests and concerns. There are high ethics, and interest in ideas that expand the mind out beyond the material world, such as religious to themes or spiritual ideas.

Sextile: the mind invokes goodwill and friends
Here with this aspect, there is a good alignment of the person's core social dynamics (the Midheaven point) and Jupiter. This brings real insights about his or her social dynamics. So this person can encounter and work well with people who help them in life. The soul is wholesome, with a good sense of social responsibility, so people trust this person.

Trine: thinking seeks ways to be of service
Here with this aspect, there is a very good alignment of the person's core social dynamics (the Midheaven point) and Jupiter. This aspect leads to a very positive attitude, with a social conscience in regard to their duties. This person can work towards their goal without infringing on others, and has no problem with authority. They can set themselves a fulfilling goal, and keep busy working on it.

Square: the thinking is self-centred and ambitious
Here with this aspect, there is a misalignment of the person's core social dynamics (the Midheaven point) and their thinking (Jupiter). Instead of a breadth of mind, there is instead a narrow, ego-centric mindset. This person has an ambitious attitude, which is blind to the needs of others, and undervalues other people.

JUPITER TO MIDHEAVEN continued

Opposition: the mind looks to its childhood for security

Here there is a no interaction of the person's core social dynamics (the Midheaven point) with the clear thinking of Jupiter. So with this aspect, this person finds it difficult to step into a mature social dynamic. Their family is important as a refuge; and childhood memories are a source of comfort. A sense of inner constriction exists, as a reflection of this internal blockage.

Inconjunct: poor understanding of one's social context

Here with this aspect, there is a poor alignment of the person's core social dynamics (the Midheaven point) and the clear thinking of Jupiter.. So, the person feels socially awkward, and struggles to properly integrate themselves into their social context.

JUPITER TO ASCENDANT

Conjunct: The thinking is flexible and ethical
This aspect brings the person (their ego-sense) into a good relationship with Jupiter's capacity to give a broad, optimistic mindset. The result is a person whose attitudes are generous, helpful, honest, optimistic, and sanguine. There is enjoyment of travel, and good ethics.

Sextile: the thinking is affirming and positive
This aspect brings the person (their ego-sense) into a very positive relationship with Jupiter's capacity to give a broad, optimistic mindset. This aspect creates an open-minded, flexible thinker who is a positive type, someone who can use opportunities as they arise.

Trine: an enquiring and jovial mind
Here the trine brings about a very similar result to the Sextile, leading to someone who is an open-minded and flexible thinker interested in learning, but also expansive in a good-humoured way.

Square: thinking is self-centred and dislikes boundaries
This aspect indicates that the sense of self (the ego-sense, represented by the Ascendant) has little capacity, when thinking, to access more enlightened, insightful attitudes (Jupiter's higher capacity). The result is narrow thinking, and a self-centred attitude with an inclination to extravagant, and a sense of being restricted somehow by life. The influence of a parent in this person's life can be excessive, as this person is often too happy to just coast along as a replica of someone else. This person has to become empowered by acting out of their true self, (one client had to stand up for their own truth by struggling against the influence of a tyrannical father).

JUPITER TO ASCENDANT   continued

Opposition: thinking is self-centred and dislikes restrictions

This aspect indicates that the ego (or the sense of self) represented by the Ascendant, when thinking, has very little capacity to experience enlightened, insightful ideas about life (Jupiter's better capacity). In essence, a narrow, unwise, self-centred thinking is the result. But negative Jupiter influences are the mildest of any planetary negative; so the result is a self-centred person who cruises along, attaching themselves to other people whose energies will be of use, but in a sanguine, unobtrusive way. There is a naïve wish for personal freedom in regard to work duties and to forming deeper relations to other people, as well as a tendency to extravagance.

Inconjunct: the intellect is unaware of others and insecure

This aspect, very similar to the Opposition, indicates that the sense of self (the ego-sense), represented by the Ascendant, in regard to thinking and attitudes in general, is narrow, unwise, and self-centred. This person is extravagant, naïve and undisciplined. They will 'bite off more than they can chew', in regard to projects and ideals. Their thinking expands into vague large ideas, leading to plans that cannot be properly completed. Or this aspect causes the body to have an expansive frame or to easily gain weight.

SATURN TO URANOS

Conjunct: the will has a weak sense of purpose
Saturn is conjunct to Uranos only every 45 years. But this aspect when it occurs, leads to some inner tension, due to indecisiveness about whether to go forwards or to stop. So this person can make an impulsive break from a project that they have committed to, as the orderliness and coherent sense of purpose from Saturn is countered by the unpredictable impulses of Uranos.

Sextile: an active will to seek knowledge
This aspect is very positive; it invokes the positive (future) Uranian energies. It creates a deep respect for knowledge, and the capacity to use it. There is an inherent interest in truth, to be free from ignorance. This person is efficient and disciplined, but could arouse antagonism through knowing and sizing up a situation ahead of others. There is a wish to make changes, but not to disruptively upset traditions or patterns of behaviour. So idealism is balanced with pragmatism. Vocationally this aspect indicates teaching.

Trine: an active will to be personally challenged
With this aspect, one enjoys complex mental challenges at work, and the will can push the person on, almost beyond the body's capacity.

Square: the will is frustrated, feels disempowered
Here there is an inner tension causing outbursts of anger, because there is a conflict between freedom and duty. So this person can be quite unruly, but can then be dutiful and obedient. The inner disempowerment is projected outwards, creating resentment of authority. In romance, this person seeks a partner who will give approval of their being (especially if the south lunar node is in Leo).

SATURN TO URANOS continued

Opposition: a frustrated will vacillates between social upheaval, and social acceptance

Here, the coherent sense of one's life purpose, from Saturn, is weakened by negative, unpredictable impulses from Uranos. So this person is caught in an inner contradiction, at times conforming and working out of a sense of duty, but at other times feeling the urge to independence.

Inconjunct: the will is frustrated and finds security in the past

Here, the coherent sense of one's life purpose, from Saturn, is obscured by negative, unpredictable energies from Uranos. As with the Opposition, there is stress from the conflict between freedom (or what one views as freedom) and what is understood to be one's duties.

SATURN TO NEPTUNE

Conjunction: the will is intuitive even idealistic
This aspect merges a psychic, or spiritually-aware consciousness with the subtle intuitive sensing of one's life purposes. This results in a capacity for valuable insights; insights which can be integrated in the reality of this person's life.

Sextile: a high social ethic is present in the will
Here the intuitive promptings about one's life purposes (or karma-sensing) are strengthened and refined by positive Neptune energies. So this person has great self-discipline, and can go without things when seeking a higher goal, and is able to integrate higher ideals with pragmatic reality. There is a good objectivity about life and there may be interest in a spiritual path. The person is humanitarian, and interested in social work. In romance, that partner is attractive who affirms this person's social goals.

Trine: social ethics & spiritual ideals are in the will
Here the intuitive promptings about one's life purposes (or karma-sensing) are imbued with a spiritual awareness, and thus ennobled by positive Neptune energies. This is a very fine aspect. The person is very reality based, and can develop the impulse for renunciation, especially to achieve spiritual goal. There is a commitment to high personal spirituality and a real interest in helping other people.

Square: confused intentions and a distorted mind
Here the intuitive promptings about one's life purposes (or karma-sensing) of Saturn, are blocked, and replaced by distorted ideas from negative Neptune energies. This aspect causes a serious distortion between reality and one's own world-view, so people with this aspect can feel that the world is opposed to them (paranoia). This leads to unrealistic expectations and goals, or to incorrectly assessing the reality of a situation. (One client found it very hard to know if she was still dreaming or now awake.) This aspect also makes a person suspicious of others, leading to an anxiety tendency. People with this

SATURN TO NEPTUNE   continued

Square, continued
aspect need to avoid illicit drugs even more than other people, as these can activate negative psychic influences with very negative outcomes. A similar outcome is possible from allopathic medicines, too. There is a lack of confidence, and difficulties in social interaction. Being involved in 'occult' practices could result in a kind of obsessive condition. But any positive angles to Saturn or Neptune in the chart will help to moderate this.

Opposition: the will's intuitive function is blocked, causing insecurity and phobias
This aspect occurs only every 35 years. Similar to the Square, the intuitive promptings about one's life purposes (or karma-sensing) of Saturn, are blocked, and replaced by distorted impressions from negative Neptune energies. This aspect makes this person feel that the world is a dangerous, frightening place, and they become suspicious of others. There is a fear of failure, and relationships can be very unpleasant, as this person will often be taken advantage of. In strongly negative circumstances, phobias are strong and possibly criminal tendencies may be present. Negative Neptune energies permeate the subconscious Saturn influences, which underlie the will and hence our the limbs (the organs of our will). This leads to sleep-walking (one client would get up and clean her teeth at night, whilst fast asleep).

Inconjunct: the will's intuitive function is blocked, causing insecurity, and inner confusion
Similar to the Opposition, the intuitive promptings about one's life purposes (or karma-sensing) of Saturn, are blocked, and replaced by distorted impressions from negative Neptune energies. With this aspect, fantasy becomes a nervous condition, with fear and irrational anxieties (one client reported panic attacks that had no known cause). Psychosomatic illnesses are possible, and also a psychotic tendency is possible. Such inner distortions may cause illness later in life. There may be also a martyr complex, so there is the chance of being utilized by a spiritual or religious society or movement.

SATURN TO PLUTO

Conjunct: a resolute, intense will
This aspect only occurs every 33 years. Saturn's influences lead to semi-conscious sensing of our will and our own life-path. Pluto here strengthens these influences. This person's will can be fired up to change the world in some way. The Saturnine capacity for endurance and determination is also strengthened.

Trine: a will for orderliness and to find success
Pluto here strengthens the Saturnine capacity for endurance, and makes the person a hard worker, and quite formidable because of a strong will to succeed. This person is very controlled, a serious type, well-structured and informed. He or she has an inner sense of where they are going in their life, and precisely how to get there.

Sextile: the will is self-disciplined and plans ahead
With this aspect, the person is orderly, can endure difficult times, makes inner growth happen and has self-discipline. This aspect confers good self-discipline, and this person likes to plan and organize their career. But they might find it difficult to tolerate shortcomings in others.

Square: the will resists the common good
Here Saturn's influences, active in the semi-conscious sensing of the wisdom (or karma) behind our own life-path, is blocked by Pluto, and can be degraded into a ruthless self-centred will; or at least it can lead to a cold and hard person. This person is usually a bad loser who avoids community and social obligations. They seek to get control at work, as status is a high priority, and they tend to have resentment of those with success. The attitude that 'the world is against me' is common.

SATURN TO PLUTO continued

Opposition: the will invokes domination by others
Here Saturn's influences, active in the semi-conscious sensing of the wisdom (or karma) behind our own life-path, is blocked by Pluto. Their underlying will is rigid, self-centred, resistant to ethical uplift and can invoke power plays of some kind.

Inconjunct: the will's intuitive function is blocked, causing rigidity, and inner obstacles
Here similar to the Opposition, Saturn's influences, active in the semi-conscious sensing of the wisdom (or karma) behind our own life-path, is somewhat blocked by Pluto. This person feels that they face opposition from the world and must work very hard to just keep things running smoothly. The soul has a kind of inner sclerosis, hence resistance to change.

SATURN TO ASCENDANT

Conjunct: the will is dutiful and accepts burdens
This person is mature beyond their years, and has responsibilities early in life. They may find it hard to relax, and possibly are a worrier. They are reserved, very reliable, conservative and shy, needing more confidence.

Trine: the will is reality-oriented
Here Saturn's subtle promptings about one's life purposes are assimilated by the self (its secondary aspect, the Ascendant). This aspect allows this inner awareness to flow on into one's life; making this person a realist, a pragmatist and a hard worker.

Sextile: the will is conscientious
Here Saturn's subtle promptings about one's life purposes are assimilated by the self (its secondary aspect, the Ascendant). With this aspect, one is a reliable loyal friend, a serious type, and a practical person. In a fine chart, this person has a strong sense of ethics.

Square: a frustrated will resents restrictions
All the negative aspects between Saturn and the Ascendant indicate a weakened capacity of the will to respond to the self (which is reflected in the Ascendant). This aspect creates the very independent person who can show this in two ways. One way is to be openly rebelling against authority, and too sanguine; the other way is to appear conservative, but attract friends who are rebellious. The drive to freedom is suppressed, so they seek out others with this freedom.
But people with this aspect are disturbed by social injustice, sometimes very strongly so.

SATURN TO ASCENDANT continued

Opposition: poor karma-sensing impedes social interaction

A person with this aspect often becomes a hermit and must learn to form social contacts. This person may invoke harsh people into their life. Often this person seeks older persons in their life as friends (or as a partner).

Inconjunct: the will lacks an inner guidance

This creates the solemn, serious type who lacks self-confidence.

SATURN TO MIDHEAVEN

Conjunct: the will is duty-bound
This creates an excessively strong sense of duty and an inflexible mind, but a respect for authority, and a capacity to persevere. Vocationally, this person has an aptitude to be a teacher.

Sextile: the will is disciplined
This aspect creates a very good inner discipline, but the person can be a loner.

Trine: the will is disciplined and self-focussed
With this aspect, one is very orderly and systematic, but also a loner. In later life this person retreats into an unusual social group.

Square: the will has barriers to societal interaction
This creates a withdrawn person, who feels that others impede their freedom. They need to resist the 'hermit' tendency.

Opposition: the ego-sense is blind to the social nexus
This aspect creates the hermit, whether outwardly in life or just inwardly. This person feels inwardly empty, and needs much emotional support; they make themselves very busy with others to deal with this problem.

Inconjunct:
a hesitant will which fears societal interaction
Similar to the Opposition, the person has difficulty with authority figures, and reacts to the lack of sensing an inner guidance by creating a very structured world around them, nervous about social interaction.

URANOS TO NEPTUNE
(occasional, slowly changing aspects)

Conjunct: psychically sensing the threshold
Neptune is a kind of doorway or threshold between the normal mindset and the paranormal, so for psychic souls this aspect enhances their sensitivity. But for others this aspect creates an unconventional attitude, even a somewhat eccentric mindset.

Trine: open to a psychic sensing of the threshold
This angle only occurred from 1939-43. R. Hand states that it gives the ability to deal with psychic experiences, and an interest in esoteric ideas.

Square: ungrounded interest in unconventional ideas
This angle only occurred from 1953-56. R. Hand states that it leads to people with strong interest in new social ideas and ideals, but who have an unrealistic attitude about these.

URANOS TO ASCENDANT

Conjunct: an uneasy seeking of inner freedom
This aspect of Uranos to the ego's reflection, (the Ascendant) results in an unconventional, free spirit, who may also be quite tense, as the freedom urge is not integrated fully.

Sextile: a well-integrated urge for inner freedom
This aspect leads to an outspoken person, with their own ideas, which they defend and push. They also adopt new ideas, and generally are good communicators.

Trine: the freedom urge dominates
This aspect creates the rebel, who is sanguine and adaptable.

Square: a frustrated freedom urge
This creates the very independent rebel, who is sanguine and creative. But this person may not be able to manifest their creativity properly and thus seeks out others who can.

Opposition: a non-integrated urge for freedom
This aspect also causes an urge for freedom. But this person attracts unreliable, uncommitted and odd partners.

Inconjunct: a destructive urge for freedom of action
With this, there is an urge for freedom which is not integrated into the self-sense, so there is conflict for this person with their environs. This person needs challenges both for a hobby and at work. Relationships are harmed by an excess of this need. A tendency to accidents can also be present.

URANOS TO MIDHEAVEN

(The brief notes following here owe much to the outstanding books of Robert Hand and Robert Pelletier; see Recommended Books list)

Conjunct: being a free person is a key social focus

This aspect leads to a very individualist type, and sometimes they play the joker.

Sextile: seeks freedom socially but responsibly

With this, the person is strongly individualistic, quite original, but often a loner, yet someone who can commit to a higher or unusual belief.

Trine: a free person personally and socially

With this, the person wants few possessions, is sanguine and very much an individual.

Square: a socially negative freedom urge

This aspect leads to the eccentric, negatively suggestible person. They usually get right away from their childhood home.

Opposition: a socially negative urge for freedom

The main feature here is a strong need for emotional freedom, without regard as to how it relates to people around one.

Inconjunct: a socially negative urge for freedom

The main quality here is that the person is a rebel.

NEPTUNE TO ASCENDANT

Conjunct: sensitive but inwardly confused
This aspect creates people who seek to understand themselves via other peoples' reactions. There is a tendency to feel a lack of self worth, and also an excessive sensitivity to the environs. These people can be psychic, yet not in touch with their own yearnings. They can be drawn to get involved in acting.

Sextile: psychic aware & compassionate
With this aspect, the person is very sensitive to other people, and may have a psychic tendency. There is a natural interest in helping people. As a child there is a strong fantasy life.

Trine: spirituality and awareness of spirit
With this, Neptune's higher spiritual influences are integrated into the ego, making the person imaginative, sensitive, and often psychic. This person can also seek out wise people.

Square: ego-sense undermined by inner confusion
This aspect leads to people who are easily misunderstood, and very sensitive to others' feelings. There can be a martyr tendency, and a lack of self-confidence, causing them to withdraw from challenges. They are too reserved regarding authority figures.

Opposition: social interaction is undermined by inner confusion
With this there is much confusion in relationships, or it may cause a search for a wise teacher, but this can lead to unwise New Age groups and guru worship.

NEPTUNE TO ASCENDANT   continued

Inconjunct: the ego-sense is undermined by an inner vulnerability
This aspect leads to a feeling that one has to compromise with others to succeed socially, and hence there can be a resentment to people. Possibly there is also a martyr complex, and medically, very often an acute sensitivity to chemicals.

NEPTUNE TO MIDHEAVEN

(The brief notes following here owe much to the outstanding books of Robert Hand and Robert Pelletier; see Recommended Books list)

Conjunct: unclear threshold impressions create social uncertainty

With this aspect the person is very sensitive but confusion is caused by the impressions they receive. They can be depressive, or at least have a tendency to be discouraged. At its most positive it causes psychic, religious or mystical interests; very often eastern mysticism attracts these people.

Sextile: spiritual intuitions create social vulnerability

With this, the person is passive, solitary, and a dreamer who usually has a spiritual-esoteric awareness. They are too open to others' feelings and this leads to shyness; there can be a recluse tendency.

Trine: spiritual intuitions heightens social conscience

This very positive aspect creates the idealistic person who dislikes possessions, but is very caring. They often like to care for animals, and are very humanitarian; they are also shy due to a heightened sensitivity.

Square: unclear threshold impressions weakens the ego-sense and creates social confusion

With this aspect, one is very insecure, and suffers from exposure to any negative mindset. This person is very empathetic, and often psychic, but they may misunderstand others' auric energies, becoming confused.

NEPTUNE TO MIDHEAVEN   continued

Opposition: unclear threshold impressions weakens the ego-sense which seeks support

This aspect is similar to the Square. But in addition, one parent may have been too weak to properly guide this person, who may seek a parental type of partner.

Inconjunct: unclear threshold impressions weakens and distracts the ego-sense

With Neptune in this position, the person lacks self-confidence, and is very sensitive to the environs. If they are brought up in negative environs, their soul-life as an adult may be harmed. This adult may seek to explore spiritual metaphysical ideas, to the detriment of their career potential.

PLUTO TO ASCENDANT

Conjunct: intense, fiery ego-sense
This aspect creates a very intense person, who is very serious, and gets over-involved in projects. This person also goes through phases of inner growth, and this causes a choleric tendency. There is a power dynamic here; so there will be either a positive use of this capacity, or domination urges will arise.

Sextile: the ego-sense is acute
With this, there are very intense relationship dynamics, owing to a somewhat charismatic quality in the person. It also indicates a gift for psychology.

Trine: intense ego-sense needs moderation
Pluto in this aspect makes the person stubborn in regard to their own ideas, and has intense emotions, as well as a drive for reform.

Square: an intensified ego-sense which impairs personal interaction
With this aspect Pluto creates negative power dynamics; there are fights over issues of power, and this person is intense, brooding and stubborn.

Opposition: intensified, aggressive ego-sense
Similar to the Square, this aspect leads to power plays, for example in relationships, and thus to conflict. In general this creates an intense personality.

Inconjunct: intense, but non-integrated ego-sense
With this aspect, Plutonian forces cause this person to attract extreme or odd people into their life. This person is also quite competitive; the nature of this tendency and its strength depends on whether there are some negative Mars aspects in the horoscope.

PLUTO TO MIDHEAVEN

(The brief notes following here owe much to the outstanding books of Robert Hand and Robert Pelletier; see Recommended Books list)

Conjunct: the ego-sense is socially dominating

This aspect leads to the person who seeks to make an impact on others. This is an intense person, who has phases of choleric behaviour, or is at least irritable. One parent may be very dominant, and this person may use emotional blackmail in their social interaction.

Sextile: a strong ego-sense, but socially integrated

Here, power dynamics are integrated into the sense of self in a positive way; this person is ambitious, and enjoys advising people.

Trine: a strong ego-sense which gives social & vocational advantages

This aspect also confers positive power dynamics, where the person seeks to use their own resources in order to get ahead, and may also learn many skills.

Square: an intensified ego-sense which impedes social interaction

Pluto in this aspect leads to an ambitious person, whose power dynamics must be moderated by concern for others' freedom. They seek to change and reform the world, but their intentions may not relate to what is actually appropriate for everyone.

Opposition: the ego-sense is weakened by social & subconscious influences

This aspect causes early childhood experiences to have strong impact. Often one parent is very influential. Prejudice and suppressed fears exist in the subconscious soul-life of this person.

PLUTO TO MIDHEAVEN   continued

Inconjunct: socially, the ego-sense attracts domination

In this aspect Pluto's empowering quality is negative to the Midheaven point, which determines one's social dynamics, so people try to dominate this person, who becomes quite secretive, and has a tendency to be under-handed. (The lunar south node in Scorpio can make this stronger.) This person may also become very withdrawn.

****

Chapter Five   The Planets in the Houses
What a planet's position in the houses means.

HOUSE ONE
the sense of self (the ego).

MOON
This placement produces a strong need to be appreciated; this person's basic mood is the need for personal recognition, and he or she is sensitive to every change in the environment. This person constantly goes through phases, and they like having upfront, direct expression of their moods. This person is too affected by moods in personal interaction; they also reflect the mood of others and hence can easily merge into a group of people.

<u>Negative</u>: The mother has an excessively prominent influence. Also the moon here can cause the mysterious phenomenon of sleep-walking, indicating that the residual power of the self (ego) is too weak during sleep, in regard to the influence of lunar energies.

MERCURY
Here Mercury causes the person to have a curious, but rational intelligence. The intellect is quick and flexible, and this person can be a good public speaker.

<u>Negative</u>: A talkative person who is restlessness, with a nervous tendency. If Mercury itself is ill-aspected, then speech defects are likely, or the person may be too egocentric in his or her thinking. This kind of intellectuality can lead to nervous problems.

VENUS
The person is charming, socially-skilled, and very aware of his or her appearance, and consequently can work as an image consultant. The person is attractive physically as well as being tactful, artistic and kind. This person enjoys being kind to others.

HOUSE ONE   continued
the sense of self

VENUS   continued
<u>Negative</u>: Often this causes flattery, sensuality, and laziness, especially regarding helping others or in regard to one's own self-development. There is a need to be liked by all.

SUN
Since the sun represents the sense of self or ego, in the first house it empowers the ego, resulting in the executive type, (unless the sun is ill-aspected). Courage, enthusiasm and energy are all typical qualities here.

<u>Negative</u>: If the Sun itself is ill-aspected by Pluto, Jupiter or Mars there is arrogance and a show-off tendency.

MARS
Mars here leads to the energetic, self-assertive, courageous and daring person. This person enters into activity with a strong determination. This person is determined, has leadership ability, and good recuperative powers. But note these strong personality traits may not manifest at all if there is a substantial block to the person being assertive. This blockage could be due to a predominant south lunar node, inducing a self-undermining resistance to assertiveness. (See the last chapter for more about this.)

<u>Negative</u>: Seeks conflict, is impulsive, aggressive, choleric, reckless and accident prone (especially prone to accidents of the head.)

JUPITER
Here this planet gives frankness, honesty, generosity, and a healthy, vigorous energy. This person likes travel, is often sporty, and possibly has executive potential. Jupiter here often results in a real common sense; and in a fine chart, this person has wisdom.[27]

---

[27] A fine chart is viewed as the indicator of a soul who has evolved well in their past lives.

HOUSE ONE continued
the sense of self

SATURN
In this house Saturn has several significant possibilities. Often this person has to deal with earnest adult issues at an early age. Depending on how this planet is placed in the chart over-all, it can create a feeling of inadequacy, but awareness of this can be a spur to this person becoming an achiever. In a fine horoscope it will bestow an intuitive capacity, and make the person conscientious, with an ability to calmly accept substantial life-challenges. There may be a desire for power or social status, which has to be carefully monitored. Often this person as a youngster appears older than their age, but takes on a younger way of being as the years go by.

Negative:
The person may deny their own yearnings, feel ill-at ease socially, and have a cautious, melancholy tendency.

URANOS
This leads to the unconventional person who must follow their own independent urges, even if these are not soundly based. They are restless, have a great need of freedom, hence somewhat rebellious. They are often creatively innovative (working as inventors or in technology). There is an innovative leadership quality, but they may be highly-strung and need to overcome being wilful.

Negative:
Can be erratic, untactful, autocratic, and demand their freedom in an anti-social way, and be generally rebellious.

NEPTUNE
The refined, gentle, vague, imaginative person; a dreamer who is very sensitive, becoming aware of 'atmospheres'. All this causes mood changes to occur. This person does not really perceive their own personality clearly, nor do others; the result is a glamorous quality, a

HOUSE ONE continued
the sense of self

NEPTUNE continued
charismatic appeal, but based on illusions. There is often a self-confidence problem. Neptune generally weakens the self-sense, hence these people can be swayed by others, and can put on a different persona when they wish to. The capacity for fantasy is strong. They endeavour to avoid causing any hurt to others, this can be due to an inherent empathetic quality which Neptune instils, or it can be due to a strong compassion which this planet brings about in a fine chart.

<u>Negative</u>:
Unreliable and subject to excessive a day-dreaming tendency. The problem of being 'ungrounded' or naïve about life and relationships is acute if Neptune is ill-aspected.

PLUTO
Here Pluto can powerfully enhance the ego-sense, creating an intense person who has an extreme tendency, and who seeks to be empowered in their world. But if Pluto is well-aspected the result is a person who seeks to change their world wisely. There can be sudden endings and equally sudden new beginnings, especially in relationships. Sometimes Pluto here causes an inferiority complex, causing this person to be internally conflicted, lacking confidence; but if their temper is stirred, this person can become very angry.

HOUSE TWO
talents & abilities, and the sense of self-worth.

MOON
Here there is a strong urge to hold on to possessions as well as an impulsive buying tendency. This person likes to keep objects for a long time, and also forms strong attachments to people, and hence become possessive of friends. This person can move between generosity and thriftiness. Women can be significant for this person, in relation to material gain or loss. The challenge here can be the need to establish a permanent set of values in life and also to decide clearly which abilities to use for their career.

Negative:
They may be too possessive or rather selfish regarding objects, or too sanguine regarding their career path.

MERCURY
One gains financially through communications, media, sales skills, or writing. Generally one is business oriented, and can make quick decisions.

SUN
This person can have the ability to attract money and access resources. There is generally a desire for material success, or the ego has a strong focus on really defining life-values, and on clearly perceiving which inherent talents that can lead to a career.

Negative:
This can include clinging to possessions or friends, and struggling to achieve clarity about what talents one possesses, in terms of a vocational choice.

VENUS
A good position for Venus, as here it can bestow financial success, including making the person a 'lucky' winner. Vocations associated with the arts or beauty are favoured.

HOUSE TWO
talents & abilities, and the sense of self-worth.

MARS
This person wants complete control over their own assets; if they see a desirable object, they must get it. Vocations can include engineering or the military or possibly medical surgical work.

Negative:
There can be impulsive buying, and disputes over ownership of objects.

JUPITER
This person is financially fortunate (unless Jupiter is negatively aspected or Saturn is a predominant influence in the horoscope). Or this person can wisely sense what aptitudes they possess and how to use them. This person has a sense of an inner abundance. Here Jupiter can make one likeable, in such a way as to attract money. One earns money in connection with travelling or banking.

Negative:
This person may accumulate possessions for their emotional well-being, or be a showy big spender, or lose money through being too casual about finances.

SATURN
Here the challenge (or life-lesson) is to establish one's true life values ! In a fine horoscope this confers the ability to discern spiritual life-values; and this usually means a vocation which enables this person to be of help to other people. But in a less fortunate horoscope, there are impediments to doing this. Generally there is the will to work hard to gain benefits and obtain possessions.

Negative:
One may be too possessive about possessions or too conservative regarding using one's own resources. If Saturn itself is ill-aspected then there is anxiety about money, or difficulty in choosing a vocation, because one struggles to discern one's own talents and aptitudes.

HOUSE TWO   continued
talents & abilities, and the sense of self-worth.

URANOS
In this house Uranos makes the finances subject to sudden or unpredictable events. One seeks original ways to earn, and spends money impulsively, because the urge to be apparently 'free' is satisfied by spending money. Vocationally, it is better to be a self-employed person.

Negative:
This is a bad position for speculative financial activity.

NEPTUNE
This person can be disinterested in financial security, or have an intuitive sense as to how to access wealth. In a fine chart this gives the ability to sense ways to develop an inner (or outer) resource to become something of value to the world, spiritually.

Negative:
This person may use money naively, and will have to learn to use money or resources wisely. Gambling losses are indicated, and if Neptune is ill-aspected in the chart then severe losses of assets can happen, perhaps by being duped.

PLUTO
In house two Pluto creates intense wishes for possessions, or for a goal to be achieved by really utilizing one's resources. Money and possessions are important because of the power they give. This person must have control over their own assets.

Negative:
One can accumulate many possessions, but if Pluto itself is ill-aspected, there may be substantial losses.

HOUSE THREE
the mind (thinking & speech), also siblings and the local neighbourhood.

MOON
This results in a good sense of what is right or bad for oneself (one client already at 14 years of age, sensed exactly which allopathic medicines they were allergic to). But this person's opinions can vary a lot, reflecting the changeableness of the moon. This person can be gifted at expressing their moods, but in a dialogue may speak (i.e., think) without really consciously responding to the other person. Usually here is a strong connection to siblings, and the needs of the family.

Negative:
The moods influence the thinking too much, and one can be a dreamy, woolly thinker. If there is insecurity, one withdraws into a private world. If the moon is seriously ill-aspected, the mind may be unstable.

MERCURY
The planet of intelligence in house three means that the intelligence is high, and one is a good communicator, a good secretary and may work in journalism. The mind is curious, restless, sanguine, but eager to learn. Travel usually appeals.

Negative:
The negative traits here will depend upon how Mercury is aspected; it can include untruthfulness or sarcasm or rigid thinking.

VENUS
This makes the person fond of lovely decor items, and gives a charming self-expression. There is artistic capacity or interest in the Arts; usually they are fond of music and painting. The person is close to their siblings, and diplomatic, with a capacity to be tactful.

Negative:
A tendency to flattering, sensuality, to being mentally lazy, and making compromises in serious conversation to maintain harmony.

HOUSE THREE continued
the mind (thinking & speech), also siblings and the local neighbourhood.

SUN
With the sun here, the ego is focussed on thinking and expression of ideas. Self-expression is needed, especially through communicating with other people. This placement assists the person to be a good speaker, observant, and often with scientific ability.

MARS
In this house Mars energizes the thinking and speaking, that is the communicating with others, so this person can communicate effectively. This person is forthright and likes to argue or debate with others. There can be many short journeys, and a close relative may work where iron (steel) is prominent in the workplace (e.g., surgery or the military).

Negative:
The speech may be too opinionated or too harsh. This person can find different opinions an irritation; arguments with siblings occur. If Mars is ill-aspected, then travel can lead to accidents or annoying hindrances; or there can be friction between siblings.

JUPITER
Unless Jupiter is strongly ill-aspected, the childhood home will be harmonious, as one's siblings are supportive. This person can have a lot of common sense, enjoys intellectual expression and also travel. In a fine chart, there is interest in many subjects, and higher education brings good results.

SATURN
Here the planet gives a more serious intellect, and a patient, subtle mindset. But a depressive tendency is possible, and also little rapport with relatives. One may be rather lonely or deeply self-aware as a child, leading to a tendency to withdraw from social activity. The mindset is often conservative, but by mid-life a more flexible attitude arises.

HOUSE THREE continued
the mind (thinking & speech), also siblings and the local neighbourhood.

SATURN continued
Negative:
This person can have anxiety about unfamiliar situations, and have a very rigid mindset.

URANOS
Here this planet produces an inventive or intuitive mind, but possibly also an eccentric and inconsistent mentality. Hence some ideas cannot really be put into practical life as they are impractical. This person could have an inspirational type of thinking (e.g., sudden hunches) or, if Uranos is ill-aspected, an odd way of speaking which shows a problem with having an inner freedom. This person can have a resourceful and original mindset, a wry sense of humour and a capacity to be an inventor.

NEPTUNE
This leads to someone who can get the over-all picture of a situation easily; this person has a strong imagination and gets 'hunches'. In a fine chart, this indicates an artistic and very perceptive person who is an intuitive thinker. Such a person can also grasp spiritual teachings and possibly bring inspired thoughts into the world as a writer, or in their speech. (Note that if Neptune is retrograde, a strong psychic ability is very likely.)

Negative:
This person could choose to communicate in a way that is fascinating and charismatic on the surface, to impress others. The intelligence can be subject to a lot of day-dreaming and untruthfulness. If Neptune is ill-aspected then actual deceit is likely; and even mental health issues, especially psychosis.

HOUSE THREE continued
the mind (thinking & speech), also siblings and the local neighbourhood.

PLUTO
When this person gets interested in a subject, they get deeply involved in it. They usually have constantly changing, evolving views about the life. They can also have a penetrating perception of others minds and in a dialogue can bring other people to a greater self-awareness. (If Pluto is retrograde, then a strong psychic ability is very likely.)

Negative:
This person can want others to agree with their viewpoint too forcefully, causing social difficulties. They can focus too much on issues to do with the role of power or authority and what their rights are. If Pluto is ill-aspected to Neptune or Mercury, then the intelligence will be in turmoil; there can be serious mental health issues, including psychoses and fixation.

HOUSE FOUR
the core feelings and the home.

MOON
This person is very dependent upon their family roots. The past is a major theme in their life; they can be fond of antiques, and interested in history and genealogy. They hold on to old toys, and don't want the childhood home ever to be sold. Their moods about their adult home-life and their own feelings go through phases. There is usually a strong attachment to their mother. They can enjoy nurturing others through making a secure home.

<u>Negative</u>:
They can be too self-centred, and too dependent upon the family of their childhood. If this house is governed by Cancer and the moon is here, then an unsettled childhood home-life can be really traumatic.

MERCURY
This leads to a good memory, and clarity about one's emotional dynamics. The person is usually clear about the type of house they want. The home may be used as an office.

VENUS
This person wants an aesthetic home, and specifically needs to make it beautiful, to feel at peace there. This person is close to their parents, especially the mother. If Venus is well-aspected the emotions will be tranquil and harmonious; there is usually also an interest in the Arts.

SUN
The Sun here leads to the urge for a secure home-base to retreat to; a home where one is in charge. (If Leo governs this house, the home must be splendid.) Unless the sun is ill-aspected, the emotional life is at peace and healthy; and there is a strong interest in ensuring that the emotions are <u>integrated</u> into the sense of self, but not <u>dominating</u> the self. If the sun itself is ill-aspected the emotions may be subject to unclear dynamics which are self-undermining. Vocationally, real estate is a possible profession.

HOUSE FOUR   continued
the core feelings and the home.

MARS
This person wants to be in charge of their home, and they like the home to be exactly as they want it. The emotions may be too intense and they have a tendency to dominate others.

Negative:
There can be strife and tension in the home life, or anger carried in the emotions which derive from childhood stress. The mother is dominating, perhaps even aggressive. If Mars is ill-aspected, then fires in the home are possible.

JUPITER
The home is a relaxed place where an expansive hospitality is easy to achieve. The core emotions are expansive and this person dislikes being 'cramped' by anxieties or by cautious attitudes, either in oneself or from friends. In a fine chart, there is a subtle wisdom in the heart.

Negative:
The home can be a chaotic place where orderliness is hard to achieve. Emotions can tend to get the upper hand, bringing a disorderly or frivolous element to the personality.

SATURN
With the solemn planet Saturn here, there is a need placed on this person to be aware of, and to freely express, their emotions. But often there will be an inner impediment to doing this. However, in a fine chart, the intuitive faculty that Saturn bestows, does enable the emotions to be clearly cognized. There may be some anxiety about old age, and this person may have older people in their home. Often this person is fond of antiques, and will be happier living away from the birth-place.

Negative:
The saturnine impediment to sensing or expressing one's feelings can be acute. Negative aspects to Venus or the moon will show how this manifests.

HOUSE FOUR continued
the core feelings and the home.

URANOS
This person's childhood home may have been unstable, with major changes in family circumstances or moving many times to different houses. (One client as a child had to move 20 times in one year). One parent can be away often. This sort of uncertain home life can lead to emotional stresses in adult life, such as feeling inhibited or unfree if one is the owner of a house.

Negative:
One may rebel against close family ties in order to feel at ease, but this results in a veiled layer of unhappiness. One can feel unfree if visitors just 'show up' without prior notice.

NEPTUNE
Here Neptune bestows on the emotions a sensitive, intuitive capacity. It also leads to musical or artistic talents, and an inherent idealism in the heart. The home should be a tranquil, uplifting sort of place. In a fine chart, there is also a psychic tendency, a capacity to sense (in the heart), all sorts of 'atmospheres' and the real feelings of other people.

Negative:
There can be confusion about how one feels, because other peoples' feelings are sensed, but not differentiated from one's own. One may be too self-sacrificial or too idealistic in the domestic scene. This person is often indecisive because the values of significant other people, or of spiritual groups, reduce their capacity to decide what is best for himself or herself.

PLUTO
The home is a focal point of one's life, and one needs to be the authority there. The core emotions have a prominence in the personality, or there is a struggle to integrate these.

Negative:
A dictatorial parent is possible, especially if Pluto is ill-aspected; disputes over the issue of power in the adult home are likely.

HOUSE FIVE
romance, children and one's energies, as used in romance or work or in creative interests.

MOON
There is interest in theatrical activity, and it is beneficial for this person to express their emotions and attitudes. Fertility is high, especially if the moon is a strong feature in the chart. Women and children are predominant in one's life. This person is fond of children, romantic, and charming.

Negative:
This person may bond a child to themselves far too closely. There are unsettling, changing moods in romance.

MERCURY
With Mercury here, the thoughts are expressed in personal, individualized manner. There is a natural connection to children, and the thoughts can focus greatly on romance.

Negative:
One can be very opinionated, or lascivious.

VENUS
The planet of love in this house of romance means that this person is usually very romantic, and attractive. But artistic interests are also usually prominent. Young people can feature strongly in one's life.

Negative:
One can be sensual or even lascivious, and self-focussed.

SUN
This placement means that this person has to be creative; they must be themselves. They will seek social, congenial occasions. This person is usually popular, has success in romance, and may be an entertainer.

Negative:
A show-off tendency or a domineering urge is likely, especially if the sun is ill-aspected.

HOUSE FIVE continued
romance, children and one's energies, as used in romance or work or in creative interests.

MARS
This creates a compulsion to express oneself, and to be involved in art and drama. The desires are strong; the urge to be self-expressive or to be in a romance situation is powerful. There can be an athletic ability.

Negative:
One can be rash and reckless, and sensual.

JUPITER
To this person sport and outdoors activity is especially enjoyable. Romance brings relaxed, pleasant times. In a fine chart, the creative or artistic capacity is assisted by an intuitive skill.

Negative:
An urge to gambling, and undertaking challenges in a big way, beyond what is prudent.

SATURN
This person is reserved in romance, due to a need to maintain high standards or high image, and she or he is often attracted to older partners. They may be either too duty oriented in regard to parental activity, or very intuitive. Empathy with children may have to be consciously developed. In a fine chart, the urge to creative activity is felt as a spiritual necessity, and romance can be undertaken in a platonic way.

Negative:
This person could be cold, and inhibited, rejecting romance as an inappropriate activity, though yearning for it. Infertility can be caused if Saturn is ill-aspected. In health, a sclerosis tendency is possible.

HOUSE FIVE continued
romance, children and one's energies, as used in romance or work or in creative interests.

URANOS
In this house, Uranos leads to seeking adventures in romance, and seeking 'freedom' with one's personal creative energies. This is done in either a constructive or rebellious way.

Negative:
One is too rebellious, the result of an unclear urge for 'freedom'. Hence one is unwilling to be restricted in a relationship, as the urge for 'freedom' impairs the capacity for commitment.

NEPTUNE
This person is fond of drama, and over-dramatizes life. They are also definitely romantic, but over-idealize their partner. Often sacrifices are made for their partner, which are not appreciated. Or there is a liaison made with an unfree person (e.g., someone already married or about to go overseas). This person is compassionate, and enjoys helping others, but this can lead to taking a troubled person into their life, whose needs become a real burden. In a fine chart, this placement can result in spiritually insightful creativity.

Negative:
If Neptune is ill-aspected then secret love affairs could occur, or sexual perversions are possible.

PLUTO
With Pluto here, there is enjoyment of gambling, one is willing to take risks, both in financial and emotional areas of life. Sometimes this person succeeds financially in a risky venture. This person takes romantic affairs very seriously, yet they can also become celibate. As a child, playing is taken too seriously. There is some talent in acting, and spontaneously expressing oneself is often a beneficial.

Negative:
One can be too possessive of the partner, or have sexual problems. If Pluto is ill-aspected then power-plays occur in romance and in theatrical activity.

HOUSE SIX
daily work and health

MOON
There is a strong connection between the health and the moods in the workplace. It is hard to work in a structured way, but one is empathetic with colleagues at work. Vocationally, this placement indicates home services, health care, food services.

Negative:
If Moon is ill-aspected, one is prone to colds and the 'flu. Negative moods, especially at work, can lead to digestive problems. This person, more than most people, should not eat when tired or emotional.

MERCURY
This person is analytical at work, and enjoys some mental challenges when working. However a sanguine attitude at the workplace can cause difficulties; but working as a courier or telephonist can be a good solution here. Otherwise jobs involving teaching and writing are attractive.

Negative:
Anxiety or excessive sanguine work attitudes or excessively analytical demands take a toll on the digestive system.

VENUS
Here Venus offers good health, and popularity at work. So this is a good placement for mediators, agents and arbitrators, as well as artists and counsellors. This person likes to create and maintain harmony at work, and works well with others.

Negative:
There can be some laziness regarding work, or a too emotional attitude in the workplace. If Venus itself is quite ill-aspected, then some bickering is likely to occur with work colleagues, and in terms of health, too many sugary foods are consumed.

HOUSE SIX continued
daily work and health

MARS
Here Mars generates much activity in the workplace; there is a mechanical flair, leading vocationally to such professions as, mechanical engineering, surgery or the military speech. But working as a speech therapist is also possible. Another effect of Mars here, in a fine horoscope, is the capacity for really substantial socially beneficial initiative, in whatever vocation is chosen.

Negative:
There can be difficulty in co-operative activity, or even outright hostility.

SUN
The focus of this person is their daily work (or daily routine if not in the workforce). Work is something they enjoy, and they have high standards in what they do. The more this person is fulfilled in their work, the better is their health; they enjoy learning new work procedures.

Negative:
If the Sun, or this house, is ill-aspected the health is not so robust.

JUPITER
This is a good placement for Jupiter, as one can expand one's skills whilst working. There is a capacity to learn at work, both in terms of the work skills but also about oneself and life. Dull, repetitive work is particularly off-putting, and may impact on the health.

Negative:
If Jupiter is afflicted, then one can be lazy or too undisciplined at work. In terms of health, liver disorders are likely (alcohol is especially bad for these people). This is especially possible if this person over-indulges; one very likely outcome of a negative Jupiter is being overweight.

HOUSE SIX continued
daily work and health

SATURN
At work, this person seeks to be responsible and methodical, and is able to undertake challenging exacting work. Already in childhood they may have more responsibilities than other children. Their health may be delicate in early years, but improves later on in life.

Negative:
If Saturn ill-aspected, then a chronic health problem is possible.

URANOS
This person has a sanguine tendency at work, liking a job that brings changing environments or varying tasks. The Uranian dislike of authority can manifest in the workplace.

Negative:
One can be scattered and possibly also highly-strung at work. But if a very volatile, changing type of work is chosen, the health can suffer.

NEPTUNE
This placement means that the body is sensitive to outside influences, such as some foods, chemicals and drugs. Allergies are common and psycho-somatic illnesses are possible. Work relationships can be subject to problems caused by either a psychic tendency or an emotional sensitivity. But the urge to be of service to others is quite strong, so vocationally this is a good indicator for doctors and nurses, and therapists of various kinds.

PLUTO
This brings a regenerative, intense connection to work. This person wants to be really immersed in their work. There is a potential for counselling work, and for investigative, under-cover work.

Negative:
The health may suffer from over-work habits; and if Pluto is ill-aspected then issues around dominance and power-plays in the workplace are likely.

HOUSE SEVEN
marriage, and other long-term significant people.

MOON
Since the moon governs the life-forces, in this house it gives awareness of the mood and general state of one's close long-friends or partner. This same ability is also the cause of a need to be close to someone; likewise, close long-term friends are chosen because of their empathy to oneself. An early marriage is likely because of the need for closeness, but this is not always the best reason for marriage.

Negative:
If the Moon is ill-aspected, then an unstable partner is a possible choice (subconsciously). This person may experience hostility from women.

MERCURY
This person finds intelligent people attractive, and hence the marriage partner needs to be able to share in meaningful conversations. This person is sociable, and likes to debate ideas and issues with friends. The partner is often younger than oneself.

Negative:
Business dealings can be subject to problems, and the marriage can be subject to bickering and disputes.

VENUS
This person is socially graceful, and often has a happy marriage, which can also bring financial benefits. There is a yearning for a partner, and a natural empathy with the partner.

SUN
With the sun here this person gains self-knowledge via personal relationships; especially from how others react to their own will. A good social position, and an active interaction with others, is sought for. Important life lessons come from adapting to the wishes of others. Vocationally, counselling is a possibility.

HOUSE SEVEN continued
marriage, and other long-term significant people.

MARS
This brings a tendency to a premature marriage; if Mars is well-aspected then this person can expect to find a partner they can harmonize well with, and who can spur this person on to achieve their potential. But if Mars is ill-aspected then either they or the partner may be aggressive, and arguments often occur.

JUPITER
Here Jupiter indicates a faithful and harmonious partner, as well as possibly having material gain through marriage. There is a preference for long-term connections to people which offers some deeper insights and sharing of ideas.

SATURN
With this placement there is often an age disparity between the two people, and the partner is conscientious and responsible. There can be an attitude with this person that marriage is mainly a serious social responsibility. But with a well-aspected Saturn, there can be a wise, intuitive choice of partner, harmonizing with deeper karmic dictates.

Negative:
There may be difficulties in facing and verbalizing one's own emotional vulnerabilities; or the partner could be emotionally rigid. Often there is a search for a 'parenting' partner, and marrying primarily for security. An allergy tendency can occur when Saturn is here.

URANOS
This planet here causes the person to be attracted to unusual unconventional people. This is a quintessential Uranian dynamic, derived from a suppressed yearning for so-called freedom and is a highly problematic basis for long-term relationships. But this

HOUSE SEVEN continued
marriage, and other long-term significant people.

URANOS continued
dynamic can – as often in planetary aspects – manifest in the **other** person, not in this person. Then the other person's yearnings disrupt the partnership for this person as they insist on having their freedom in the relationship.

NEPTUNE
The effects of this placement are dreamy, ungrounded ideals of a 'perfect soul-mate' and also lack of self-assertion in relationships. Both these tendencies can easily result in unsatisfactory relationship dynamics. This person may also be attracted to an unfree person (e.g., someone who is married), or they may make great sacrifices for a partner. But in a fine chart there are, in regard to love and marriage, strong, but properly grounded, ideals.

Negative:
There is a kind of neon glow around the theme of 'a partner' in this person's mind, so this person may not perceive themselves nor the partner clearly, leading to substantial disappointment later on.

PLUTO
Relationships become the major source of self-knowledge, and of changes which lead to personal growth for this person. They can attract dominant persons, who attempt to change their life. Relationships can be very intense, and often involve power struggles. Marriage can bring substantial change to where this person lives.

Negative:
If Pluto is ill-aspected then aggression and power plays can occur in the relationship. This person can keep their deeper hopes and concerns about a relationship hidden.

HOUSE EIGHT
intimations from spirit realities (consciously or subconsciously influencing the soul), also sexuality, the partner's income, and the end of life

MOON
This placement causes strong moods and feelings, and these go through regular cycles of change. For this person, women are important, for they pass on something of value, whether financial or otherwise. Being of service to others is an inherent urge, but this person may also be too vulnerable to the wishes and demands of other people. There is a psychic tendency, due to the extended nature of the life energies, not the conscious ego. Hence there is interest in, and perhaps experiences of, the after-life. This can include sensing the soul of a deceased child.

VENUS
If Venus is well-aspected, financial gain comes from marriage, or from an inheritance which is connected to a woman, or the marriage partner. With Venus here, there is often an emotionally-based psychic sensing. But in a fine chart, there can be an ability to more consciously perceive spiritual realities.

Negative:
If this house has negative aspects (from Venus itself or the zodiacal ruler of the person's 8th house), then laziness, or being possessive of friends, or overindulgence in food is likely, and possibly a heavy sensuality.

MERCURY
The planet of the logical mind placed here gives a penetrating intellect, possibly attracted to esoteric topics. This person is capable in handling other people's money. In a fine chart this gives an ability to communicate very well, as the mind is acutely discerning.

Negative:
Coarse sensuality leads to early sexual desires; one can also be sly or sarcastic.

HOUSE EIGHT continued
intimations from spirit realities (consciously or subconsciously influencing the soul), also sexuality, the partner's income, and the end of life

SUN
With the self (or ego) focussed here, there is an interest in being really aware of what life is about, what it can offer. Spiritual influences from across the threshold exert an influence on this person, but with varying degrees of awareness, depending on the person's own nature. Also this person is gifted at taking care of public assets. In the chart of a spiritually focussed person, there is also interest in esoteric topics, and in personal development.

MARS
Here Mars gives strong desires and a strong driving force. This person can be skilled at helping people arrange their lives, including their finances.

Negative:
There is strife over the partner's finances. If Mars is ill-aspected a possibility exists for loss of assets through a fire. If this house or Mars itself is afflicted by Neptune (also possibly Uranos) then an unwholesome form of psychic capacity or experiences are likely.

JUPITER
This person is resourceful, and handles money well; they also can gain through an inheritance, or their partner contributes assets. In a good chart, there is interest in esoteric topics and in the healing profession. In a fine chart there is a capacity for deep intuitive insights about spiritual realities.

Negative:
These include being dishonest or extravagant, and possibly a weakening of the ego-sense through dubious mystical-occult techniques.

HOUSE EIGHT continued
intimations from spirit realities (consciously or subconsciously influencing the soul), also sexuality, the partner's income, and the end of life

SATURN
This placement brings about life-lessons involving using or managing other people's monies or assets. But since Saturn creates a subconscious sense of one's karma, here in the house of the threshold to the spiritual realms, it often leads, in childhood, to important experiences about death. This person as a child can have a fear of death; one client reported being sleepless as a child, because, she said to herself, "You can't bake a cake without breaking the egg'. This appears to mean that the child sensed that release of the soul from the body required the body to die.

Another client stayed awake at night worrying, without any basis, that 'Mum may die'. Another client dreamt of her father's death three days before he died. In adulthood, this anxiety manifests more clearly as awareness of the spiritual realms as very real and relevant to life. It also can cause karmic life-lessons involving the partner's assets or income. In a good chart, the person is competent in administration of inheritances and in legal matters.

Negative:
A desire for power over others, including the use of sexuality, to achieve this. There may be a tendency for sexuality to be repressed un-freely, or to be excessive; this is more likely if the south lunar node is in Virgo.

URANOS
With Uranos here, changes in life tend to occur suddenly. The partner's income can be subject to unpredictable upsets. There can be dreams that are 'predictive', i.e., they depict events that come true a few days later. A psychic tendency is very likely, and this includes receiving spiritual insights gained during sleep. (If the sun is in Scorpio, psychic impressions of **odours** can be detected.)

HOUSE EIGHT continued
intimations from spirit realities (consciously or subconsciously influencing the soul), also sexuality, the partner's income, and the end of life

Uranos continued
Negative:
Sexuality can be subject to erratic, intense eccentricities. Included in this is, providing Uranos is ill-aspected, that when a close associate dies, this person can feel as if the deceased lives on in their own desires and yearnings. Unwholesome psychic dynamics are likely, and can be triggered off by such techniques as a Ouija board.

NEPTUNE
Here Neptune creates a very strongly psychic condition; this includes out-of-body experiences, and strange dreams. Even as a child this person is usually interested in spiritual topics. As a child they can have odd fears, especially of death, because this house acts as a doorway between the physical world and the spiritual.

But this awareness of 'the Beyond' (even though veiled) induces stresses for a child, who may play out going to a funeral. In a fine chart, this placement brings about a wholesome clairvoyant tendency. In the area of desire and romance, there can be potent fantasies.

Negative:
Legacies may become involved in complicated problems. If Neptune is ill-aspected, it is essential that this person avoids ego-weakening activities, such as hypnosis, psychedelic drugs and occult experimenting. Very rarely, this person can be subject to comas or trance-like states, as a result of severe illness or mishap. It is suggested that they advise doctors of this (perhaps also wearing a medallion), so that medical staff do not assume that their death has come.

HOUSE EIGHT continued
intimations from spirit realities (consciously or subconsciously influencing the soul), also sexuality, the partner's income, and the end of life

PLUTO
The transforming or undermining power of Pluto manifests here very strongly. So this person goes through periods of intense and substantial change; they are impelled towards inner growth. As a child, they may be overly concerned about death. They will use all their resources to get on with the present goal. This is a good placement for the rejuvenation of the body; it can recover very well from illness. An inheritance often provides financial freedom. In a fine chart, this brings an inherent need to realize the higher self, and interest in the spiritual. In any event, a psychic or clairvoyant tendency is common.

Negative:
The negative modes of Pluto here include a morbid interest in death, or being fanatically religious or degenerately sensual.

HOUSE NINE
one's attitude to religious-spiritual values, to relationships and also travel.

SUN
With the ego focussed in the house of education and ideas, this person is keen to learn, and will probably keep on being educated (or self-educated) long after leaving school. Understanding of life is gained through interaction with people of different cultures. Linguistic abilities are common. Vocationally, being a teacher, lawyer or travel related jobs are likely.

MOON
This placement brings significant dreams, and enjoyment of travel. This person's worldview is coloured by their moods.

Negative:
A restlessness which hinders learning and seeks refuge in travelling is likely and also changeable views about life and the world.

VENUS
This person's engagement with knowledge and travel is coloured by their emotions; but this person does well in studies which they find enjoyable. Their mind relates to things and concepts not from logic, but by feeling how they interlink to create a wholeness, or a harmony or beauty. This person is also usually attracted to the Arts. Teaching is also a likely profession, for this person enjoys educating others. Travel can have a strong emotional appeal; and the partner may be from a distant country.

MERCURY
This creates an active mind, with an interest in higher education and possibly in the study of spiritual ideas. In a fine chart, there is an ability to logically present intuitive ideas. In a good chart there is a teaching skill that can communicate ideas in a stimulating way.

Negative:
The mind seeks to interfere in other people's ideas. A very sanguine yearning to travel is common.

HOUSE NINE   continued
one's attitude to religious-spiritual values, to relationships and also travel.

MARS
Here Mars produces strong opinions, a restless mind, but enjoyment of travel.

Negative:
There can be aggressive convictions, religious fanaticism, and nightmares.

JUPITER
This person is studious and often inclined to higher or holistic ideas. This person is interested in travel and is tolerant of different ways of being. In a fine chart there is interest in esoteric ideas. Vocationally this indicates working as a writer, educator, publisher, or in the law.

Negative:
One exaggerates, is fond of ostentatious display, or has a confused and unwise view of life.

SATURN
Early in life this person is dogmatic or rigid in their attitudes and world-view, but later on they usually become more tolerant. In any event this person is not inclined to accept new ideas without due consideration. In a fine chart, there is interest in inspiring others as an educator, or even a pronounced intuitive, philosophical mindset. Vocationally, this indicates working as an educator, or publisher (usually in non-fiction).

Negative:
Often a Saturn influences create the narrow-minded person, slow to adapt. They can be fanatical, and dislike foreign travel.

URANOS
This person has unorthodox ideas about life, but is a resourceful, free thinker, who sees the world differently to most.

HOUSE NINE continued
one's attitude to religious-spiritual values, to relationships and also travel.

URANOS continued
Negative:
The mind works erratically, producing inconsistent ideas, even a fanaticism. There can also be difficulties when travelling in foreign lands.

NEPTUNE
This placement produces the compassionate, impressionable, religious or mystical soul; a dreamer or mystically inclined person who senses the spirit. In a fine chart this placement leads to clairvoyance or at least a psychic tendency, and often the ability to able to clearly explain spiritual truths. In a normal chart, the person is prone to odd dreams and forebodings, and is an idealist who seeks ways to reform society.

Negative:
If Neptune is ill-aspected then caution is advised in regard to legal matters, as deceit from solicitors themselves is possible, and legal processes can be subject to complications. But care is also needed with regard to many spiritual-mystical exercises as these can weaken the ego-sense and will be harmful; substance abuse is especially damaging. In a chart with Neptune ill-aspected, a deceptive, atavistic clairvoyance is likely, which brings serious confusion.

PLUTO
This causes the person to be restless, eager to travel, and to have an intense interest in really comprehending a subject. This person has very strong opinions, and will defend them. They like to discover new aspects of the mind, and are gifted in psychology.

Negative:
There is a fanatical attachment to ideas and one may try to force one's opinion on others.

HOUSE TEN
one's social reality: usually career and marital status.

MOON
The reputation this person has (socially or professionally) is very important to them. There is an underlying mood that one must be an achiever. The mother is very influential in areas governed by house ten. Some vocations prominent here include the food industry, shipping and nursing.

MERCURY
This indicates that one will seek further education in order to further one's career path. The career will revolve around public speaking, or communications or travelling. There can also be multiple jobs or a tendency to frequent changes of occupation.

VENUS
Venus here induces positive responses from business or career colleagues. Working in Public Relations or in the Arts is likely, (and the diplomatic service).

SUN
This placement indicates a need to achieve a social position, by being successful. In a good chart this suggests an authoritative person who obtains public recognition; many people in civic positions (including politics) have this.

MARS
Even as a child this person wants to get ahead in vocation, and as an adult is willing to work hard to get there. Vocationally, this indicates a career in the military, or in mechanics and engineering.

Negative:
One has to learn to co-operate with authority figures. There can be friction with one's father.

HOUSE TEN continued
one's social reality: usually career and marital status.

JUPITER
Indicates success in one's career, through a leadership capacity, leading to managerial positions which bring success. The career often entails service to the less fortunate. In a fine chart, there is a wish to serve the spiritual purpose of life through one's profession; this includes being a dedicated educator (for children or adults).

SATURN
This person in his or her career will be self-reliant, ambitious, conscientious and hard-working. There is usually an urge to be recognized as authoritative in the career. If Saturn is well-aspected then success comes later in life. Teachers often have this placement. In a good chart, this person will be choose a career that is in accordance with their life-context (or karma), but the pathway can still be a demanding one.

URANOS
This person will seek an unusual occupation, and also his or her career may change direction dramatically. A hobby may become a new career and they may have two simultaneous careers; in any event being self-employed is often the preferred option. The career may involve large groups or the public.

NEPTUNE
Here this planet can bring about a unique career, or strange events occur in one's career. This person changes jobs quite often. When this person is young, they can be unsure what career to choose. In a good chart, a unique career path can be created. In a fine chart, there can be an inspirational career, for this person has a unique ability connected to high ideals.

But such a person may not receive recognition for their special achievements, and also they may become socially isolated through having such high career goals. Often compassionate work choices are made, such as nursing.

HOUSE TEN continued
one's social reality: usually career and marital status.

NEPTUNE   continued
Negative:
If Neptune, or this house in general is ill-aspected, caution is needed to protect the career from scandal, as odd dynamics and unexpected enemies may be operative. There can be a career goal based on 'a special mission' which doesn't succeed (possibly for good reasons) and one then becomes disillusioned with a 'blind' world.

PLUTO
Pluto here makes one self-assertive and very determined in one's career. This person may want to reform the world, and generally gets really involved in the career; so they are the workaholic type. If Pluto is well-aspected this person can bring new (and potentially quite valuable) perspectives to their field of work.

Negative:
There could be a dominating employer, or one could be fanatically determined in the work. Power-plays and rivalry may occur between oneself and colleagues in the workplace.

HOUSE ELEVEN
life-goals and groups of friends.

MOON
This placement makes one socially oriented, with changing life goals. Women are helpful to this person, helping in regard to their life-goals. There is strong need for friends, but this person must be able to trust them. Changing moods affect both life-goals and friendships.

Negative:
There can be deceptive friends, or intense friendships which then suddenly end. Also superficial attitudes about life are likely.

MERCURY
This placement gives interest in social reforms, and possibly Utopian ideas. This person likes to give effort to deciding about their life goals.

VENUS
If Venus is well aspected, this person will be sociable and have many friends. Their goals in life will reflect a compassionate heart, or artistic interests. Friends can bring good fortune into one's life.

SUN
This placement indicates that one's goals and life objectives are attained through one's friends. Often a friend will say something that opens a really important window on the topic of life-goals. There is an inherent need to integrate oneself into group activity. This person is socially oriented and has skill in group-interaction dynamics; they can easily be either a good team-player or a leader.

MARS
Here Mars provides a lot of initiative for achieving of goals; but friends often are of value in achieving a goal. This person will vigorously defend their own decisions, and they are generally good organisers.

HOUSE ELEVEN continued
life-goals and groups of friends.

Mars continued
Negative:
Other people seem to oppose one's own life goals, hence disputes with others about plans can easily occur.

JUPITER
This makes a person sociable, and hence someone who attains their goals through their friends. This person is also fortunate in regard to friends including some socially prominent ones (unless Jupiter is ill-aspected). In a fine chart there is an ability to make wise choices in regard to goals in life, and the choice of friends.

SATURN
Saturn here often means that this person has only a small circle of friends, but these can be deep friendships, and one feels a sense of duty to them. In a fine chart, there is a strong intuitive capacity to find the right life-path.

Negative:
If Saturn is ill-aspected, friends could cause a lot of trouble, so care must be taken when choosing close friends. Likewise, the decisions about life-goals may be not in harmony with one's reality (karma).

URANOS
Eccentric people are chosen as friends, friends must not limit one's actions, and goals in life can be unclear, inconsistent, and often change.

Negative:
There can be eccentric, unreliable friends, and impulsive friendships which end in hostility.

HOUSE ELEVEN continued
life-goals and groups of friends.

NEPTUNE
In a fine chart, Neptune here enables one to formulate noble and idealistic life goals. But often some effort is needed to formulate one's goals. A yearning for a group of loyal friends can be quite strong.

Negative:
If Neptune is afflicted, unreliable friends are chosen, and this person has unrealistic goals for their life (a 'dreamer of dreams').

PLUTO
With this placement, friends have an important, self-transformative influence in one's life. Friends can also suddenly leave, and may never re-appear. A strong urge to reform society is common, and one can be quite perceptive with social dynamics.

Negative:
One must be careful about a tendency to dominate friends, and colleagues in social initiatives.

HOUSE TWELVE
the subconscious soul-life (wishes, ideas, or intentions, etc)

MOON
The Moon here causes shyness, sensitivity, and a dislike of new environments. This person can work well alone, and is self-sacrificing. This person often works as a nurse or doctor, or in jobs where help to others is paramount; this is a must for these people. They may feel reluctant to discuss their own moods and feelings, even though these are strong, because they want to be really understood in such a conversation.

Negative:
There can be secret affairs, and possibly ill-will from women, regardless what gender the client is.

SUN
When the sun, which activates the ego-sense, is in this subdued house, this person is not an up-front person, and has to make effort to avoid living a lonely life. In a good chart, this person is compassionate and hence drawn to being of service to others. Vocationally, this person is drawn to work in a therapy centre, medical centre or possibly a sanatorium or retreat of some kind.

Negative:
If the Sun is ill-aspected then this person can undermine their own best interests. There can be a lack of self-confidence, and a self-pitying tendency.

VENUS
This leads to a very compassionate person, who is kind to those in need, and generally sensitive; peaceful, secluded locations appeal.

Negative:
There is a lack of discrimination in regard to desires. This can lead to clandestine liaisons, which result in hostility from women.

HOUSE TWELVE continued
the subconscious soul-life (wishes, ideas, or intentions, etc)

MERCURY
Here Mercury leads to a subtle mind, capable of analytical thinking. This person likes to work in seclusion, and dwell on past experiences a lot. If Mercury is retrograde (see last chapter about retrograde planets) then this person is even more introverted, replaying past dialogues over and over. The logical mind is constantly active, analysing life. But in a fine chart this situation can lead to a very perceptive, sharp intelligence.

Negative:
This person may find if difficult to openly say what they are thinking – to their own detriment. If Mercury is ill-aspected then past ideas or past experiences can be viewed in a mentally distorted way.

MARS
Mars in this subdued placement makes this person introspective and feeling that they are not able to really deal with challenges in life. But often they find that they do have to face considerable problems alone. A feeling of being incapable pursues this person; this is a situation which can lead to resentment against those who do succeed. There can be a feeling of tiredness, which is not a medical condition but comes from a frustrating conviction that one cannot succeed.

JUPITER
This indicates a very compassionate person, who has a lot of common sense and in a good chart, even real wisdom. If this person thinks about a problem at night, they can wake up in the morning with valuable insight into that problem. It is often said that help can mysteriously come to this person when they most need it.

Negative:
If Jupiter is ill-aspected then foolish decisions can be made, and extravagant ideas are attractive.

HOUSE TWELVE   continued
the subconscious soul-life (wishes, ideas, or intentions, etc)

SATURN
Saturn subconsciously provides, to some degree, intuitions that admonish one to be aware of the purpose and intentions of one's life (karma). So placed here in the house of the subconscious, the challenge is how to find life's mission ! Because for this person this subtle sensing is blocked. There is also a sense of being inadequate. This in turn causes a feeling that the world is against oneself, and also a dislike of restrictions (whether physical or social).

The father may have been distant, either physically or emotionally, increasing the demand on this person to generate their own discipline and goals (to 'be their own father'). Isabel Hickey concludes that this person "must serve others or suffer misery". But in a fine chart, this placement indicates a capacity for research into spiritual themes.

URANOS
When this person is young, they tend to suppress their own feelings to achieve peer approval, but this can lead to secret resentment. This person has a yearning for an exciting, unusual life; and usually there is interest in unusual or even spiritual themes.

Negative:
If Uranos or this house is ill-aspected, then a strong urge for a chaotic immature 'freedom' causes problems. If this urge is unrecognized, and thus suppressed, then compulsive behaviour patterns arise. Hostility can occur through people with mental health issues.

NEPTUNE
In this house, Neptune has a strong influence; especially towards a psychic ability, or at least a natural awareness that spiritual realms are a reality. A psychic tendency dominates the ego, because there is only a vague periphery to the aura, leaving this person exposed to

HOUSE TWELVE   continued
the subconscious soul-life (wishes, ideas, or intentions, etc)

NEPTUNE   continued
(and often drained by) other persons' auric forces. That is, other people's moods live on in this person. So this person is empathetic, and therefore often compassionate, working with less fortunate persons in institutions. There is also an artistic potential, especially for dancing or eurythmy. Vocationally, nursing or healing activity attracts. In a fine chart, this placement suggests a strong capacity for understanding of life and for spiritual perception.

Negative:
Claustrophobia is common and often the fantasy-life is too potent, giving rise to un-grounded ideas and dreamy views of life. There can be many secret enemies, or one can be subject to deception.

PLUTO
Pluto's influence in the subconscious is subtle; it basically strengthens tendencies and urges that are in the deeper layers of the soul, and hence are not consciously perceived. If a person has substantial stress points in their soul, Pluto here can lead to the possibility of mental health issues, because these anxieties or suppressed yearnings are also stirred. One result of the resulting stress is psychosomatic pain. Any therapy which could raise such anxieties or yearnings into consciousness can have a powerful impact.

Negative:
If Pluto is ill-aspected, it creates a tendency towards dominating others and power plays in social interaction. There can also be a tendency to actions which are not fully meaningful; this is the manifestation of hidden inner pressures.

****

Chapter Six

The Planets in the Signs: the qualities they create in the soul.

This chapter gives an over-view of the significance of a planet's position in each zodiac sign. Before interpreting a chart, the zodiacal placement of Venus, Mars and Mercury should be noted, as this determines the underlying quality of a client's personality (see the last chapter for more about this). The zodiac sign in which a planet is positioned at birth, confers the qualities belonging to that sign on the part of the soul - or the psychological dynamics, if you prefer - in which that planet is active.

The reader is advised to gain more knowledge about the qualities created by a planet's position in the zodiac, by noting how clients reflect this. Further reading on this theme is valuable; see the list of recommended books in the last chapter.

The four dynamics of a planet in a zodiac sign

The ancient Greeks established that there are four types of dynamics that the planets can have in a zodiac sign. But these are only of peripheral weight in assessing a chart.

A planet can be a 'ruler' of a sign; this means that the qualities of that planet are most pronounced in that sign (in the birth chart).
A planet can be 'exalted' in a sign; this means that the qualities of that planet are quite compatible with that sign.
A planet can be 'in its fall' in a sign; this means that the qualities of that planet are not compatible with that sign.
A planet can be 'in its detriment' in a sign; this means that the qualities of that planet are not very compatible with that sign.

We shall start with noting once again the influence of the Moon in the zodiac signs, but also refer to what was said on pages 35-39, where the emphasis was on the Moon signs as very powerful, but inherently less conscious in their impact than the influence of the sun signs.

MOON in the SIGNS

ARIES
This fiery sign influences the lunar governed life-forces, which greatly form our temperament, so as to create a predisposition for power, and hence success in the career. In women this adds a more assertive quality; but here both sexes have a choleric tendency. The temperament is naturally upfront and good in a crisis. The father may have particularly strong impact.

TAURUS (exalted)
This gives a stable resilience to the life-forces, which produces a robust health, and very earth-connected quality. Usually this person is a warm-hearted person, and likes parenthood. But there can be some moodiness, and a dislike of changes, as well as being attached to things, especially things that have been around a while.

GEMINI
This sanguine sign here results in a sanguine and witty temperament, and this person seems to stay young for long time. This person's sanguine nature dislikes burdensome or solemn duties. Duties and commitment are also not liked, as they give an unfree feeling; relationships are therefore a source of inner conflict. Work that requires quick thinking and negotiating are appealing.

CANCER (ruler)
With the moon here, this person is very sensitive, has a deep bond to the mother, and is generally quite maternal. Lunar Cancerians have a very acute sense of hearing, so they especially dislike loud noises. They may brood and sulk, possibly displaying an emotional blackmail tendency. These are nurturing people, so they like to start up an initiative but are happy to let others continue it. This person is very loyal and caring to the family, and takes on a parenting role in relationships.

MOON in the SIGNS   continued

LEO
There Leo's sense of pride means that this person's temperament is inherently often stubborn, and liable to become really annoyed if she or he feel insulted or unappreciated. They are selfless for loved ones, but these people must show appreciation. Their appearance is important, from childhood onwards, they are often looking in a mirror. This person can quickly appraise other people, is usually a good organiser, and can have leadership tendency.

VIRGO
This person is naturally drawn to having integrity and decency; such people make good teachers, or accountants. But the negative side of Virgo can cause this person to never quite finish a job or to be satisfied with how a task is done, as they are too pedantic and too critical. Earthy things, like gardening is appealing.

LIBRA
This person has a natural predisposition for glamour, for artistic environments, especially for music. Their inherent mood is to be gentle and non self-assertive, due to an innate urge to maintain harmony between people, and to avoid conflict. It goes against their nature to assert themselves, but they have a natural skill at being sociable.

SCORPIO (fall)
The life-energies in these people make them intense, this gives them strong recuperative powers, and a temperament which lets them size up other people very quickly. But despite a generally calm personality, their moods are intense, and fiery outbursts can occur. They are jealous and possessive of their partner and close friends, and like to have authority. It may be difficult to learn to forgive, and forget.

MOON in the SIGNS   continued

SAGITTARIUS
This person is by temperament, adventurous, socially naïve, often making indiscrete remarks. Their natural tendency is to need their freedom or independence, and they are often involved in sports. There is a tendency to be contradictory in what they like, for many things, or people are not quite right; somehow not quite what this person wants. They can be quite choleric, but also generous.

CAPRICORN (detriment)
These people are naturally predisposed to be somewhat shy, and vulnerable, yet they are practical and sensible. They are self-disciplined, cautious, hard working, very considerate and have a wry sense of humour. The emotions may be strong, but it is their temperament to repress these. They can be melancholic. There is a dislike of new people, of unexpected, unplanned events, or sudden suggestions about things to do. Socially they don't impose themselves on others, as if insecure about their own worth; so they can undermine their own success.

AQUARIUS
These people are generally sanguine; it is their natural urge to be in communication with others, so they are pleasant conversationalists and at ease in discussions with people who have different views on life (like solar Aquarians, but then it is more conscious). They have a bright mind, and in a good chart, they are humanitarian. They are often somewhat detached with their emotions, and can leave a situation without any apparent regrets. They need to be free inside a relationship, preferring unconventional friends.

PISCES
The lunar Piscean is a sensitive (sometimes psychic) person who is very considerate, often idealistic and gifted at creatively visualizing, so they can get the over-view of any project or dilemma. A loyal friend and quite perceptive, they are sought out for solace by friends in trouble; but often too much so, burdening their own life. Likewise,

MOON in the SIGNS   continued

PISCES   continued
they are too sensitive to criticism and any bullying or harshness that life brings. Teenage years can be stressful as their emotional needs and dreamy ideals cause difficulties. They often like dancing. With their temperament being infused by Piscean rapport with fantasy worlds and spiritual things, they have an inner rapport with children.

****

VENUS IN THE SIGNS

ARIES (detriment)
Here the feelings are enflamed, leading to strong passions and intense wishes. This person's feelings will be impetuous, sometimes stormy, and easily self-centred, at times this causes social problems. But they can be popular, as they have initiative and enthusiasm, and their friends are quite clear about what this person is really feeling.

TAURUS (exalted)
The emotions here have depth and don't dissipate quickly; so this person is loyal in love and friendship. This person is usually calm and somewhat phlegmatic, liking pleasures and comfort. There is often an artistic ability or appreciation of the arts and beauty; lunar Taureans can be gifted at singing.

GEMINI
The emotions are infused with Gemini's sanguine nature, so this person does not like to make a commitment in relationships (or in other areas of life). The emotions are drawn to change and variety, and to witty interchanges. Friendships arise from intellectual bonding, and literary pursuits are attractive.

CANCER
This person has strong emotions, and is deeply in need of affection (although this need may be kept private). This person is sympathetic and affectionate, and their affections have almost a maternal quality. There is usually a close emotional connection to the mother. In a relationship, this person bonds very closely and is hurt by betrayal and feels very deeply a lack of love in their life.

LEO
This is the warm-hearted, sympathetic, generous person, who likes lavish expression of affection. Pride is a noticeable feature in their feelings, so friends need to be appreciative and to reflect well on this person; if friends prove to be disappointing, they are cast off. Leo here confers a dramatic element to this person's feelings. Artistically, colourful or lavish spectacles draw their interest, so being involved in drama or opera appeals.

VENUS IN THE SIGNS   continued

VIRGO   (fall)
Here the feelings are drawn towards propriety, being prudent and being decent; but they are also often critical of their partner or friends. The passions are restrained, and there is a distinct confrontation with desires. This is either because karmically this person has worked hard to overcome them and has very high standards; or this person has failed to fully acknowledge their desires, and is caught in a struggle with them. Orderliness and neatness are common features here, as well as being helpful to others.

LIBRA   (ruler)
Here Venus bestows a gentle calmness and kindness; the feelings strive towards harmony between people. The arts are prominent, this person being fond of beauty in its many forms including fine clothing and decor. They are often artists and can have very refined perception of both beauty and inner goodness. But they do have to guard against letting others dominate them in personal relationships or at work.

SCORPIO   (detriment)
The passions can be strong, leading to hasty or unwise partnering; if Venus (or Pluto) is ill-aspected this can lead to lascivious behaviour. Life is experienced on a deep emotional level, so the bond to close loved ones is taken very seriously, and a deep, meaningful mutual bond is expected. This can lead to jealousy if the partner is affectionate to friends. Artistically, deep poetry and soulful music is attractive.

SAGITTARIUS
The breezy sanguine tendency of this sign makes the feelings of the lunar Sagittarian rather fickle as regards love. Typically they are not at all sentimental, and they often have to decide between two possible partners, and their partner must not cramp their freedom. They are drawn to travel and outdoor activities. In a fine chart, the emotions resonate to spiritual or religious ideals.

VENUS IN THE SIGNS   continued

CAPRICORN
The emotions are kept under control, and displays of affection are often not approved of. This coolness can have a socially negative impact. But the feelings can be very strong and run deep, hence this person rejects bubbly, frivolous ways of relating to people. The passions can be also very strong, but kept private, as the Capricornian enhanced sense of self needs to process the impact of this. In a poor chart, the capacity for warmth and empathy can be negligible, and the passions may be lascivious. In a fine chart the opposite occurs.

AQUARIUS
Here the feelings reach out to form bonds with others, especially through conversation. It is said that Aquarians, both lunar and solar, are cool people with detached feelings, and this is commonly found; but some can in fact be strongly and deeply emotional. Still, even these Aquarians will want freedom in a relationship, and are drawn to the strongly intellectual and unusual person.

PISCES   (exalted)
The emotions here are especially predominant; in a fine chart, affection and loving-kindness ray out from this person. They like to help people, and are very fond of the Arts.   They yearn for romance and seek an idealistic relationship. But this can be a trap, for ungrounded romantic ideas, and little inclination to defend their own rights, means that they can become callously misused.

****

MERCURY IN THE SIGNS

ARIES
This fiery sign confers the impulsive, quick kind of intelligence to Mercury's energies. So this person engages easily in conversation, but is not given to reflective, contemplative thought. This person likes to 'duel' mentally in conversations, and can become argumentative.

TAURUS
Opinions are stubbornly held to, but the thinking is logical and clear. The mind is rather ponderous, but not dull, Taurus here gives a kind of phlegmatic way of thinking. This person responds to artistic experiences and relaxed pleasurable times.

GEMINI   (ruler)
Here the thinking is sanguine, but clever and inventive, and also good humoured. This person is very talkative, and fond of new ideas going to see new places. Negative aspects to Mercury can lead to superficial, hazy ideas or to somewhat hectic, nervous speech.

CANCER
The mind is tactful, discreet and whilst quite adaptable to new ideas and places, any old ideas and values, especially gained in childhood, can be retained because of the emotional significance they acquire. The intellect is influenced by the feelings, and this person's feelings tend to look back to the past.

LEO
In Leo, Mercury takes on an authoritative stance, liking to get understanding of the over-all situation and making this perspective clear to everyone. The mindset is kind and generous but at times the temper can flare up. The mind can also be stubborn and dogmatic.

MERCURY IN THE SIGNS continued

VIRGO (ruler)
Here the intellect looks at life in a prudent, analytical and meticulous way. It does confer academic ability, including in linguistics and scientific research, but the mind can be too critical of others and rather pedantic. In their studies, they are good at grammar and vocationally, often work in accountancy.

LIBRA
The Libran features of indecisiveness and gentleness show in this person's thinking. Their mind is prone to being indecisive, and to avoiding giving support to proposals that could lead to conflict. This can make them slow in analysing problems, yet the intellect can be quite powerful. The artistic quality of Libra leads to an intellectual interest in artistic or aesthetic topics, such as architecture, but this person is also inclined towards psychology and mathematics.

SCORPIO
Here the intellect has a veiled, sharp edge to it. There is an enhanced capacity to perceive the workings of other peoples' minds, and an acute analytical power. This leads to a skill in psychology, investigative work and problem solving. But care is needed to avoid appearing devious through keeping one's own mental processes too close to the chest. This person can be sarcastic and too suspicious of others.

SAGITTARIUS (detriment)
The large-scale view of life that Sagittarius confers tends to reduce the intellect's capacity for patient, detailed analysis of problems. But on the other side, it makes possible an interest in deeper ideas. In a fine chart this leads to interest in scientific, philosophical or even spiritual ideas. A blunt way of speaking leads to a lack of discretion, but these people do have an honesty and forthrightness in their speech.

MERCURY IN THE SIGNS   continued

CAPRICORN
The persevering, dutiful nature of this sign bestows here an intellect which is acute, determined, careful, economic, patient and often ambitious. So this person can be an excellent teacher or scholar or researcher. The mind can be too solemn and too meticulous. The powers of concentration are high and this combined with the above qualities can make for capable business executives.

AQUARIUS   (exalted)
The mind here has originality and delights in new and unconventional ideas. There is often a humanitarian nuance to the thinking, which can be acutely perceptive, but this person often stubbornly holds on to a conclusion or viewpoint despite evidence to the contrary. They enjoy exchanging ideas and learning of how other people experience life.

PISCES   (detriment)
The intelligence is not so skilled at detailed critical assessment, but instead is quite imaginative, so these people can be good entertainers, story-tellers or writers. They can also be psychic; but not necessarily consciously so. In essence there is an intuitive mentality which makes the person sensitive and highly imaginative, but too exposed to the wishes, fears and ideas of other people.

MARS IN THE SIGNS

ARIES (ruler)
Mars in the fiery sign of Aries intensifies the way these people expresses their driving force. So they are competitive, almost combative, self-assured and enterprising. But a tendency to anger, impatience and being impetuous has to be moderated, to avoid clashing with others. They usually have a high energy level, and a dislike of being thwarted.

TAURUS (detriment)
This placement creates a more patient, thorough nature, but one which can be very stubborn and easily moved to jealously and possessiveness. This person can be a patient, skilled craftsperson or a reliable, thorough manager in commercial and industrial enterprises. A person with this more phlegmatic driving force has to be aware of the need to acknowledge annoyances and resentments or else a seriously strong fit of anger can suddenly occur.

GEMINI
Mars here stimulates the sanguine tendencies, making this person mentally resourceful, alert and witty. In their feelings, this person is attracted to new places, and always ready to jump into action – but that action can soon lose its appeal, in favour of a newer stimulus.

CANCER (fall)
The emotional intensity of this sign merges with Mars' driving force, leading to highly emotive responses to life. There will be a strong reaction to criticism, to whatever is irritating, and there is a tendency to hold a grudge. The digestive system is vulnerable in this person as the emotive highs and lows impact negatively on it. But when feeling cheerful, this person is affirming and supportive.

MARS IN THE SIGNS

LEO
The leonine qualities are naturally reinforced as both sign and planet are fiery. So this person's driving force is alert to challenges, leadership opportunities, and has a sense of pride in accomplishment and with regard to their image. The desires are intensified and energy levels are usually high. A strong sense of drama and leadership capacity is usually there.

VIRGO
These people are gifted at skilled, exacting work that requires energy be directed towards meticulous careful tasks, including surgery and pharmaceutical work. They can be pedantic and too critical of others.

LIBRA   (detriment)
This placement brings difficulties, as the primary element of the Libran - the need for harmony and a partner (either personal or business) - is intensified. This leads to ardently seeking romance, and a yearning to work with a partner vocationally. But then an unclear martial urge to be competitive can mar the cooperation with a business partner, and ill-advised romantic liaisons are likely.

SCORPIO   (ruler)
The Scorpio person naturally has a more intense inner life (their thoughts, feelings and yearnings), and here this is fired up, leading to intense passion, and generally strong emotions; yet this may not be obvious to the observer at first. The will is determined and the mind is acutely perceptive. This person can be revengeful and quarrelsome, so anger can be a problem, or grudges can be held silently for a long time. But in a fine chart, this placement leads to discernment, resourcefulness and courage.

MARS IN THE SIGNS continued

SAGITTARIUS
The soul responds energetically to ideas, especially big ideas and initiatives where the 'bigger picture' and challenges abound. This person seeks freedom of movement and of thought, and brings enthusiasm and energy to life. In a good chart, this includes a natural generosity and sociability and being attracted to deeper ideas especially ideas that can become practical ideals.

CAPRICORN   (exalted)
This sign's focus on persevering and long-terms goals is fired up with this placement. So this person is capable of scaling the heights through their ambition, their courage, their high organizing ability and managerial skills. They are determined and resourceful but discreet, and can be subject to intense, but hidden, passions.

AQUARIUS
This person is determined and ambitious but very original, seeking to have his or her own ideas triumph, or at least acknowledged. An intellectually gifted person who is a good speaker and scholar, but at times this is a person who holds onto his or her ideas stubbornly. Yet this person is also subject sudden impulses and new viewpoints. In a good chart there is interest in humanitarian work or ideas that reform society.

PISCES
Piscean sensitivity and self-surrender tends to clash with the fire force of Mars, leading to retreat from aggression, and uncertainty as to how to deal with demanding people (furtive behaviour needs to be avoided). Moods can vacillate between gentle non-assertiveness and being gloomy and unsure. At its best this means the person is sensitive and compassionate and seeks a vocation that alleviates suffering.

****

JUPITER IN THE SIGNS

ARIES
The thinking and the will are brought into an especially enhanced Sagittarian mode with this placement. So this person has a keen interest in more grand and challenging ideas, whether in literature or in social and business enterprises. There is ambition and optimism, networking is a natural talent that greatly helps to further this person's pioneering goals, and can lead to high positions in government or business circles. There is a danger of being too grand, and too optimistic. In a fine chart there is interest in deeper spiritual ideas and how to help society with these.

TAURUS
Here Jupiter's focus on thinking and initiative, merge with the earthy orientation of Taurus, producing the person to whom ideas are of interest if they are practically applicable or serve pleasure and general comfort in life. This person is usually generous, relaxed, warm-hearted and attractive to the opposite sex.

GEMINI
The mentally scattered, short-attention span (i.e., sanguine) influence of Gemini weakens Jupiter's energies of wisdom and clarity of thought. This person can be humanitarian, benevolent and witty, but has trouble with deeper, reflective thinking. But there is skill with words and hence public speaking, leading to success in tertiary education and a vocation in business, finance or teaching.

CANCER
The expansive nature of Jupiter lifts the Cancerian energy into a deep sympathy with those who need nurture. So this person is sympathetic and often has a maternal, compassionate nature. Often the work undertaken by this person helps other people in terms of either the body (nursing, nutrition, healing) or the soul (counselling, therapy).

JUPITER IN THE SIGNS

LEO
The awareness of one's own image, generosity and the leadership drive are all enhanced here. So in a good chart, this person will be 'big-hearted', benevolent, drawn to civic duties or at least likes to be of help to charities, or to youth groups, and can be financially successful. In a fine chart there is a kind of 'heart-wisdom'. In a more difficult chart, extravagance and pomp and over-dramatizing can all occur.

VIRGO (detriment)
This placement weighs down Jupiter's capacity to bestow an expansive, relaxed, even wise way of thinking. This person is meticulous, often too fussy and too cautious. The Virgoan focus on ethics is there, but so too is a very critical attitude; and in some people, there is a problem with self-confidence.

LIBRA
The effect of this placement depends greatly on whether Jupiter is ill-aspected or not. In a positive chart, this makes the person gentle, refined, artistically sensitive, and interested in culture and the arts. This person can also succeed financially and raise funds for organisations. In a fine chart there is also a potential for deep artistic insights. But if Jupiter is ill-aspected there is indecisiveness and clumsiness in social relations, self-indulgence and possibly difficulties in legal processes.

SCORPIO
With this placement the thinking is drawn towards a more perceptive or more shrewd understanding of life, so this person is a good researcher, a skilled analyst. The personality can persevere, be given confidential information or be attracted to mystical views. There can be strange friendships and association with powerful people. This person can very quickly take advantage of possibilities in life.

JUPITER IN THE SIGNS continued

SAGITTARIUS   (ruler)
The outgoing nature of Sagittarius merges with the transcending nature of Jupiter to produce results that, in a good chart, make this person's mind interested in ideas that are big, idealistic, challenging, and even philosophical, religious or spiritual. This person will also be generous, affable and honest. But in a chart where Jupiter is ill-aspected, this person will be reckless, naïve, or seek to convert others to their superficial views.

CAPRICORN   (fall)
The effect of this placement is particularly dependent upon whether Saturn is ill-aspected. In a good chart, this person has a serious, thoughtful mind, the will is ambitious and the emotions are held in a prudent, restrained mode. This placement can then lead to considerable success in life. But in a difficult chart, this person is frugal and rigid in their views, emotionally unresponsive, too cautious and intolerant of human failings.

AQUARIUS
Here the thinking becomes humanitarian, tolerant, and aware of justice versus injustice. This person has an original way of thinking and a strong interest in social issues. Their will is industrious and has a clear social ethic. In a fine chart, the thinking becomes intuitive, and interested in higher ideas or religious values.

PISCES   (ruler)
This placement allows Jupiter's impetus towards clear thinking to move up to high ideals and visionary thinking which grasps the overall picture; in a fine chart this is deepened into a keen interest in religious or spiritual, metaphysical ideas, possibly direct spiritual perceiving. This person is compassionate, hospitable, unassuming; but they may avoid defending their own rights and invoke people who like to dominate others.

****

SATURN IN THE SIGNS

Note: Saturn's influence is very powerful and significant in regard to how we live our life. For every person is subject to impulses in the subconscious where an awareness pulsates in the will as to what our purpose in life is (our karma); that is, what we should both achieve and struggle against in life. These influences are due to admonitions coming from Saturn. But we need to note that because its energies are located in the subconscious, Saturn's influence is also quite subtle. There are two modes by which Saturn influences us through its position in a zodiac sign.

A Negative: It creates blindness about some aspect of our human nature. This leads to a deficiency, or an imbalance, regarding this part of our being, making us feel cautious and inhibited, or experience very restrictive circumstances. Through this dynamic, we are being impelled to progress in developing themselves. We could call this a stern or negative, karma-regulating influence, enforcing what we are not able to recognize.

B Positive: It bestows perception about our self and our abilities. This can bring about substantial insights into our personality, and insight as how to best move forward in life, meeting our obligations and furthering our development. We could regard this as the capacity to sense what our karma requires of us.

ARIES   (fall)
Saturn in this sign, in mode A, causes the person to feel inhibited in regard to their own initiatives, thus to 'blow hot and cold', and to be easily angered. They have to struggle to perceive the social impact of their more self-centred behaviour, their ambitions and intentions.

In mode B, although here planet and sign are not very compatible, the finer aspects of Mars can have some impact. Then this person is able to have patience and discernment as to how to place their own will into the world, by intuiting how to integrate their own personality into the world around them.

SATURN IN THE SIGNS continued

TAURUS
In mode A, this person has to struggle to intuit how to keep the urge for sensual pleasures, for material possessions, and for a predictable, routinal niche in life, in the right balance with regard to their own best interests.

In mode B in this sign, Saturn reinforces intuitively the Taurean urge for sensible, secure arrangements in life, and it also instils the impetus to avoid a too dull, phlegmatic way of being. It can also refine any involvement in sensual experiences, and affirm the urge to be meaningfully welcoming and hospitable.

GEMINI
In mode A in this sign, Saturn's influence makes manifest this person's incapacity to interweave their emotional needs and wishes with clear thinking, and here Saturn does this by inhibiting this ability. But in all of its inhibiting actions throughout the zodiac, Saturn's influences are intended to impel a person to struggle to balance out their (karmic) deficiency, and thus acquire the missing ability.

In mode B, Saturn's intuitive power gives stability and consolidation to the thinking capacity. This person can take on mental challenges that require disciple and focus, in particular literary studies, or legal and mathematical problems. But the intellectuality is not inclined towards intuitive ideas or imaginative thinking.

CANCER   (detriment)
In this sign, Saturn's influence is primarily negative (that is, mode A). Saturn's intuitive promptings, active in the subconscious, are muffled, because the planet and this sign, with its inner link to the moon, are incompatible; the moon and Saturn are direct opposites.[28] So this placement causes the person to be emotionally unclear, and

---

[28] The infant with its rounded-out, 'moist' qualities is lunar influenced; the old person with their more 'dry' and angular features are Saturn influenced.

SATURN IN THE SIGNS continued

CANCER continued
from this confusion, all sorts of uncertainties arise for them. This person needs as a child to be especially affirmed and loved; this lessens their emotional insecurity on into adulthood. Otherwise, a tendency to a feeling of abandonment, melancholia, suspiciousness and self-pity manifest. A result of these problems is often loneliness and seeking comfort in many possessions or by clinging to the past.

In mode B in this sign, Saturn's intuitive prodding strives to give understanding of the role of emotions and vulnerability in the person. But this mode would require considerable factors in the chart to be effective, including perhaps the south lunar node in Cancer (and the current sun sign or rising sign being in Cancer).

LEO (detriment)
In mode A in this sign, Saturn's intuitive promptings about the underlying purpose and direction of one's life are muffled, so this person can be autocratic and arrogant, inhibited in their will, and not warm-hearted.

In mode B in this sign, Saturn's intuitive impulses strengthen (or bring about important challenges regarding) the leonine sense of selfhood, of being ethically a leader of others. So this person is, or gradually becomes, responsible and loyal, and can determine their own pathway in life. (This positive mode would need the sun and Saturn to be well-aspected.)

VIRGO
In mode A in this sign, Saturn's intuitive promptings are poorly 'heard', leading to a rigidity of the primary features of the Virgoan; this person is very efficient and orderly, but too critical of others or themselves, too prudent, too cautious and a worrier. This person can also be quite melancholic, pedantic and even somewhat servile.

In mode B in this sign, Saturn's intuitive impulses have only a limited outcome, leading to a precise and meticulous person whose patience allows them to work well in scientific and medical research areas. Yet in a fine chart, if Venus is not ill-aspected, there are high standards of personal morality.

SATURN IN THE SIGNS continued

LIBRA (exalted)
Saturn in mode A in this sign prods the person to realize that socially clinging to a kind of island mentality is self-defeating. To suppress the yearning for partnership with others, for significant other people in our life, is harmful. The challenge is to realize that those whom karma brings into one's life need to be affirmed and their involvement welcomed. The tendency to indecisiveness also is encountered, in order that the person may learn to overcome it.

In mode B, Saturn strengthens, or impels the person to strengthen, understanding of what the presence of other people in their life really means. For this person the mystical saying, 'we are one another', becomes an underlying guiding thought, in a general social sense. In a fine chart, there is a high sense of social responsibility, and interest in helping bring harmony to society. This placement also strengthens appreciation of art, and the capacity for tact and sociability, which consequently brings about success in one's career.

SCORPIO
Saturn's intuitive promptings here lead to a stronger self-sense, equally spread through the will, the thinking and the emotions; but of a Scorpio kind. So the over-all consciousness (or 'soul-life') is subtly enhanced. Now, the outcome of this is determined very much **by the personality itself**; namely whether this person has a difficult or a fine chart. That determines how well the subconscious promptings from Saturn are received or 'heard' by the sign. Whereas with the other zodiac signs, it is a question of whether the planet itself is ill-aspected or well-aspected.

So in mode A in this sign, the intensity of the Scorpio personality is fired up in his or her over-all makeup, but in a dubious way. This causes an intense and problematical sex nature, and an intensely self-centred, often ruthless or devious nature, as well as being jealous and subject to bouts of anger.

But in mode B, Saturn here, in enhancing the over-all sense of self, encourages an ethical will and a responsible, balanced emotional life, hence making this person very determined, shrewd and resourceful, which can lead to success in their personal and career goals. This person is also capable in crises.

SATURN IN THE SIGNS   continued

SAGITTARIUS
Saturn's intuitive promptings (or admonitions) in this sign produce almost exclusively positive results, as the intuitive energies from Saturn have a natural affinity to the planetary ruler of Sagittarius, which is Jupiter, whose energies are predominantly benign and at their best encourage the quest for wisdom. So Saturn here is operative almost only in mode B; this brings out an interest in learning, in religious or spiritual ideas, in maintaining high ethical standards, in being humanitarian and kind, and making sure that one's moral principles are always honoured. The few negative outcomes include, being too upset by harm to one's personal reputation, and being rather conservative.

CAPRICORN   (ruler)
When Saturn is in this sign, it simply intensifies the features of Capricorn itself, because it is completely attuned this sign, being its the ruler. Also, the sign of Capricorn is very deeply linked to this planet. So, there is not a mode A and a mode B dynamic here, which are based on how well or how poorly the planet harmonizes to the sign). Instead, the outcome of this placement is determined by the actual nature of the Saturn influences in this personality, that is, whether these are negative or positive.

But we note also that Capricorns have an enhanced ego-sense, and an enhanced sense of their 'mission' in life and how all this is placed in a flow of time going from the past towards a very focussed-on future. So this placement means that the person will manifest strongly all the normal Capricorn qualities, of being ambitious, practical, persevering, severe, good organisers, emotionally restrained. Naturally, the best Capricorn features will manifest strongly in a fine chart and the hardened, ego-centric, anti-social features will be there in a poor chart.

AQUARIUS (ruler)
When Saturn is in this sign, it intensifies the features of Aquarius itself, as Saturn is the ruler of this sign (and also of Capricorn). So here the person has subconscious Saturn admonitions towards being true to their nature and destiny (or karma), giving in effect an enhancement to the main features of the Aquarian personality;

SATURN IN THE SIGNS   continued

AQUARIUS   continued
intelligent, very fond of dialogue and of new ideas, defending the rights of others, supporting humanitarian initiatives, being a loyal friend, and being a bit too stubborn.

PISCES
Saturn here is active only in mode A; the gentle and very sensitive, and often psychic Piscean is dampened right down. For Pisceans respond to the subconscious Saturn admonitions, about sensing and being true to their destiny (or karma), in a way that makes them fearful. The Piscean translates these solemn and earnest promptings into a need to be very cautious, to refrain from asserting oneself. For the Piscean's sense of ego is usually not strong, so she or he easily surrenders their own wishes and become obedient to authority. They can be fearful and moody, and with their emotional life under pressure to be self-restricting, inclined to make a poor choice of partner.

****

The Outer non-classical Planets: Uranos, Neptune & Pluto

We cannot give details about these outer planets in the signs here, as insights from Rudolf Steiner's work into the significance of the three outer planets, Uranos, Neptune in a horoscope is negligible. And naturally there are no insights from Rudolf Steiner about Pluto, as this was not discovered until five years after his death. Insights from modern astrology about the significance of these planets, is sketchy at best, because of the very limited opportunities to research this. Uranos stays in a sign for a period from about 7 to 14 years (depending on when it is going retrograde).

With Neptune this takes 14 years, or longer if in retrograde, and naturally this means that entire generations have one of these planets in the same sign in their horoscope. Pluto is in a sign for 15 years to about 30 years, and was only discovered in 1930, so huge numbers of people have it in the same sign in the horoscope. So the only interpretation possible is generational, not personal, and based on very limited years of observation.

Chapter Seven
The Rising Sign and signs on the cusps

To interpret a horoscope, you must of course integrate the Rising Sign into the personality's dynamics; the rising sign is almost as strong an influence in determining the personality as the sun sign. The soul qualities brought about by the rising sign are obvious, they are on the surface, but remember these traits are not in the person's core qualities; those derive from the sun-sign. The rising sign in a horoscope actually determines what zodiac sign is on the cusp of, (or governs), each of the 12 houses in that person's horoscope. This sequence of zodiac signs is very important; it determines very greatly how the person experiences the 12 facets of life, which each house governs. As we noted in Chapter One, the House system which seems to me to be the most accurate, is the Placidus system.

The Placidus system is the most widely used system in the western world, and once you become familiar with interpreting horoscopes you will see why; it defines the person's life very accurately. But various alternative systems are used, for a number of reasons, see the last chapter for more about the different House systems.

Whatever sign governs a house in each horoscope, gives a vital 'colouring' to the psychological dynamics of that house. Here we present the essential significance of the zodiac sign for each house. This is a complex area, and the counsellor is advised to read further on this theme.

Note that the description of the Rising Sign qualities, that is, the sign that governs the first house, assumes that it is free to give its very strong colouring to the personality; but it may not be ! There may be influences from the past which are blocking this. Then the person's life may centre around the effort to manifest these dynamics. (This is dealt with in more detail in the last chapter.)

It is useful here to refresh our memory as to what the Houses govern:

The Houses

House One: the sense of self (the ego).

House Two: talents & abilities and our life-values. These together help form our sense of self-worth.

House Three: the mind (thinking & speech), also siblings and the local neighbourhood.

House Four: the core emotions and also the home.

House Five: romance, children and one's energies as used in romance or work or in creative interests.

House Six: daily work and health.

House Seven: marriage, and other long-term significant people.

House Eight: intimations from spirit realities (influencing the soul consciously or subconsciously), also sexuality, the partner's income, and the end of life.[29]

House Nine: one's attitude to religious-spiritual ideas values, to relationships and also to travel.

House Ten: one's social reality: usually career and marital situation.

House Eleven: life-goals and groups of friends.

House Twelve: the subconscious soul-life (wishes, ideas, or intentions, etc)

Note: when interpreting a chart, the **house location of the ruler** of the rising sign (e.g., the Mercury for Gemini) must be born in mind; the theme of that house will determine the focus of that part of the person's life which that planet governs. Thus, since Mercury governs the intellect, and if Gemini is the rising sign, and Mercury is in say, the house seven, then this person's mind will focus naturally on close, long-term relationships.

---

29. The 8th House acts as a threshold, through which spiritual influences flow into humanity.

IF THE RISING SIGN = ARIES

House One governed by   Aries
As with all rising signs, the qualities that a zodiac sign gives here are very similar to those it gives as if it were the sun sign; they are just not as strong. So here this person will have a competitive, assertive and somewhat fiery nature, the ability to see an idea and then to act quickly to get it happening. There is also a good sense of direction and an inherent ability to get things done. But bear in mind that anyone getting to know this person will discover that 'behind' these features of their rising sign, are the features of this person's sun sign. (This applies to all the other rising signs.)

House Two   Taurus
Every person naturally tends to draw on their talents and abilities to determine his or her vocation; and this is what house two governs, as well as our life-values. When house two is governed by the sign of Taurus, then this person has an interest, as regards their career, in the earthly world of financial markets, real estate, or in other activities that bring pleasure and security. But Venus, the ruler of Taurus plays a role, so there is also an interest in the arts, and in that which brings beauty, harmony or pleasure to people (wealth is partly governed by Venus).

So the aspects to Venus in this horoscope are important; these determine how well or poorly this person accesses and applies their abilities. But is important to note that if in any horoscope, the moon is also in the rising sign (and especially if the sun sign and the rising sign are also the same), then **this** zodiac sign will tend to over-ride how this person approaches such a core activity of determining which of their abilities they shall use in their work, and in what way.

House Three   Gemini
The house of how we think and speak, (and of siblings and the local scene), when governed by this sanguine sign, makes the person naturally a witty and intelligent person, a good speaker and clever thinker. Again, the aspects to this sign's ruler (Mercury) determine how well or poorly this person communicates and thinks.

THE RISING SIGN = ARIES   continued

House Four   Cancer

The house of our core emotions and our home life, when governed by Cancer, makes these two aspects of our life especially vulnerable. So this person with a Cancerian emotional vulnerability in this house, needs their home to be a place of the safety and comfort; if it is not, they will feel stressed. Likewise the core emotional qualities will be a focus point for this person. These two aspects of life can be stable and secure, or the opposite, depending on whether the moon is well-aspected or ill-aspected.

Now, our home life is firstly that of our childhood; but the parenting which we received then strongly affects us, on into our adult life. This occurs more strongly than we realize, because the parental influences remain highly operative, but in the subconscious. However, it is important to note here that the fourth house is linked to the person's parents; more precisely to the opposite-gender parent. (Some astrological traditions link this house to the mother, but this is, in my view, not correct: see the last chapter for more about Houses and the 'archetypal zodiac' versus the Houses.)

This applies of course to the fourth house in all horoscopes, not just the sequence for the Aries-rising person which has Cancer here. This means that the core dynamics of that parent – their stresses, self-worth issues, anger, view of life as worthwhile or burdensome – are perceived by the young child, even if not very consciously. And the child does make conclusions about, and have reactions to, these dynamics. These responses live on, undetected, into adulthood.

The strength of these responses varies according to the degree of self-integration of the person; some people are potently directed by these, other people can surmount them. Moreover, the inner life of the opposite-gender parent is either good or bad, depending upon how well or badly the moon is aspected in, <u>not</u> the parent's chart, but in <u>the client's own chart</u>. If the moon is significantly aspected in this person's chart, then the same-gender parent will have manifested the dynamics of those aspects.

House Five   Leo

When the house of our personal energies, and how they are manifest in romance, with children, or in creativity, is ruled by Leo, one's way of being in these three areas of life depends very much on whether one acts from a sense of pride and confidence or from a feeling of

THE RISING SIGN = ARIES   continued

House Five   Leo   continued
inferiority. The negative or positive dynamics involved here are determined by aspects to the sun.

House Six   Virgo
The house of health and daily work, when ruled by Virgo, makes the person fastidious in regard to orderliness and cleanliness in these areas. With a Mercury influence here, there is also a need for work that challenges the person to be efficient and mentally engaged, so aspects to this planet are important.

House Seven   Libra
This house governs the most important relationships (marriage and long-term associates), and the rule of thumb for the seventh house in all horoscopes, with regard to choice of partner, is that 'opposites attract'. One reason that opposites attract is that they provide the experience of a missing element, an element which exists in the other person's personality. From this experience, we are giving ourselves the possibility to acquire these qualities, to round out our personality. And the zodiac ruler of house seven is the opposite of the zodiac ruler of house one.

So with Aries rising, the opposite sign, which will be in house seven, is Libra. The Libran partner appeals to this person because they offer an experience of that missing element of their own personality, namely quiet self-reflection and mildness. But also Librans have no aggressive, abrasive qualities, so they don't antagonize the competitive, fiery nature of Aries. (See the last chapter for more about choice of partner and the rising sign.)

House Eight   Scorpio
As we have noted, this house concerns intimations of spirit realities, sensual desires/the type of partner (and the partner's income), and also the end of life. With Scorpio governing this house, the Aries-rising person has a more intense awareness of life's experiences, more intense yearnings and desires. So there is a heightened involvement with, or arguments around, sensuality and the partner's personality (and their income), depending on how Pluto and Mars are aspected.

THE RISING SIGN = ARIES   continued

House Nine   Sagittarius
This house concerns one's attitude to religious-spiritual values, to relationships and also to travel. With Sagittarius governing, this person has an expansive worldview, they like to travel and can easily accept big ideas. With Jupiter being important here, civic issues and philosophical ideas – even spiritual ideas – appeal, but often without this person feeling any need to ponder them in detail.

House Ten   Capricorn
The focus of this house is one's social reality: usually the career and marital status, and with this sign governing it, much depends on the aspects to Saturn in the horoscope. If these are good, then the career and conduct in regard to significant others are appropriate, and the person is conscientious in both. If these are bad, then life-lessons await in regard to these themes in life, associated with a lack of perception as well as low confidence and inadequate social awareness.

However, it is important to note here that the tenth house is linked to the person's same-gender parent. This applies of course to the tenth house in all horoscopes, not just the Aries-rising sequence person. (Linking this house to the father, in my view, is incorrect: see the last chapter for more about the 'archetypal zodiac' underpinning the Houses.) As with house four, the childhood parenting has an ongoing impact on the person, and here the inner life of the same-gender parent is either good or bad, depending upon how well or badly Saturn is aspected in, not the parent's chart, but in the client's own chart.

If Saturn is significantly aspected in this person's chart, then the same-gender parent will have manifested the dynamics of those aspects. If Saturn is badly-aspected that parent was absent either physically or emotionally, or was deeply insecure. The after-effect of this is, that the client may restrict their own choice of career and partner.

House Eleven   Aquarius
When the house of friends and life-goals is governed by Aquarius, then the Aries-rising person seeks out friends who are intriguing, perhaps even eccentric. In terms of life-goals, there is also interest in

THE RISING SIGN = ARIES   continued

House Eleven   Aquarius   continued
projects that help the less fortunate or reduce injustice in the world. Aspects to Uranos and Saturn provide important indicators as to how this person functions here.

House Twelve   Pisces
This fiery person, with Pisces governing the house of the subconscious, has a veiled softer, more feminine nature, which is often quite intuitive. If there is a weakened Mars in the horoscope, the person feels a lack of guidance and confusion about their life plans, (one client said to me, "I'm always facing the 'what-ifs' dilemma). With a well-aspected Neptune, these people can have valuable dreams, whether offering insights into their life, or even predictive dreams which indicate events of the future. But with a badly aspected Neptune, this inner spiritual guidance is lacking.

RISING SIGN = TAURUS

House One   Taurus
As with all rising signs, the qualities that a zodiac sign gives here are very similar to those it gives as if it were the sun sign. So this person enjoys the earthly pleasures of life. There can be a capacity for singing and the arts in general, and there is a phlegmatic tendency in thinking and with decision making. Physically, this person often has a slightly cow-like look around the eyes, or a thickened upper shoulders area.

House Two   Gemini
This person's use of their talents in earning an income has an intellectual focus. They are good speakers and salespeople, and they like their work to be 'sanguine'; that is, offering changing tasks and interesting goals. They could have two jobs at once, or turn a hobby into a job. But money will be a focus of the mind, and clever ways found to earn it. The house of position of Mercury (and its aspects) will tell you in what area of life, income is earned (for example, if in house three, through intellectual activity, but in house six, through service to others, perhaps in health or nutrition.

House Three   Cancer
This emotional sign governing house three, makes the thinking and therefore this person's speech, subject to their feelings and general sensitivity. So emotional responses can warm up their thinking, making it empathetic, or cause the mind to over-react subjectively in socially difficult situations. Aspects to the moon are critical here.

House Four   Leo
When Leo governs this house the person's attitude to their own core feelings and their home is determined by how much self-confidence they have. If they are confident, then a fine home, even a lavish one, is desired. The opposite-gender parent's own self-image affects this person's attitude, as an adult. Moreover, the inner life of the opposite gender parent is either good or bad, depending upon how well or badly the sun is aspected in, <u>not</u> the parent's chart, but in <u>the client's own chart</u>.

If the sun is significantly aspected in this person's chart, then the same-gender parent will have manifested the dynamics of those aspects. If the sun is ill-aspected then this parent was probably

RISING SIGN = TAURUS   continued

House Four   Leo   continued
insecure about themselves, and may pass that on to this child. But as we noted earlier, some people can overcome their childhood responses.

House Five   Virgo
When the restrained and orderly Virgo energies influence this house, then romance and a potential partner are subject to cautious prudence and critical analysis. Helpful, but careful, parenting is the norm, and social events are approached in a well-planned and capable way. Aspects to Mercury indicate how well or poorly this person applies himself or herself to romance and being creative, and parenting.

House Six   Libra
With Libra governing here, the person seeks harmony, even aesthetics, in their workplace and in the relationships with work colleagues. There is also a strong drive to work together with one other person. In this way their sense of whom they really are, is given a chance to develop more. This person's health is linked to the aspects of Venus; if it is ill-aspected there can be an excess desire for sugary foods, harming the health.

House Seven   Scorpio
One reason that opposites attract is that they provide the experience of a missing element, an element which exists in the other person's personality. So to the placid Taurus-rising person with their phlegmatic (or laid-back) nature, and a strong sensuality, a dynamic perhaps even charismatic Scorpio type is attractive. This dynamic can drive them early into relationships and sometimes this creates difficult, turbulent situations, especially if Mars or Pluto are ill-aspected. But if these planets are well-aspected, then a very good partnership is likely for this person.

House Eight   Sagittarius
This person has an outgoing, active interest regarding sensual desires and the type of partner and also regarding ideas or experiences that involve things 'beyond the threshold', i.e., religious

RISING SIGN = TAURUS   continued

House Eight   Sagittarius   continued
or spiritual topics. In a fine chart, with Jupiter well-aspected, this can lead to deep insights, and their relationship dynamics are sound, (and the partner can bring financial benefits). But negative aspects affecting Jupiter, Mars (or Pluto) can lead to difficult outcomes in all areas that this house governs.

House Nine   Capricorn
The themes of higher education, travel, and spiritual-religious ideas, sense of duty and of having a mission or goal in life. But Saturn's influences here induce either a self-limiting caution and anxiety or an insightful, pragmatic interest, depending on how this planet is aspected.

House Ten   Aquarius
The Taurus-rising person is drawn to unusual, but humanitarian vocations. But as we noted earlier, the 10th house is linked to the person's same-gender parent, and the inner life of this parent is either better or worse, depending upon how well or badly Uranos and Saturn is aspected in, <u>not</u> that parent's chart, but in <u>the client's own chart</u>. If Uranos and Saturn are significantly aspected in this person's chart, then the same-gender parent will have manifested the dynamics of those aspects. If ill-aspected, then this person may be influenced by that parent's tendency to eccentric or nervous responses to life.

House Eleven   Pisces
This person is loyal and sympathetic to groups of friends, and has life-goals that are likewise focused on caring for others. But the choice of friends and life-goals are influenced by the aspects to Neptune and Jupiter. If these are negative, then the decisions here can be unwise, often ungrounded (naïve, idealistic).

RISING SIGN = TAURUS continued

House Twelve   Aries
The placid Taurean has her or his sense-of-self, which Mars energies help to manifest, placed under a veil. For them, being assertive is difficult; to express any choleric quality is a challenge. If as a result, anger builds up and is not given expression, then it can either slowly burn away, causing illness or resentment; or it can suddenly explode. Aspects to Mars can say more about how this person responds to this dynamic. (Jeanne Avery recommends undertaking art or craft activity with an iron (steel) instrument, to 'drain off' any anger energies.)

****

RISING SIGN = GEMINI

House One   Gemini
Similar to having Gemini as the sun sign which has Mercury as it ruler, this person will be sanguine, often witty and intellectually focussed. As with every rising sign, the house location of its planetary ruler tells a lot about the main focus of the person's life. The mind of the Gemini-rising person is focussed on the theme of whatever house Mercury is located in the horoscope.

House Two   Cancer
Here, those abilities and talents are drawn on, that enable this person to work in a field where they can nurture or in some way assist other people, in a caring manner. Their finances are therefore linked to how well they can apply their abilities to this kind of work. Aspects to the moon will assist or hinder this person accessing these abilities.

House Three   Leo
Here the leonine sense of pride in one's social image and in one's achievements is linked to this person's ability to think and speak, and therefore to how well they communicate with other people. If the sun is well-aspected, this person can have a commanding quality in their speech and in the actions which follow on from their resolute, confident way of thinking.

House Four   Virgo
The home must be orderly and sensibly laid-out, so that it functions efficiently; the emotional energies should also be orderly and 'sensible', so that the otherwise sanguine Gemini can have a more stable quality to their feelings (and especially in their home). But the opposite-gender parent's way of being is a factor to consider, regarding house four. If Mercury is significantly aspected in this person's chart, then the opposite-gender parent will have manifested the dynamics of those aspects. Here the question is whether Mercury in that parent's horoscope predisposed them to being very critical of this person or to being mentally stimulating.

RISING SIGN = GEMINI

House Five   Libra
In the area of romance and using energies creatively, the Gemini-rising manifests a gentle, soft quality, so they seek harmony in their creative activity and a loyal, kind partner. But they may not sufficiently affirm to themselves their own needs in romance. With Venus as the ruler of Libra, and also since it is the planet of love and of the Arts, the dynamics in these areas of life depends strongly on how well or poorly aspected is Venus in the horoscope. If well-aspected, this person has enjoyable romantic and or artistic times; if ill-aspected then this person tends to opt out of really engaging with these areas of life, and all that they require of a person for success in these endeavours. In a fine horoscope, Libra here opens up the way for inspired artistry.

House Six   Scorpio
This person can apply themselves with intensity and determination to their daily work. They can have a somewhat charismatic quality in working with others. Here the aspects governing Mars and Pluto are important. If these are good, then this person can be capable but not dominating in their workplace. If these planets are ill-aspected then, power plays and manipulation, as well as arguments are likely.

House Seven   Sagittarius
As we noted earlier, one reason that opposites attract, is that they provide the experience of a missing element, an element which exists in the other person's personality. The outgoing, confident, optimistic qualities of Sagittarius appeals to the Gemini-rising person when it comes to choosing a mate. The relaxed, expansive, generous, good-humoured qualities of this sign provide that missing element to their own nature. But attractive too, is the capacity which the Sagittarian has at times for deeper intellectual discussions. The aspects to Jupiter are therefore important; poor aspects can invoke an unreliable, superficial Sagittarian.

House Eight   Capricorn
Capricorn's cautious, conscientious nature impacts here on sensual desires/the type of partner and on ideas or experiences connected to a sensing of spiritual realities, (which owing to Saturn's link to

RISING SIGN = GEMINI

House Eight   Capricorn   continued
Capricorn will include here intimations about one's karma).[30] The aspects to Saturn itself determine whether there is in regard to these themes, a self-limiting, solemn and anxious response, or a response to a mature, insightful dynamic which harmonises with life's purpose. These aspects also influence the role played by the partner's income.

House Nine   Aquarius
This person is drawn to studies and also travel experiences which open new horizons and provide ongoing mental stimulation, through the Aquarian urge for independence. From the influence of Uranos they can receive sudden flashes of insight, and are drawn to careers where this kind of mindset is an asset.

House Ten   Pisces
A vocation which gives opportunity where seeing the 'bigger-picture' is essential has strong appeal, especially if the work is of service to others, alleviating suffering and misery. Additionally, with this house the same-gender parent's influence has to be considered; it can be pivotal. If Neptune is significantly aspected in this person's chart, then the same-gender parent will have manifested the dynamics of those aspects. If Neptune is ill-aspected, then that parent was disillusioned in their own vocation, or at least an impractical person. This can impact on this person's decisions about their life, making un-grounded 'visionary' ideas alluring.

House Eleven   Aries
Here, an enhanced sense of one's own self intensifies this person's search for life goals, and a desire for groups of friends. This can bring strong, competitive friends into their life. The sanguine nature of the Gemini-rising person can weaken the interest in trying to clearly define one's goals in life. If Mars is ill-aspected, then aggressive friends appear, and the link between them is disturbed by arguments.

---

[30] That is, from beyond the threshold demarcating this world from spiritual energies.

RISING SIGN = GEMINI

House Twelve   Taurus
This placement in the house of the subconscious puts the awareness of feelings, and emotional responses to sensory impressions, under a veil. This causes the emotional life and artistic awareness to be less consciously registered by this person, so they have to struggle to access and acknowledge what they really sense or are feeling. Sensitive emotions, a latent artistic talent, or a heavy sensuality can be ignored. Aspects to Venus in the horoscope will indicate more clearly the dynamics that apply here.

****

RISING SIGN = CANCER

House One   Cancer
Similar to having Cancer as the sun sign which has the Moon as its ruler, this person will be strongly emotionally oriented. Easily the most compassionate or empathetic of the 12 signs, the Cancerian and Cancer-rising person must feel loved and secure in order for themselves be loving and supportive. As a child, lacking a matured selfhood, this person is difficult to parent, as any discipline imposed on them makes the child feel as if really abandoned. They are closely linked to their mother, their childhood home and old possessions.

House Two   Leo
This person's decisions as to which abilities to access to earn an income is directly linked to their sense of self-worth, which is a hallmark of Leo. Consequently, the aspects to the sun or other features of the horoscope which influence self-confidence, shows how well or poorly this is done. The house position of the sun greatly determines the area of life where income earned.

House Three   Virgo
Here, the mind has the Virgoan focus on clarity and orderliness, thus moderating the Cancer-rising's emotionality. There can be a gift at communicating, including writing. Aspects to Mercury will show whether being critical and pedantic, or being clear and concise triumphs in this person's thoughts and communicating.

House Four   Libra
The home life has to be aesthetic and harmonious, even artistic and the core emotions must also be, so far as possible, free of disagreeable tensions. But regarding house four, the opposite-gender parent's way of being is a factor to consider. If Venus is significantly aspected in this person's chart, then the same-gender parent will have manifested the dynamics of those aspects. Here the question is whether Venus in that parent's horoscope predisposed them to being submissive to other people and too laid-back, or to being warm and enthusiastic about the possibilities in life.

RISING SIGN = CANCER continued

House Five   Scorpio
If the soul of this person is burdened by potent inner turmoil, making them withdrawn, insecure and self-centred, then both in romance and how they use their personal energies in recreation, will be a source of ongoing trauma for them. They can pick partners who have negative Scorpio traits, and who 'burn' them, emotionally. But if there is a generally positive feeling towards life, then a charismatic, dynamic Scorpio person with a good nature will be attractive. Aspects to Mars and Pluto are significant here.

House Six   Sagittarius
Daily work that offers challenging tasks based on ideas which require an adventurous, outgoing response to succeed, appeals to this sensitive person. Aspects to Jupiter need to be considered; negative aspects can lead to interest in working with the disabled, as this helps them to work out their own inner conflicts.

House Seven   Capricorn
One reason that opposites attract, is that they provide the experience of a missing element, an element which exists in the other person's personality. To the emotional Cancer-rising person, a stable Capricorn partner will be a good choice, able to be a calming, reliable, supportive quality. But if, through the moon having negative aspects in their chart, this Cancer-rising person is especially emotionally delicate, then the Capricorn mate they choose will have the negative emotional qualities of this sign, such as being emotionally immature and needy, self-centred, and they may also be judgemental and somewhat cold.

House Eight   Aquarius
A strongly individualistic response occurs to this person's sensual desires and the type of partner and also ideas or experiences connected to a sensing of spiritual realities. But the Cancer-rising's sensitive, empathetic nature does play a role here, often leading to difficulties about sensuality versus love. This person is also affected by influences raying from spiritual sources (or 'beyond the threshold'), causing flashes of insights. But if Uranos is poorly-aspected, then these influences can lead to psychic problems.

RISING SIGN = CANCER   continued

House Nine   Pisces
With Pisces here, the empathetic, emotive tendency of this person causes them to respond emotionally to religious-spiritual ideas and values. Hence many have a strong religious tendency and often a strong involvement in charitable activity. There is interest in directly mystical experiences. In a fine chart with positive Neptune aspects, mediumistic activity, which weakens the ego-sense can be avoided, and instead, wholesome, consciously spiritual study taken up.

House Ten   Aries
This person has a determined, self-aware attitude towards their social (marital) status and their vocational choice, and how they perform at work. As always with house ten, the same-gender parent's influence has to be considered; it can be significant. If Mars is significantly aspected in this person's chart, then the same-gender parent will have manifested the dynamics of those aspects. If Mars is poorly aspected in this person's chart, then the same-gender parent will have manifested the dynamics of those aspects. If Mars is ill-aspected, then that parent was angry or frustrated, which could hinder their child's approach to the themes of this house. If Mars is well-aspected then they had a positive outlook, helping this person to be confident in their vocational and social status.

House Eleven   Taurus
The Cancer-rising person seeks as a life-goal, to have a secure, comfortable niche in life. This person will seek out well-to-do friends who also have a pleasurable, even luxurious lifestyle. Friends are warmly welcomed, and enjoyable gatherings with them is an important part of life for this person.

House Twelve   Gemini
With Gemini governing the subconscious, the emotive Cancer-rising person has their logical, intellectual capacity somewhat veiled. Hence feelings can easily over-rule their intellect, causing confusion in moments when the emotions run high. Hence if Mercury, which rules Gemini, has some negative aspects, this person's logical processes can be strongly impeded.

****

RISING SIGN = LEO

House One   Leo
Similar to having Leo as the sun sign which has the sun as it ruler, this person will be strongly self-aware, and inclined to initiatives where their own personality can shine, as it were. At best, this person is warm-hearted and generous, very appreciative of kindness or praise, but otherwise, arrogance and dominating the social situation is common. Often this person has a leonine style of hair, reminiscent of a lion's mane. The house position of the sun determines the main focus of their life; but this is affected by the aspects to the sun in the horoscope.

House Two   Virgo
This person can usually assess their talents and abilities quite well, and use a strong analytical skill in their work. Such professions are chosen as teaching, and managerial positions, where giving advice and training of other people is required. The placement of Mercury amongst the houses indicates the area of life where they work.

House Three   Libra
The Leo-rising person is helped in achieving their goals, because Libran qualities bestow on this person's way of speaking an harmonious quality which is experienced by listeners as very agreeable. This is a very good position for those in Public Relations work, and for those whose creative work needs to appeal to the public. Since Venus rules Libra, and this house also governs the way of thinking, this person's mind has a natural interest in, and perhaps a gift in, the Arts.

House Four   Scorpio
A quietly strong, yet intense, quality lives in the heart of the Leo-rising person, because Scorpio energies bestow their strength in the feelings. But in house four the opposite-gender parent's way of being is a factor to consider here. The question is, what are the aspects governing these Mars and Pluto in that parent's horoscope? If they are significantly aspected in this person's chart, then the same-gender parent will have manifested the dynamics of those aspects.

If one or both are ill-aspected, then this person will have turbulent emotional dynamics, including manipulative power-plays from Pluto

RISING SIGN = LEO   continued

House Four   Scorpio   continued
or irritated anger from Mars. The home life is also governed by the same forces, and hence subject to the same dynamics.

House Five   Sagittarius
This person's creativity is outgoing and optimistic, liking challenges, and invoking pleasant and successful outcomes. In romance a mirror of this Sagittarian joviality is sought for in a partner, but if Jupiter is ill-aspected then both in romance and general creative activity, there is a naïve optimism, which is blind to the grounded reality. With negative aspects to Jupiter, gambling can become a problem.

House Six   Capricorn
This placement of Capricorn enables this person to carry out very strenuous, arduous work. There is a high capacity for persevering at work and to endure hardships in the job, because of a saturnine sense of duty and a heightened urge to be conscientious. If Saturn is ill-aspected then this person can become over-worked by their employer, as they cramp their own lifestyle to meet the needs of the workplace.

House Seven   Aquarius
One reason opposites attract, is that they provide the experience of a missing element, an element which exists in the other person's personality. That partner is appealing to the Leo-rising who demonstrates a spontaneous and flexible, non-dominating way of being. This is the Aquarius type, who will also allow the Leo-rising to be in charge (up to a point, as Aquarians value their own freedom). The partner's appearance and general nature must also reflect well upon the Leo-rising.

If Uranos or Saturn are ill-aspected, the Leo-rising can choose the wrong type, an Aquarian with an exaggerated eccentrically spontaneous nature. Then there will be a clash of 'freedoms', that is a false, immature urge for freedom and authority that causes arguments.

RISING SIGN = LEO   continued

House Eight   Pisces
Here Piscean sensitivity is the main influence on this person's sensual desires/the type of partner and also on ideas or experiences connected to a sensing of spiritual realities. So these areas of life are subject to either ungrounded, idealistic attitudes or to strongly ethical goals, even spiritual values. In a fine chart with Neptune well-aspected to the sun, spiritual insights are possible. In a chart with Neptune ill-aspected, many problems associated with choice of partner and involvement in ill-advised spiritual groups is likely.

House Nine   Aries
The Aries forces intensify the determination of this somewhat fiery person, when it comes to their religious or spiritual ideals. The Aries self-awareness and determination also drives them to consider what a further education could allow them to achieve, either for themselves or for others. But if Mars is ill-aspected, then being too zealous or aggressive for a cause or an idea is a problem.

House Ten   Taurus
Vocations that involve the arts or provide comfort and pleasure to people is attractive to the Leo-rising person, but he or she is at pains to ensure that it results in something that reflects well on them. As always with house ten, the same-gender parent's influence has to be considered, as it can be significant. If Venus is poorly aspected in this person's chart, then this indicates that the same-gender parent will have manifested the dynamics of those aspects, and this can impact on the Leo-rising person, affecting their decisions.

House Eleven   Gemini
With this placement, there is interest in groups of friends who are good conversationalists. The Leo-rising person is a loyal friend who enjoys a lot of socializing. In a fine chart, these friends need to be strongly intellectually stimulating. The life-goals of the Leo-rising are subject to change, as different ideas fall in and out of favour.

House Twelve   Cancer
The Leo-rising's emotions are veiled to herself or himself, and so their own emotional responses can cause them considerable stress. Their feelings are also their vulnerable point, for they are quite

RISING SIGN = LEO continued

House Twelve   Cancer   continued
emotionally sensitive, but they never want this to be realized by others, and they resent this trait in themselves. It is a classic Leo-rising (and Leo sun-sign) tactic to actually keep their emotional hurts very secret; only their closest loved ones find out when there is something upsetting them.

****

RISING SIGN = VIRGO

House One   Virgo
Similar to having Virgo as the sun sign, this person will have typical Virgoan traits of orderliness, neatness, emotional reserve and especially the inclination to make a practical analysis of tasks and people, often being too critical in their assessment. Since Mercury is the ruler of Virgo, the mind of this person will activate its analytical approach into whichever area of life is governed by the house where Mercury is found in the natal horoscope.

House Two   Libra
With the Libran quality of needing someone else around, to be able to sense their own self, this person tends towards using abilities that, in the workplace, are more successful if they work with a partner. With Venus exerting a major influence in this house, the Virgo-rising person, in earning an income, is drawn to using their abilities and interest in artistic things or activity that brings harmony to others. They also need to feel harmonious in their work, or have an aesthetic environment at the workplace to be happy at what they are doing.

House Three   Scorpio
There is a strong, determined quality in the thinking and speech of the Virgo-rising, so as a communicator this person can be very effective. But the Scorpio intensity, operative in the mind, can cause communications to be too abrupt, even abrasive. If Mars or Pluto are ill-aspected, then power games or the urge to dominate through thoughts and speech can occur.

House Four   Sagittarius
The core emotional nature tends towards optimism and the home will be large and comfortable, even opulent, with grand proportions, if possible. But in house four the opposite-gender parent's nature is a factor to consider here. The question is, what are the aspects governing Jupiter in that parent's horoscope? If they are significantly aspected in this person's chart, then their opposite-gender parent will have manifested the dynamics of those aspects, and this impacts to some extent upon this person. A common outcome of an ill-aspected Jupiter is that the emotional nature is wilfully blind to reality, choosing to believe in an ungrounded ideal.

RISING SIGN = VIRGO   continued

House Four   Sagittarius   continued
This would have lead the parent into various mistakes or disappointments, effecting in turn this person, causing them to be too cautious about life, for example.

House Five   Capricorn
In the area of romance and how their personal energies are used in any creative activity, the Virgo-rising person is subject to the cautious, prudent, and duty-bound nature of down-to-earth Capricorn. If Saturn is poorly aspected there may be an unconscious inclination to choose a partner who is insecure and emotionally cold. In a good chart, where Saturn is neutral or well-aspected, a caring and insightful partner is chosen.

House Six   Aquarius
The somewhat rigid and conservative Virgoan qualities are over-ruled by the impetuous and outgoing Aquarian influences, leading this person to seek work where originality is valued and where a sanguine work style is possible. Uranos exerts an influence here, so aspects to this planet in the horoscope will also affect the way of working; but also the dynamics around this person's health. Negative Uranian energies induce flighty or tense states of being at work, and this can impact on the health.

House Seven   Pisces
One reason that opposites attract is that they provide the experience of a missing element which exists in the other person's personality. So in the choice of partner, the pragmatic, earthy nature of this person finds the non-rigid, imaginative Piscean person an attractive complement. For the Virgo-rising, such a person provides a welcome counter-balance to their nature. In a good chart, this works out well. But if Neptune is ill-aspected, an un-grounded, dreamy idealism naively expects to find a perfect partner. In this situation, a partner can be invoked who is a self-deceived, unreliable person.

House Eight   Aries
Here a determined Aries energy is the main influence on this person's sensual desires/the type of partner, and also on ideas or experiences connected to a sensing of spiritual realities. This fires up

RISING SIGN = VIRGO continued

House Eight   Aries   continued
their interest in a partner quite early in life, but the over-riding Virgoan influence lessens the vehemence of this. If however Mars is ill-aspected, then relationships can be marred by disagreements, and the partner's income can be the cause of arguments.

House Nine   Taurus
Here the earthy Virgoan energies are reinforced by Taurean influences, so interest in higher education, and in religious, spiritual or philosophical ideas is viewed with a very grounded attitude, and linked to a practical goal. Artistic or agricultural activity can be appealing, and successful, as is comfortable travelling.

House Ten   Gemini
With Gemini here, this person's career interests are oriented towards vocations that offer intellectual stimulation, and opportunities to talk with people. As always with house ten, the same-gender parent's influence has to be considered, as it can be significant. If Mercury is poorly aspected in this person's chart, then the same-gender parent will have manifested the dynamics of those aspects, and this can impact on the Virgo-rising person. That parent may have been too critical or too sanguine, affecting the Virgo-rising person's decisions in the area of career and social status.

House Eleven   Cancer
With this placement, the emotionally vulnerable qualities of Cancer colour the attitudes to friends and life-goals. It is easy for this person to have anxiety about life and one's own life-goals. They also have anxiety about their friends (one client said, 'I wonder if friends will betray me somehow'). But the positive element is there, too; namely a loyal, kind and even maternal attitude to friends, and a goal in life is often, 'how can I alleviate misery in the world'? Aspects to the moon show whether the dynamics manifesting here will be positive or negative.

RISING SIGN = VIRGO   continued

House Twelve   Leo
The Virgo-rising person has an impediment to their ego-sense, hence to their confidence and assertiveness, when the sun-ruled sign of Leo is in the house of the subconscious. So these people are not so commonly found in a prominent position, as this is not easy for them. But they still can have influence and success, by a more discreet way of working.

****

RISING SIGN = LIBRA

House One   Libra
Similar to having Libra as the sun sign, this person is generally charming, sociable and likable. The Libra-rising person is aware of aesthetics and is often strongly artistic. There is a need for other people to interact with, and also a need to ensure that harmony prevails socially. There is especially a yearning for another person who can be a real partner, whether in a marriage and at work. Aspects to Venus will show whether the emotions are balanced and at peace, or whether anxiety around disharmony and aggression are creating the need to steer around this. The zodiac position of Venus is also important as this will have a major influence.

House Two   Scorpio
The use of abilities and talents to achieve an income is surprisingly intense with the gentle Libra-rising, as Scorpio's intensity is active here. Work that involves groups of people can be more successful than work with individuals. There can be an attitude that success is guaranteed, and if Pluto and Mars are well-aspected, this can happen.

House Three   Sagittarius
Despite the social ability of the Libra-rising, they can be quite clumsy in social situations if they speak their mind, because here Sagittarius is operative, bringing both optimism in the thinking and in speech, but also the blunt, non-tactful way of speaking. In a good chart, there is natural interest in larger, challenging ideas, including ideas of a religious or spiritual kind.

House Four   Capricorn
This placement brings an attitude that order and responsibility must be found in the home life, and likewise within one's core emotional qualities. However, in house four the opposite-gender parent's personality is a factor to consider. The question here is, what are the aspects governing Saturn in that parent's horoscope?

If they are significantly aspected in this person's chart, then their opposite-gender parent will have manifested the dynamics of those aspects, and this will impact to some extent upon this person, especially seeing that Saturn and Capricorn are the major agents of karma. If Saturn is ill-aspected then it is likely that this parent was too severe or too emotionally reserved, creating difficulties for the

RISING SIGN = LIBRA

House Four   Capricorn   continued
Libra-rising in their quest to find their own inner authority and validity.

House Five   Aquarius
When it comes to romance and being creative, the Libra-rising person allows himself or herself to leave the quiet, predictable harmony of Libra. They are attracted to unconventional, people who radiate a sense of freedom and excitement. Their creative activity can be very people-oriented, and even focussed on social justice. But if Uranos is ill-aspected invoking a chaotic immature freedom urge, then the partner chosen can be eccentric, or worse, and personal creativity can be enmeshed in a nervous, chaotic energy. If Saturn aspects invoke restrictive and anxious attitudes, then a rigid, stifling, unemotional partner can appear.

House Six   Pisces
At work this person can easily feel the idea, the over-all purpose of what is going on. They are willing to be particularly helpful, even when this is against their own rights and interests. In a fine chart, work that provides opportunity for the visionary dream of what could be achieved is appealing. If Neptune is ill-aspected then this person can be dominated at work, or entertain ideas for a job that are ungrounded.

House Seven   Aries
We have seen how one reason that opposites attract is that they provide the experience of a missing element, an element which exists in the other person's personality. The opposite of the indecisive, gentle Libra is fiery Aries, so Aries people are attractive to this person. The experience of their energies is needed by the Libra-rising, who are somewhere striving to have their own initiative stirred up by them.

But Mars forces are not easy for the Libran to acknowledge, let alone assimilate, and consequently the Libra-rising person, subconsciously aware of this, can often have a veiled frustration. If Mars is ill-aspected, then this person can get irritated or even angry in the relationship. Or the partner they select may be a particularly angry,

RISING SIGN = LIBRA continued

House Seven   Aries   continued
irritated person. This is one area where the Libran urge for harmony has to at times experience the stress of being confrontational.

House Eight   Taurus
With this dynamic, the Libra-rising generally has a deep-seated sensuality and also an artistic capacity. In a fine chart, there is a high artistic creativity. If Venus and the Moon are well-aspected then this person can reach out for a suitable partner with an appealing charm, and can integrate their desires with their social reality. If these planets are ill-aspected then the reaching out for a partner, and the integration of personal energies in relationships, can be the cause of problems.

House Nine   Gemini
There is usually a lively interest in ideas about the 'bigger picture' which religion and spiritual books offer. Ongoing education appeals, as does any travel that offers exposure to different ways of being.

House Ten   Cancer
The career chosen by this person should allow them to respond with emotional sensitivity to the needs of the public. As always with house ten, the same-gender parent's influence has to be considered, as it can be significant. If the moon is poorly aspected in this person's chart, then that same-gender parent will have manifested the dynamics of those aspects, causing them to have negative attitudes and moods. These problems can impact on the Libra-rising person, affecting their own self-confidence or their view of how they stand in the world, inhibiting their capacity to let their emotions play a role in their career.

House Eleven   Leo
Friends are many, and socializing is a priority for this person. Capable, optimistic supportive friends are chosen with confidence, or unsuitable, unreliable friends are chosen from an underlying attitude of low self-esteem: depending on aspects to the sun. Friends, who are often influential or high profile people, need to reflect well on the Libra-rising, and to show appreciation of the achievements or

RISING SIGN = LIBRA   continued

House Eleven   Leo
intentions of this person. The attitude to possible goals in life is also directly linked to aspects influencing the sun.

House Twelve   Virgo
This dynamic strengthens the reluctance of the Libra-rising person to speak their mind. The logical, organizational ability conferred by Virgo is veiled in the house of the subconscious. So as a client said 'There is a struggle to get to the point', when speaking your mind means conflict, or possibly conflict, with someone else's ideas. Aspects to Mercury, which underlies the logical mental processes, will help or worsen this problem, depending on what these aspects are.

RISING SIGN = SCORPIO

House One   Scorpio
Similar to having Scorpio as the sun sign, this person will have an intense but veiled inner life; few people will know how powerfully this person experiences their emotions and their thoughts. Their eyes often have an intense shine, and though the general predisposition is usually unobtrusive, the Scorpio-rising has a formidable capacity to assert their desires and will. Mars and Pluto are the rulers of Scorpio, and hence the aspects to these two planets will indicate how the Scorpio energies are modified.

House Two   Sagittarius
Here the attitude towards selecting one's own talents and abilities for a choice of career is usually optimistic and outgoing. There is the courage and energy to try a challenging field of work, one that offers substantial results. Aspects to Jupiter will show whether there is an excessive optimism, or soundly based decision-making. The house position of Jupiter determines to which area of life the work is connected.

House Three   Capricorn
The mind has a solemn, serious and patient quality carried by a sense of duty and responsibility, derived from Capricorn. Intellectual effort is not shirked, and a disciplined and thorough way of thinking is typical. If Saturn is ill-aspected, then mental communications can be hesitant and this person can suffer from a lack of confidence in their speech and writing. But if Saturn is well-aspected there can be a valuable, intuitive capacity in the thinking.

House Four   Aquarius
The emotions and the home life of this person are focussed on having freedom, so the home must not be a place of restrictions, rather a place where good communicating is a core value. In the emotions there is a yearning for the freedom to affirm and to express what one really feels. But regarding house four, the opposite-gender parent's way of being is a factor to consider. In this case, if Saturn and Uranos are significantly aspected in this person's chart, then their opposite-gender parent will have manifested the dynamics of those aspects.

RISING SIGN = SCORPIO   continued

House Four   Aquarius
Here the question is, if there are negative aspects, whether these planets in that parent's horoscope brought about eccentric and chaotic qualities (Uranos) or whether they brought about a restrictive, insecure, rigidity (Saturn). If so, these can these same tendencies in the child and thus place a burden on the Scorpio-rising's own fourth house dynamics.

House Five   Pisces
An idealistic glow envelops the themes of romance and children for this person, who can show a surprisingly gentle selflessness in regard to these two areas of life. The challenge will be to ensure that attitudes here are properly grounded and not subjective and flighty, leading to substantial disappointment. If Neptune is ill-aspected then these problematical attitudes are quite likely.

House Six   Aries
A strong, determined and assertive approach is taken as regards daily work. If in the horoscope of a woman, Mars is very prominent, then that woman is interested working in what is traditionally a male workplace. There is a need to learn how to work cooperatively together, even if one is the manager or supervisor.

House Seven   Taurus
We have seen one reason that opposites attract is that they provide the experience of a missing element which exists in the other person's personality. The opposite of the subtly intense Scorpio is the phlegmatic, laid-back Taurean, who is therefore a good partner for this person. The Taurean person can also meet both the sensual desires of the Scorpio and also provide a reliable, calming supportive role.

House Eight   Gemini
The bright but changeable intellectuality of Gemini colours this person's attitude to their desires, the paranormal and also any psychic-spiritual insights. It also tends to lead to a selection of a partner who can offer interesting conversations.

RISING SIGN = SCORPIO   continued

House Nine   Cancer
If religious or spiritual ideas do appeal, then this person naturally forms an emotional attachment to them. Ideas that are nurturing to others are also attractive (unless the moon is ill-aspected); and there is a natural empathy with ideas that are currently surging in society or ideas that help the socially disadvantaged. When travelling, this person finds journeying by water appeals to them.

House Ten   Leo
Pride in career achievements (and social status) is a hallmark of this person, and they easily put themselves into the limelight and work well in positions of responsibility. The aspects to the sun are significant here; if these are negative then the ego-sense is hindered, and the necessary self-esteem to really achieve is lacking. Additionally, with this house the same-gender parent's influence has to be considered; it can be pivotal. If the sun is significantly aspected in this person's chart, then the same-gender parent will have manifested a good self-confidence and will instil that into this person. If the sun is ill-aspected, then that parent was very likely lacking in confidence, and may have weakened this person's capacity to enter the workforce with confidence.

House Eleven   Virgo
Friends are chosen on the basis of their capacity for intelligent conversation, but this person needs to refrain from criticising these friends (or from attracting critical people to themselves). In a fine chart, the goals this person sets are socially aware and focussed on being of service to others, or oriented towards an organized, efficient way of being. Aspects to Mercury are important here.

House Twelve   Libra
This placement causes the emotions to be veiled over, and since Scorpios have an intense inner nature, this emotive obscurity makes them want to keep their feelings under lock and key, as exposing them could lead to awkward surprises for themselves. Often the key to harmony is to resolve the conflict between obvious potent desires over-ruling unacknowledged emotional needs and vulnerability. If Venus is ill-aspected then a too potent sensual drive can be a problem, especially as it is veiled. In a fine chart, if Venus is well-aspected, then quality artistic skills or insights are possible.

RISING SIGN = SAGITTARIUS

House One   Sagittarius
This is similar to having Sagittarius as the sun sign, but the rising sign's qualities are not as deeply grounded in the personality as those of the sun-sign. This person is fond of their freedom and of challenges, especially ones which are the result of grand and even daring ideas. But this person is also prone to making untactful remarks. Although usually generous and optimistic, there is a naïve trust in others because of a tendency to be ungrounded.

When let down by others, the Sagittarius-rising person never wants to acknowledge that they should have been more realistic. Worrying and being anxious or pessimistic are traits that are especially disliked by this person. All these qualities are influenced by the Jupiter, the planetary ruler of this sign, and so aspects to this planet are significant here.

House Two   Capricorn
The way this person's abilities and talents are utilized to earn income can be prudent and cautious, even lacking in self-confidence, if Saturn is ill-aspected. But if this planet is well-aspected then, considerable insight can be present in doing this. However, if in the horoscope the moon is in the rising sign (and the sun sign and the rising sign are the same), then this zodiac sign will tend to over-ride how the person approaches this core activity of determining which of their abilities they shall use, and in what way. For the Sagittarius-rising person, this means a more adventurous (or naïve) approach will predominate here.

House Three   Aquarius
The thinking is drawn to new ideas, and this person experiences ideas flashing into their mind. Thoughts that focus on humanitarian ideals or new ways of getting things done are attractive, but effort has to be made to avoid having a mindset which is too sanguine or too chaotic. Relations to people in the immediate environment and to siblings are also subject to lots of changes or sudden initiatives.

House Four   Pisces
A sensitive, somewhat vulnerable quality pervades the core emotions and also the home life of this outgoing person. Any troubles affecting the home life are felt deeply, as a peaceful, even uplifting,

RISING SIGN = SAGITTARIUS continued

House Four   Pisces   continued
kind of home-life is wanted. In house four the opposite-gender parent's way of being is a factor to consider. The question here is, what are the aspects governing Neptune and Jupiter in that parent's horoscope? If they are significantly aspected in this person's chart, then the opposite-gender parent will have manifested the dynamics in the aspects affecting those two planets. If these are ill-aspected for that parent, then this person may find difficulty in dealing with the more harsh or depressive side of life.

House Five   Aries
The intensity of Aries fires up this person's dynamics in romance and in creativity or recreation. Horse riding and sports in general are attractive, and a challenging quality in romance is attractive. This latter can mean that a dynamic, energetic person appeals, but if Mars is ill-aspected, then an aggressive and self-centred person appears, who triggers off irritation or anger in the Sagittarius-rising person.

House Six   Taurus
Work needs to be a source of harmony, or inner contentment, for this person, and an aesthetic environment is preferred. Work that seeks to bring about a more enjoyable or more aesthetic world for others is also appealing to this person.

House Seven   Gemini
Opposite personality types are attractive because they provide the experience of a missing element, an element which exists in the other person's personality. So in a fine chart, with excellent Jupiter qualities, an adaptable, sanguine Gemini is invoked as a good marriage partner to the determined, focused Sagittarius-rising.

The sparkling, witty Gemini way of speaking really draws the interest of this person. Ideas are of interest to Sagittarians (whether as rising sign or the sun sign), and also to Gemini people, with Mercury as the ruler of this sign. They love talking, sharing their ideas. But the Sagittarius-rising person has to beware of being attracted to a Gemini type who only has superficial ideas about life.

RISING SIGN = SAGITTARIUS   continued

House Eight   Cancer
The outgoing Sagittarius-rising person can have a subtle psychic capacity, active in the temperament or predisposition (hence semi-consciously). So the role of this house as a kind of threshold to the 'beyond', to subtle psychic experience, is heightened, and in this way the outgoing, decisive Sagittarius-rising person gets 'hunches'. They are also more emotionally affected by their partner's moods than most people.

House Nine   Leo
The way this person gets their life furthered by higher education is connected to aspects to the sun. If these are good, they step forward into learning with confidence; if the sun is ill-aspected, then the opposite applies. The same dynamic applies to how they represent their own view on life; if there is a strong self-confidence, these people have a natural teaching or sales ability.

House Ten   Virgo
In career activity, this person is naturally an organized and efficient worker, often with a sense of being prudent and aware of the social responsibility of what they do. They are also aware of their social image and irritated if they are not respected in their work. Additionally, with this house the same-gender parent's influence has to be considered; it can be significant. If Mercury is significantly aspected in this person's chart, then the same-gender parent will have manifested an intelligent way of thinking and analysing and will encourage that into this person. If Mercury is ill-aspected, then that parent was very likely subject to unclear thinking or communicating, and may have weakened this person's capacity to use their mind in the workforce with ease and clarity.

House Eleven   Libra
This person likes to have friends who are artistic or socially very agreeable and tactful. In formulating life goals, this person is influenced by friends of this kind. But the Sagittarius-rising person often find that if their friends present a variety of suggestions, which is not uncommon, they then have trouble deciding on their own pathway.

RISING SIGN = SAGITTARIUS continued

House Twelve   Scorpio
The intense inner experiencing of feelings and yearnings, typical of Scorpio, are here veiled. This hinders this person from awareness of these dynamics in their own inner soul, pushing them more towards the external world of activity and challenges. If aspects to either Mars or Pluto are strongly negative, then there could well be some strong complexes (such as phobias or anxieties or fixations on themes) which can work away in the subconscious, disturbing the inner harmony of their personality.

****

RISING SIGN = CAPRICORN

House One   Capricorn
Similar to having Capricorn as the sun sign, which has Saturn as it ruler, this person will be cautious, particularly self-aware and goal-driven. He or she will also be looking ahead of the flow of time, putting themselves into the future. This is often done at the expense of properly living in the present experience. The Capricorn-rising is emotionally reserved and yet may possess strong emotions.

There is a deep need to be wanted and treasured by someone, despite their own somewhat repressed feelings. There is also a need for the world to recognize them, because of a sense of having an important task to carry out. But also this person can subject herself or himself to a harsh way of life, because of an inherent sense of duty. This person may pick as a partner someone who later on betrays them severely.

House Two   Aquarius
In selecting abilities or talents for their career, this person is drawn to an unusual vocation, or one in which there is a lot of freedom in terms of initiative and scheduling. If Uranos is ill-aspected then this results in difficult and tense situations, financially. If this planet is well-aspected, then work that needs clever insights and a focus on others, will appeal. Being able to spend money impulsively is relaxing, and becomes a problem only if taken to excess.

House Three   Pisces
The mindset is intuitive, so this person can see the over-view of situation easily, and is able to explain and get enthusiastic about clever ideas which are also practical. In a fine chart, this person is drawn to idealistic, visionary ideas, and usually can present these (in writing or in conversation) very well. Doing investigative or research work is a natural skill, and this person can work very well on their own.

House Four   Aries
The fiery power of Aries intensifies the emotions of the Capricorn-rising person, but they may still keep them veiled. Their actual power is unaffected by this however, so this person will have to learn to acknowledge their feelings, if they are to remain healthy. But, in house four the opposite-gender parent's nature is a factor to

RISING SIGN = CAPRICORN   continued

House Four   Aries   continued
consider. The question is, what are the aspects governing Aries in that parent's horoscope? If they are significantly aspected in this person's chart, then their opposite-gender parent will have manifested either a lot of initiative or anger, depending on the dynamics of those aspects, and this personality trait impacts to some extent upon the Capricorn-rising person.

House Five   Taurus
The Taurean enjoyment of leisure and pleasure becomes active here, but if Venus is ill-aspected (or in a weak position, such as being located in House 12), then this person will find that their ability to relax and feel their more poignant yearnings is repressed. Often Venus is in a negative position in charts which have prominent Capricorn and Saturn influences. If Venus is well-aspected, then this problem does not arise, and this person can be aesthetically aware and enjoy their leisure time.

House Six   Gemini
Work which demands much from the intelligence is appealing, and in the workplace, they can be witty and think on their feet very well. There is a workaholic tendency for any Capricorn, and especially if their intelligence is high and their work is intellectually stimulating and this gives a chance for an important duty or sense of a mission to be fulfilled.

House Seven   Cancer
Opposite types are attracted to each other because they provide the experience of a missing element which exists in the other person's personality. If the emotions in the Capricorn-rising person are not too repressed, (so Venus and the moon are well-aspected), then a good bond to a partner who has strong, sensitive emotions occurs (usually a Cancerian person); this is deeply satisfying on a subconscious level to the Capricorn-rising.

But the emotions in the Capricorn-rising person are often repressed, and so the choice of life partner for this person is fraught with emotional trauma, especially if Venus is ill-aspected (and the moon as well). The Capricorn-rising has a yearning in the subconscious to be wanted and valued, which becomes a potent factor driving them

RISING SIGN = CAPRICORN   continued

House Seven   Cancer
on to redress this imbalance. This inner insecurity leads them to make a choice of someone who is in need of a lot of care, (possibly traumatised or abused) or who is a dominating type. Through the suffering caused by the ensuing emotional turbulence, they become aware of their own emotional needs.

House Eight   Leo
As we have noted, this house concerns intimations of spirit realities, sensual desires/the type of partner (and the partner's income), and also the end of life. With Leo ruling here, this person's attitude to these aspects of life is determined greatly by the degree of self-esteem and confidence concerning one's rights and needs, or the lack of this. This is greatly influenced by the aspects to the sun in the horoscope. It is also influenced by the interplay of egotism and selflessness in the Capricorn-rising person; and this varies strongly according as to whether it is a fine chart or a difficult chart.

House Nine   Virgo
Attitudes to travel, further study and one's personal philosophy of life is determined by the level of intelligence and also of wisdom in the Capricorn-rising person. This is indicated in part by aspects to Mercury, the ruler of Virgo. If these are poor, then materialism and a sceptical, logical attitude prevails in regard to religion and spiritual ideas. If these are good, then a high intelligence brings good results when further studies are undertaken. In a fine chart, spiritual insights that bring real wisdom can be achieved.

House Ten   Libra
Libra here assists this person in the interface with others in their career life, bringing a sociability and charm. Their career may be connected with the arts or to bringing a more aesthetic element into the world; or the focus is on a more harmonious world in other ways. As always with house ten, the same-gender parent's influence has to be considered, as it can be significant. If Venus is well aspected in this person's chart, then the same-gender parent will have manifested a socially capable or artistic tendency. If the aspects to Venus are poor in this person's chart, then emotional, social or artistic qualities of that parent were poor, possibly causing them, as a parent, to weaken the Capricorn-rising's ability in these areas.

RISING SIGN = CAPRICORN continued

House Eleven   Scorpio
In determining their life goals, this person has to be aware of the dynamics that prevail when they are interacting with the public, or with various groups of people. They can have a charismatic intensity which used with integrity leads to success. Or they can manipulate, and be subject to manipulation, usually resulting in power struggles, causing substantial problems. Friends and associates likewise can become deceptive and harmful, or they can be dynamic and successful people, assisting this person on their pathway.

House Twelve   Sagittarius
The relaxed, jovial, optimistic and spontaneous Sagittarian attitude is veiled for the Capricorn-rising person, with their isolationist tendency and focus on strategic planning. But these Sagittarian qualities are needed by this person for success in life, giving freedom from their harsh self-imposed discipline. This means also that the influences of Jupiter and Neptune are veiled or dimmed; yet it is the insightfulness (even spiritual awareness) from Neptune and the expansiveness from Jupiter (even real wisdom) which if accessed, bring fulfilment to this person.

****

RISING SIGN = AQUARIUS

House One   Aquarius
The spontaneous, freedom-seeking Aquarian qualities are prominent here, along with a need for a circle of friends, and a talent for dialoguing with others, and rebelling against stagnation or rigidity of any kind. Stubbornness is a feature of this person, as is the need for exercise to assist blood circulation. If Uranos is ill-aspected, then a tense, nervous condition is often present.

House Two   Pisces
For this person, the approach to which abilities they should use for their vocational life, is coloured by idealism and a desire to assist the world. This attitude is enhanced by sympathy for those who are in need of help in whatever way.

House Three   Aries
The mental processes are fired up with Aries here; so this person is a capable thinker and energetic communicator (unless Mars is weakened by negative aspects.) Opinions may be too self-centred and held on to despite negative social results. If aspects to Mars indicate the urge to dominate over others, people can feel resentment which leads to arguments and opposition.

House Four   Taurus
For the Aquarius-rising person, the home is important; it must be comfortable and aesthetically pleasing. The home is artistically arranged and decorated, and it has to offer a secure, relaxing environment. The core emotions are focused on feeling at peace in oneself, and being able to enjoy the pleasures of life. In house four, the opposite-gender parent's way of being is a factor to consider.

The question here is, what are the aspects governing Venus, the ruler of Taurus, in that parent's horoscope? If it is significantly aspected in this person's chart, then the same-gender parent will have manifested the dynamics of those aspects. If it is ill-aspected, then this person may have some areas of tension in their emotional life, and consequently have to deal with feelings that are preventing just this inner peace.

RISING SIGN = AQUARIUS   continued

House Five   Gemini
With this placement, romance with someone appeals who is witty and intellectually interesting; emotional and sentimental attitudes are not so common. The children of an Aquarius-rising person are often also witty and highly intelligent. But if this person does not have traits in their personality that make them inclined towards parenthood, they can find family life restrictive and shy away from it.

House Six   Cancer
It is in the workplace that this person gives expression to their feelings. A caring attitude is naturally there, almost a maternal kindness; being active in a group situation appeals as well. But if there is disharmony at work, this person finds this directly affects their health.

House Seven   Leo
We have explored how opposite types are attracted to each other because they provide the experience of a missing element which exists in the other person's personality. Here the decisiveness and self-assurance of a Leo type is attractive to the Aquarius-rising person, who in their less self-disciplined, more spontaneous nature lacks this.

But any Leo partner must allow this person to have the freedom to give expression to their sanguine urges. The Aquarius-rising person has to guard against being drawn to an insecure and hence subtly dominating Leo type. They need to be discerning and confident when selecting a partner.

House Eight   Virgo
This person has a more cautious, restrained attitude regarding sensual desires and hence the type of partner. There is also a rather grounded, careful and rational attitude regarding ideas or experiences that involve things 'beyond the threshold', i.e., religious or spiritual topics.

RISING SIGN = AQUARIUS   continued

House Nine   Libra
Higher ideas, whether undertaken in tertiary studies or drawn from a religious or spiritual group, appeal to this person mainly if they can lead to an enhanced appreciation of beauty, or resonate in an harmonious way with this person's view to life and ethics.

House Ten   Scorpio
This person's way of being in regard to their vocational life and their marital status is influenced by Scorpio energies which intensify these two areas of life. So the Aquarius-rising person can be dynamic and even charismatic in their interface with others at work, becoming very successful. This indicates good aspects exist between the rulers of Scorpio. If however these planets, Mars or Pluto, are ill-aspected, then whatever qualities those aspects activate in the person can strongly influence this interface; this often means being drawn to manipulation or devious behaviour.

As always with house ten, the same-gender parent's influence has to be considered, as it can be significant. If these two planets are poorly aspected in this person's chart, then the same-gender parent will have manifested the dynamics of those aspects, and this can impact on the Aquarius-rising person, during childhood. That parent may have felt inwardly wounded or vengeful, causing them to treat the child harshly, damaging the Virgo-rising person's decisions in the area of career and social status (one client spoke of their old mother still hitting her sister when she was a grown-up, 45 years of age).

House Eleven   Sagittarius
This placement leads to an optimistic and outgoing approach to life-goals, which through its own enthusiasm, coupled with an alert, intelligent mindset, tends to invoke success. This person usually has many friends, because the Aquarius-rising has a warmth and generosity when interacting with their friends (and Aquarians are group-oriented in their core nature). But if Jupiter is ill-aspected, there can be a naïve, too trusting selection of friends, and an ungrounded view of their goals in life, which then leads to disappointing outcomes in these areas.

RISING SIGN = AQUARIUS continued

House Twelve   Capricorn
This zodiac sign activates, but in the subconscious, a dim awareness of one's karma; in other words, of how one's actions and plans may, or may not, be in accordance with one's purpose in life. So with Capricorn governing the house of the subconscious, this dim, intuitive sensing of the right steps to take in one's life, is more veiled. For the very sensitive person, this can create a subtle feeling of being disempowered; otherwise it leads to slight tendencies towards complexes such as phobias, or anxieties. But in a fine chart, where Saturn is well-aspected, there can be the positive effect of an enhanced intuitive capacity, guiding this person.

RISING SIGN = PISCES

House One   Pisces
The Pisces-rising person often has large eyes and a dreamy or soft expression. This person is inherently idealistic and often has attitudes and beliefs that need to be more grounded in the real world. They can have a very fine compassionate and self-sacrificing tendency, but this is also a point of severe vulnerability for them as they can easily give way to the demands of others, leaving themselves open to being bullied or voluntarily surrendering their right to live their own life. Musical ability is common, and so is resistance to giving up their ideals when faced with reality.

House Two   Aries
In the area of selecting which of his or her abilities to use for earning an income, this person does become competitive and energetic. This is one area where a challenge and resourcefulness are both liked and needed. Aspects to Mars will indicate whether this person can easily invoke this energy or whether they would rather avoid the challenge, thereby getting frustrated about the difficulties involved.

House Three   Taurus
With the easy-going and pleasure-loving qualities of Taurus governing the house of thinking and speaking, hence communicating, the Pisces-rising person is naturally sociable. The way they interact with other people is socially very agreeable. Also since Venus is the ruler of this zodiac sign, its influences add a refined, harmonious quality to the way they communicate. This further enhances their social interaction efforts.

House Four   Gemini
With this placement, the home is subject to the changeable and restless quality of Gemini. This can lead to a more frequent change of residences than generally happens, and this person also enjoys having friends come over for lively conversations. With Mercury influences activated here, the sensitive, emotional Pisces-rising person can reflect intellectually on their feelings. But in house four the opposite-gender parent's way of being is a factor to consider. The question here is, what are the aspects governing Mercury in that parent's horoscope?

RISING SIGN = PISCES continued

House Four   Gemini   continued
If it is significantly aspected in this person's chart, then the same-gender parent will have manifested the dynamics of those aspects. So, if Mercury is ill-aspected, this person may have argued with that parent, and consequently this difficulty, plus their own struggles with logical thinking, hinders a clear, rational approach to issues. If this planet is well-aspected, this person will have avoided these difficulties and may well have been encouraged to think clearly by that parent's way of being.

House Five   Cancer
There is a maternal quality to this person's approach to romance; their emotionality comes to the fore in a caring, nurturing way. In regard to children, this person is especially nurturing and family-oriented. But romance for this person also causes anxiety about possibly being rejected by a potential or actual partner; this prospect is deeply upsetting to the Pisces-rising person because of their sensitivity, and because they become deeply attached, often sentimentally, to loved ones. If the moon or Neptune are ill-aspected, these aspects will be very relevant to the problems this person experiences in regard to romance.

House Six   Leo
In the workplace, the gentle Pisces-rising person becomes a determined and assertive person, who likes to have their achievements recognized and their authority in the workplace respected. But they need to engage in their work with a sense of self-esteem, or these drives will be repressed. Aspects to the sun indicate whether their ego-sense is healthy and strong, or weakened.

House Seven   Virgo
Opposite types are attracted to each other because they provide the experience of a missing element which exists in the other person's personality. The pragmatic, rational Virgoan with their no-nonsense attitudes and capacity to make decisions in a clear and capable manner, offers the experience of this to the Pisces-rising person. And these two contrasting kinds of people can then form a good bond;

RISING SIGN = PISCES

House Seven   Virgo   continued
the efficient, grounded Virgo giving a stable direction to the idealism of the Pisces-rising person. If Mercury is ill-aspected in the horoscope, there is a tendency to form a relationship with a critical, pedantic Virgoan.

House Eight   Libra
This house concerns intimations of spirit realities, sensual desires/the type of partner (and the partner's income), and also the end of life. With Libra governing this house, the Pisces-rising person has their already strong, semi-psychic sensitivity to subtle intimations from spiritual sources heightened; this contributes to their reputation as 'visionaries' or psychic types of people.

They also easily lean towards an idealistic view of passion, and togetherness in general. The aspects to Neptune and to Venus will be very important here, to ascertain how this person will fare in relation to both psychic tendencies and to the way of being with a partner. (If Neptune itself is located here as well, no more powerful indicator of clairvoyance or out-of-body experiences exists.)

House Nine   Scorpio
The Scorpio energies intensify the attitude of the Pisces-rising person when it comes to religious or spiritual ideals and also their higher education aspirations. These themes become subject to a quiet inner determination which can intensify the Pisces-rising's capacity in these areas of life. If Pluto has strong aspects in the horoscope, then some charisma exists for this person in their interface with others. If Pluto or Mars are ill-aspected, then unhealthy attitudes creep in, leading to an obsessive interest in ideas, or a manipulative way of representing ideas to others.

House Ten   Sagittarius
Here, as with house two and house six, house ten is governed by a fire sign, so this more 'visionary' Pisces-rising person brings a lot of drive to their career aspirations, bringing to a culmination the influence of the other two houses. So a career that offers continual

RISING SIGN = PISCES continued

House Ten   Sagittarius   continued
challenges based on bold ideas is attractive. As always with house ten, the same-gender parent's influence has to be considered, as it can be significant.

If Jupiter is poorly aspected in this person's chart, then the same-gender parent will have manifested the dynamics of those aspects, and this can impact on the Pisces-rising person, affecting their decisions regarding how to place themselves in their vocational life. One result of a poorly aspected Jupiter is to be naïve, over-estimating what one can do, or what the world allows; the result of this is disappointment. A parent with this dynamic could be unhelpful in encouraging their child to engage confidently with the world.

House Eleven   Capricorn
The choice of goals in life, and of friends, for this person can be undertaken with insight into what one's karma is calling for. If Neptune is well-aspected, and Saturn is not ill-aspected, then for this Pisces-rising person generally, there will be a capacity for such insightful discernment. Likewise their choice of friends will be sensible, and probably leaning towards people a little older than they are. But if Saturn is ill-aspected, then unwise choices are made in these two areas of life. With Saturn, (the source of karma-sensing), blocked, then selections can be made which are not in accordance with their best interest. This includes depressive or judgemental people who make use of the Pisces-rising person, and life-goals that avoid the appropriate vocational possibilities.

House Twelve   Aquarius
This placement has two significant results. One is that the urge for inner freedom to truly be oneself is not easily acknowledged and hence not easily achieved, leading to inner tension (one client reported gnashing of teeth whilst asleep). Another result is a psychic condition that derives from the 'ether-body' (that is, our organism of subtle ether forces) being too diffuse. It expands out beyond the skin, and starts to receive impressions of thoughts and feelings, etc, from beyond this person. This strengthens the psychic tendency of the Pisces-rising person, but not in a good healthy sense. This person also might be subject to out-of-body experiences.

RISING SIGN = PISCES continued

House Twelve   Aquarius   continued
If Uranos is ill-aspected, then this person can have a mediumistic tendency (one client had participated in their first séance already at 20 years of age). Or sleep-talking could occur; this is especially likely if Uranos is actually located in house 12 (one such client reported laughing in their sleep). But if Neptune is well-aspected and Uranos also, then these negative conditions don't occur, instead there is a fine spiritual consciousness which unlocks deeper wisdom to this person. This is especially the case if Jupiter is well-aspected to either, or both, of these planets.

****

Chapter Eight   More features of the horoscope & how to interpret a horoscope.

First step: ensure the printed-out chart is correct
The first step is to acquire some astrology software that can calculate the horoscope and print it out for you. Naturally, there will be a learning curve if you don't already have such an astrology software, but these programs are not too difficult to understand. I have used the John Halloran program, called AstrolDelux, for many years. This is because the printed wheel or horoscope is especially clear, really easy to read, see the Appendix for more about astrology software. It is possible to just use a website which creates the chart for you, after you type in the birth data; but it is much better to acquire your own software. You can then easily modify the horoscope, if the need arises (e.g., "oh sorry, that birth-time was not am, it was pm", or "mum says it was actually 6.30 am, not 7.30am").

Note that if the town's data is in the software, then its time-zone will automatically appear correctly in the box, "Hours difference from Greenwich". And the daylight savings times for that town will also be automatically factored in by the software. But you do have to be careful when doing a chart for someone whose town is **not** listed in the software database. You will have to find out the time-zone for any town from the internet which is not in the database. In that case, never type in the **exact** time equivalent of a town's position in terms of distance from Greenwich.

In other words, if the town's data is not stored in the software, then you will need to find out the official time-zone it belongs to, for example, **+3 hrs** or **-10 hrs**. But some sites or books will give the exact technical data, such as +3.14mins. 5secs or -10.26mins. 03secs from Greenwich. You must not enter this exact, additional data into the computer! This is because the computer program only needs the official time zone, not exactly how many minutes/seconds ahead or behind of the Greenwich time zone that town is in.

Having calculated the horoscope, look at it on the computer screen, and check that all the data is correct: have the day and month data accidentally been transposed? This is easy to do, if you were working with a UK client's horoscope and then you do a horoscope for an American client. This is because in the US, the day/month are put the other way around to the UK. (Getting clients to tell you the name of the month is always a good idea.) Also check that the chart shows a meaningful longitude & latitude. It can happen that for a town which is not automatically entered by the program, you have put in a coordinate for east of Greenwich, instead of west, or south instead of north of the equator.

So, assuming that the data is all correct, you print out the chart and the page of Aspects. Then stand the horoscope page up, near to the page with the list of Aspects, and contemplate the two pages. Become familiar with the over-all pattern. Notice if any houses have a lot of planets in them. If so, this indicates where the person's main opportunities or challenges will be experienced. Also note if there is a quadrant in which most of the planets are located: that also tells you which one of the four parts of human nature (ego/soul/life-forces/physical bases of life), will be the focus for their life.

Next, to interpret a chart, I recommend observing what I call the 'four pillars' of the chart. These are the sun-sign, the rising sign, the moon-sign and also the south lunar node (and connected with this is the north lunar node).

Write down these four points on the page you will be using in the session. Then note if any planets are in retrograde. If so, write down the house number and its planet. After this, read about the south lunar node, especially the house in which the node symbol is located. Now, see whether there are any planets in conjunction with that node. And then note whether the north lunar node (abbreviated to MNN in the print-out) has three or more planets in a negative aspect to it.

Before analysing any further, it is very important to assess whether the south lunar node is really strongly affecting this person. If there are planets in conjunction with it, then they will usually be in the same sign as the node, and will thereby intensify the negative traits of that past life's zodiac influence. These planets intensify this nodal hindrance along the lines of how that planet colours that zodiac sign's influence. But if the south node is not affected by anything else, it will probably have little impact.

However, if the <u>north</u> lunar node has several planets blocking it through negative aspects, then the <u>south</u> node's influence over that person's behaviour will also be all the more powerful. For example, consider a person whose sun sign is, say, Sagittarius, and whose south node is in Libra. If their north node, (which will be in Aries, opposite of Libra), is heavily blocked, by squares or oppositions, then that person will have very little of either the fiery Sagittarian or the Aries qualities. See below for information about the significance of the lunar nodes in the houses and signs.

Also note the position of the 'Part of Fortune'; in which house it is located and also in which zodiac sign. Later in the chapter, we shall explore the significance of the 'Part of Fortune' in the houses and signs. This feature of the chart is drawn as a circle with a cross inside it. It goes back to early Hellenistic star wisdom, although, as Robert Hand has shown, there is clear evidence that the Part of Fortune is Egyptian in origin. It is very important, as it tells you what activity or experiences bring the greatest blessing or inner happiness to the client. The location of the Part of Fortune or Fortunata symbol on a chart is determined by a mathematical formula involving the distance between the position of the moon, the Ascendant and the sun.

Once you have absorbed the above qualities of the horoscope, you will have the essential perspective about the person, so now you can correctly understand in their right context, the aspects and also the house position of the planets. These latter two features are the more complex features of the chart. From these two, exact and astonishingly detailed data about the personality can be obtained.

Now look at the print-out of the aspects, and with a pencil put a small mark next to each aspect that you will need to comment on, in the consultation. You will need to mark the conjunctions, sextiles, trines, squares, oppositions and inconjunctions (also called quincunx). You can also mark the semi-squares and semi-sextiles. This includes aspects to the lunar nodes and the Part of Fortune (PF), although only the more obvious aspects are relevant to these features. In particular, of significance are the oppositions, squares, conjunctions to the north lunar node, and conjunctions to the south node. Aspects to the PF are rarely noted, but a brief notice of the impact of the opposition, square, trine or sextile may be useful.

In marking the aspects you will be studying before the client appears, note which planets are especially subject to negative aspects. In particular, the planets that are associated with the sun sign or rising sign of the client. This tells you just how much of a struggle, or just how positive, will be pathway this person will journey along, in respect of their primary signs. This also tells you how they will experience the part of their life which that house governs, where any such planets are located. So if Neptune is in house ten, but it is ill-aspected, then the way this person puts themselves into their vocational activity and social interaction, will be especially ungrounded. But in addition of course, the aspects affecting the planetary ruler of that house (that is, of the zodiac sign which governs it) are also very important.

In the consultation you speak about what the four main pillars of their personality reveal to you, and then I recommend that you consider what the aspects tell you, starting at the top of the page where the sun and its aspects are, and going down to Pluto. You need to leave out the lunar nodes and Part of Fortune until the next stage is completed. This next stage is to speak about the significance of the zodiac signs in which Venus, Mercury and Mars are located. This tells you how their influences are modified by the zodiac signs they are in. These planets govern core elements of the soul; namely the emotions, the intellect and the driving force. Then, although this is subtle, the influence of Saturn's zodiacal position can be considered.

The next step is to discuss the planetary aspects; there will be about 15 or 20 of these. The negative or challenging aspects are nearly always the most important to explain to the client (or to speak about discreetly). But of course, the counsellor will be aware that it is not always appropriate to spell out all the raw details; it depends on the client and their situation. But it is these aspects that highlight the causes of the problems that the client is dealing with.

Then the significance of the zodiacal ruler of the houses is discussed. That means, you identify the area of life a house governs and then mention how this is coloured or nuanced by this zodiac sign. Then the significance of the planets in that house is looked at, starting at house one and going around to house 12.

Then you can consider the significance of the Part of Fortune, which brings a positive note; see below for the significance of the Part of Fortune in the houses and signs. There is still the north lunar node to consider. This is best explained as a needed antidote to the south node, (and they are direct polarities) especially if the south node is a heavy, dragging influence in that horoscope. Or, if the south node is quite lightly present, then the north node becomes a helpful influence which gives to the person the finest energies of that sign, <u>so long as the person reaches up and takes these into their soul</u>, so to speak. Because these capacities are not actually present in the person, but they are being offered to them. I find what is needed here usually is a brief outline of the best qualities of that sign; although some astrologers take up this feature in a lot of detail, (there are a few books available on the subject, see the Appendix).

House Four & house Ten: which parent?
As I noted in Chapter Seven, some astrological traditions link house four to the mother; but this, in my view, is not the case. Some

astrological traditions also link house ten to the father; but this is also, in my view, not correct. Firstly, in my experience over decades, the opposite-gender parent as such is definitely associated to house four, and not the mother. Likewise, in my experience, the same-gender parent is associated to house ten, and not the father as such. (But the opposite-gender parent will be of course in fact the father, if the client is a woman). So why do some traditions link house four to the mother, and house ten to the father?

This answer is actually linked to a very deep, core feature of the horoscope, which is almost unknown today, and so has not been recognized as playing a major part in the very structure of the horoscope. I call it the ***archetypal zodiac***.

The archetypal zodiac

This confusion about house ten and hour four is linked to a primary feature of the horoscope, namely the themes of the 12 houses. We have noted earlier on, that each house has a theme; that is, each house governs a particular part of our life. But why is this? Why actually does each house have its particular theme? With this question we enter into the spiritual reality of our soul and the cosmos. It is hard to find an answer in astrological literature to this question. The research of Rudolf Steiner is able to provide an answer.

Any answers to this question, from a viewpoint which does not have the deeper perspective from Steiner, are rather vague. For example, Noel Tyl, who wrote 10 books on astrology, concludes that each house has its theme because of,

> "...the basic, *natural* distribution of the Signs and Houses showing one astrological year of the sun's motion, giving symbolic meaning to the succession of Houses for one lifetime of Man."[31]

This answer of course, looks at the situation as some kind of symbolic 'something', and thus fails to grasp the situation as a reality. The answer is found when we understand that there is a spiritual basis to astrology, that is, to our link to the cosmos. To gain this understanding this we need to know about the 'archetypal zodiac'. Knowledge of this is given in the work of Rudolf Steiner about the cosmos. He describes, from his seership, how the solar system, and hence our planet with its human life-wave, was created over long aeons by divine spiritual beings, who were active from the zodiacal stars.

---

[31] Noel Tyl, The Houses and the Signs & Planets, Vol 2, p.9, Llewellyn Pub. 1977

Rudolf Steiner's approach
Steiner describes how gradually over vast periods of time, spiritual forces rayed in from the stars, before these stars or our solar system, were physically materialized. So this creative activity was occurring on the soul and life-forces level. But gradually the earth condensed out of the ethers and then into a fiery state, then an airy state, and down into a fluidic globe, finally becoming a solid planet.[32] During these metamorphoses, the human body was being formed within its own over-arching, enveloping life-force and surrounding soul (or aura). Hence ancient astrological wisdom tells us that the body can be divided into 12 parts, each corresponding to a zodiac sign, (see illustration 10). Steiner reports that in this long evolutionary process these same forces also formed 12 sense organs, not just five or six.[33]

Steiner also indicates how our immersion in this 12-fold cosmic creative power (or as he calls it, the cosmic Word) was participating in the forming of our soul as well. (This is the Logos mentioned in the Prologue in the Gospel of St. John.) Further, to really solve this enigma of the archetypal zodiac, we need to just briefly think of the spiritual side to our existence, in terns of our existence after death. Most people interested in astrology will accept that our soul arises into spiritual realms when a person's earthly life is over. The nature of these divine realms and the soul's journey here amongst the great spirit beings who exist in them, is not the theme of this book, but we can note here that this phase of our existence means in effect that we return to the stars of the zodiac.

Rudolf Steiner refers to this, and how our soul is interwoven with the energies radiating from the zodiacal divinities. Many ancient traditions are aware of this in different ways. The North America Indian Chief, Seattle, said in 1856, in his immortal speech, "...our dead go to walk among the stars...". It is in this very long period between lives that our soul becomes inherently linked to the zodiac. Thus when we return to the Earth, there exists around our soul, forming a kind of subtle energy integument for our aura, a subtle echo of the actual zodiac. I call this the 'archetypal zodiac', see illustration 11.

So the themes of the houses in every person's horoscope, forming a 12fold environment in which the soul exists, derive from the 12 primal zodiac energies, which since primordial times, has fashioned

---
[32] For a clear introduction to his cosmogony and cosmology, see my Rudolf Steiner Handbook.
[33] This includes a sense of movement, of life, of being in the presence of an ego, of speech, of mental images and so on. See the author's Rudolf Steiner Handbook, for a presentation on this theme.

every human being. As a result, each person is embedded in a kind of after-echo of the zodiac. This surrounds our soul, creating the theme of each House, regardless of which zodiac sign actually governs a House in their horoscope.

When a reflection of the great archetypal zodiac is said to 'surround our soul', this is best thought of as a spiritual field, in the midst of which our soul exists. But here we mean the soul viewed as an aura or 'soul-body'. This aura is embedded in a tiny reflection of the archetypal zodiac.

To understand this concept more clearly, just consider what makes planetary 'transits' possible. What is a transit ? When an astrologer says, "today you have Mercury opposing (your) Uranos, and so today your mental processes will be a bit hectic", this means that Mercury in its motions around the solar system is now opposite the point where Uranos was, **when you were born**. Now, these transits really are valid; their influence is really tangible. But actually, they can only happen because in your aura, Uranos is **continually situated** in the position, and with the dynamics, that it had, on your day of birth ! We carry these planetary qualities throughout out life. So our soul (or 'astral' body) is greatly composed of these planetary forces. And likewise, our soul carries outside, all around it, the zodiac energies.

It is from this phenomenon that in every horoscope, we get the Houses with their characteristic themes; they reflect the presence of this subtle zodiac echo, see illustration 12.

10: The zodiac signs and the parts of the body. This diagram from 1413-16, France, shows the connection of each zodiac sign to the 12 parts of the body.

11: The 12 themes of the Houses are a direct reflection of the 12 signs of the archetypal zodiac in which human life is embedded

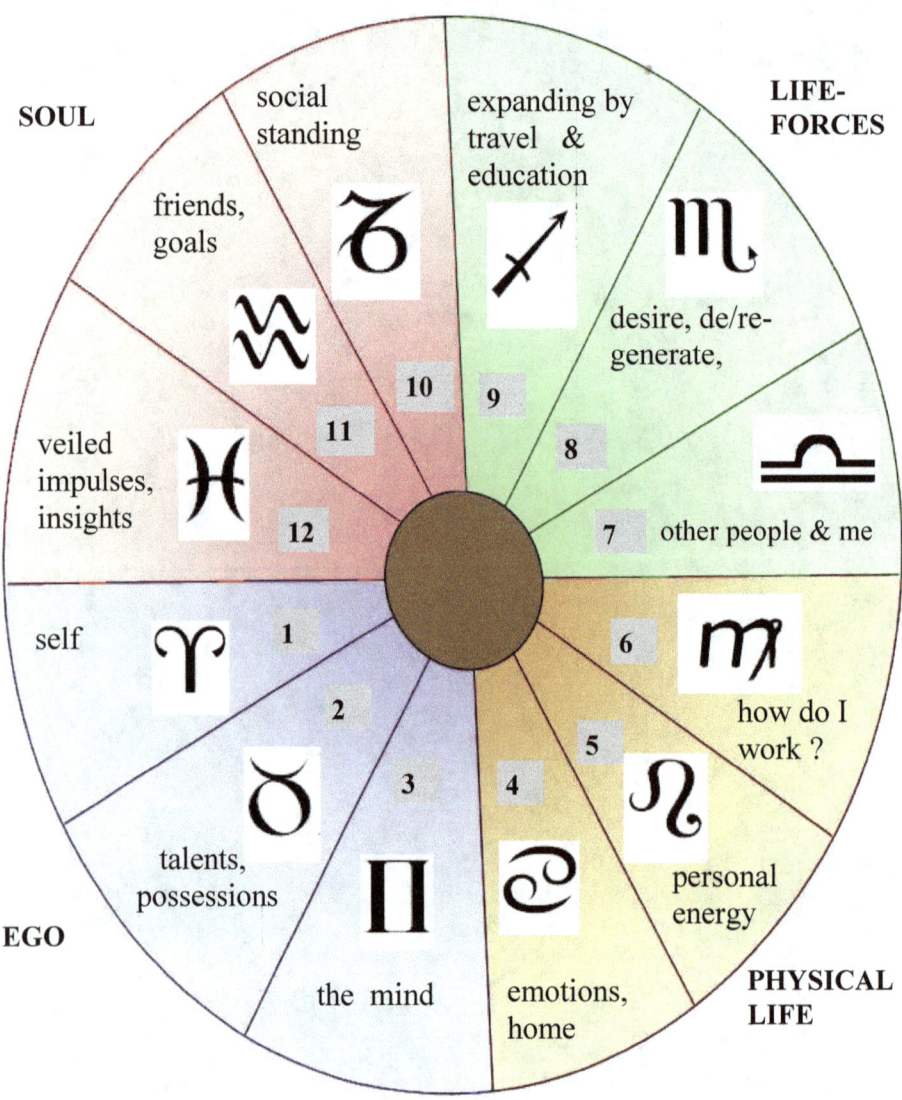

The 12 Houses with their themes, demarcate the 12 sectors, starting at the eastern horizon, governing human life. **These themes are a direct reflection of the primal zodiac signs and their qualities**, which start with Aries. But in each person's horoscope, this zodiacal sequence is not kept.

12: A human life, with its horoscope of 12 houses.
It is embedded in a background formed from the archetypal zodiac.

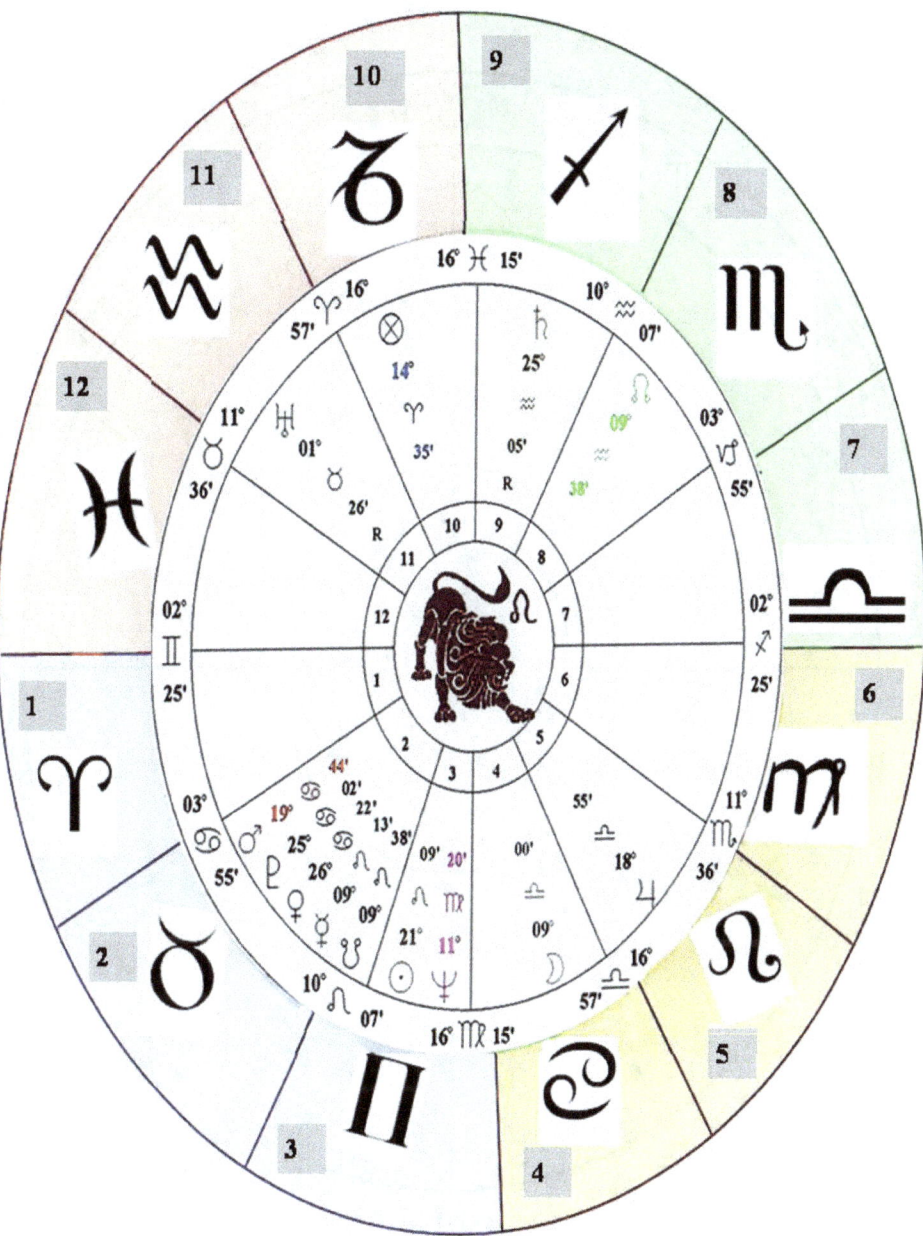

The themes of the houses derive from the 12 primal zodiac energies, which since primordial times, has fashioned humanity. Thus, each person is linked to a reflection of the zodiac, this surrounds them, creating the theme of each House, regardless of which zodiac sign governs a House.

13: An intercepted Chart

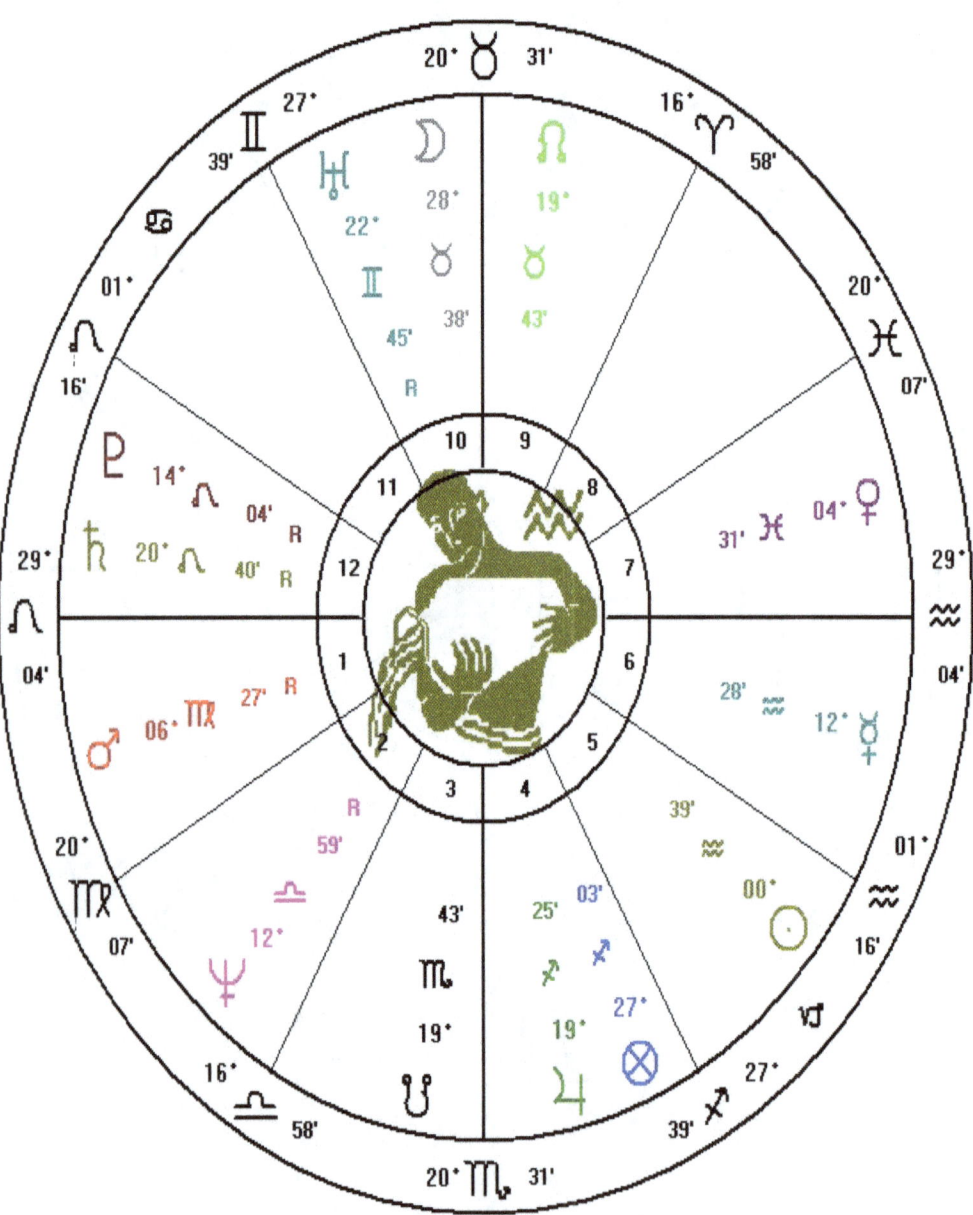

In this horoscope, house 5 is governed by Sagittarius, but inside this house, exerting a subtle influence, is the entire sign of Capricorn. Likewise, house 11 is governed by the sanguine Gemini, but hidden within this, is the vulnerable Cancerian influence.

The House system
I mentioned in Chapter Seven that the Placidus system is what I recommend. This is because I found it to be the most accurate house system to use, as do most astrologers. One reason for a few people wanting to use alternative systems is to avoid the occurrence of 'intercepted signs'. The two most commonly used alternative systems, are known as the 'whole-house' system and the 'equal-sign' system. These don't have any 'intercepted signs'. What does that mean; are intercepted houses valid or invalid?

Intercepted Signs
An 'intercepted sign' simply means that a particular house, which is governed by (that is, starts with) the sign of, say Aries, has hidden within it, another entire zodiac sign; in this instance, it will be Taurus. So the next house then begins with Gemini, whereas normally it would begin with Taurus. With the Placidus system, you do get these intercepted signs, **and so one should; these are an integral part of a horoscope**. Because these intercepted signs create dynamics which are very much an integral part of that person's psychology.

Look at illustration 13, here we see that house five is governed by Sagittarius, but within this house is the sign of Capricorn. So, the reality of this person's psychology in house five, is that there is an adventurous, outgoing approach to romance and being creative – but within this, a cautious and possibly potent karmic Capricorn dynamic will be working away. This particular client, who was a kind, loving type, actually left her child, to live with another man, and she seldom ever saw the child again. Likewise in house 11, the sanguine Gemini approach to life-goals and friends occurs, but hidden within that, is the tender, vulnerable Cancerian influence. So in this house there is a more sanguine attitude but within this, are veiled emotional energies. These two subtle influences correlate directly to the person's dilemmas and situation.

Take another example. Where Aquarius governs house five, but Pisces is inside it, or intercepted. With the Aquarian influence here, this person is attracted to unconventional people who radiate a sense of freedom and excitement. But as an undertone or veiled secondary motif, there is present also, from the intercepted Pisces, an idealistic glow and a gentle selflessness enveloping the themes of romance (and children) and being creative. Therefore the responses of this person, a Capricorn, will be quite complex, because the nemesis of the Capricorn (emotional demands) here is subtly demanding to be involved in these important themes of life.

This same person also therefore, inside House 11 which is governed by Leo, has the sign of Virgo. Through the Leo influence, friends are chosen who are capable, optimistic and supportive, if chosen with confidence. Or unsuitable, unreliable friends are chosen from an underlying feeling of low self-esteem. However, within this dynamic, through Virgo's veiled influence, friends are chosen on the basis of their capacity for intelligent conversation; but this person really needs to refrain from criticising their friends. Again this will be a dynamic that correlates intimately to the personality of this Capricorn person.

Further categories of signs and houses
We can note briefly here that the 12 signs are also categorized into three groups each of four signs. These are the Cardinal, Fixed and Mutable. These characteristics of the signs appear to me to be of little significance. The 12 houses are also divided into three types, each with four houses; that is, Angular, Succedent, or Cadent houses. This categorizing also appears to be of little practical significance.

The significance of the Lunar nodes
Note that the after-effect of the south node is in effect everywhere to be found throughout the entire horoscope. For example, consider that someone's life was that of a competitive Aries person last time, when Aries was either the sun-sign or as rising-sign. If that life went well, this will appear, **metamorphosed** in the horoscope as good aspects between Mars to the sun, or to Pluto, for example. Where the fiery Aries nature was too strong, or suffered dramatic conflict, it will reappear in this horoscope as negative aspects between these planets, creating an angry, dominating personality.

But the after-effect of the previous zodiac sign lingers on in the south node also by having some of its most prominent (and usually negative) traits lurking in the subconscious, **not** metamorphosed. And this is what is noted in the pages below; but note that in a fine chart, the south node is only a minor feature. You will want to get specialized books on this subject to study this further (see the list below). Remember that the negative qualities are the focus here. The south node is about how much of the more negative, hindering core traits of that sign are still lingering on. As they are in the lower veiled parts of the soul, in the subconscious, the client is usually unaware of these. In a fine chart, there will be very little of this; but in other charts these traits constitute one of the core factors hindering a person.

The south lunar node in the Signs

Aries
The after-echo of this is a tendency to anger rising up, or constantly having a potentially to rise, without any known causes. There is also a self-centred focus in regard to goals of life.

Taurus
The after-echo of having been a Taurean is a tendency to be laid-back, and to do things in a predictable way, avoiding innovation. In addition, there can be a clever way of doing things that make one feel empowered (although one is not really an empowered person).

Gemini
The after-echo of this past life is a tendency to be indecisive and unwilling to take on duties, and an urge to make oneself too busy.

Cancer
The residual effect of having lived a life as a Cancerian is a tendency to be far too sensitive to emotional coldness from others, and the emotions are focused on holding on to whatever is familiar.

Leo
The after-echo of a past Leo life-time is a tendency to be too proud of oneself, and of one's well-known friends, and too aware of one's social status.

Virgo
The residual effect of having lived a life as a Virgoan is a tendency to be somewhat too rigid and orderly, and also prudish or emotionally repressed, viewing the world as a source of uncleanness.

Libra
The after-echo of a past life in Libra is a tendency to be too sensitive to any kind of disharmony, and also to being very indecisive about an issue, especially when friends have different opinions on this subject.

Scorpio
The residual effect of having lived a life as a Scorpio is dependent upon how potently intense the person was back then, in their desires and convictions about life. If that life was dramatically intense, then

there will be a sense of wariness lest one is betrayed (again), or there can be a sensuality so strong, as to be problematic.

Sagittarius
The after-echo of this is a strong urge to stay free and unrestricted by anyone, or by any social customs, and a tendency to being too blunt in social dialogue.

Capricorn
The residual effect of having lived a life as a Capricorn is an ego-centric way of looking at the world, yet a very disciplined person who probably has a limited emotional response capacity.

Aquarius
The after-echo of this is a tendency to be very scattered, excessively wanting lots of friends, and to be someone who is in need of self-discipline.

Pisces
The after-echo of having lived a life as a Pisces is to have an idealistic but ungrounded undercurrent in the thinking. Also the driving force invites domination because of its gentle, non-assertive nature.

****

The south lunar node in the Houses

(The house positions of the node are often not as powerful as the zodiac sign position of the node.)

House One
The node here indicates a self-centred orientation in life. There will be lessons about involving others fully in one's life.

House Two
The node here causes a strong yearning for possessions, or other forms of greed; as well as difficulty in having a sensible view of life's priorities.

House Three
The node here generally causes the mindset to be quite earth-bound or ego-centric; or there can be an inclination to being too intellectually oriented in regard to life-questions.

House Four
The node here brings about a self-focus in the desires and yearnings, along with a strong focus on the kind of home-life that is wanted.

House Five
The node here generally causes a yearning for romance and for hobbies or creative pleasure which is all too consuming.

House Six
The node here brings about a tendency to be immersed in daily activity to the exclusion of a broader range of experiences.

House Seven
The node here generally causes a neediness for close friends and a very supportive partner.

House Eight
The node here has a subtle effect. It brings about a tendency to resist influences pushing in from beyond the conscious mind; this often manifest as a fear of death in childhood, and possibly as sexual tensions in adulthood.

House Nine
The node here indicates a strong impetus to intellectual pursuits to the exclusion of other aspects of the personality.

House Ten
The node here generally causes a strong urge to be prominent in one's career interests, at the expense of family and recreational time.

House Eleven
The node here generally causes difficulties in sorting out what one's life-goals really are. There can be either dreamy ungrounded attitudes or ideals that are too self-centred.

House Twelve
The node here has a subtle effect; it involves being resistant to sensing, and then dealing with, tensions and anxieties that are in the subconscious.

****

Books about the Lunar nodes:
Martin Schulman: Karmic Astrology; the moon's nodes and reincarnation   (highly recommended)
Celeste Teal: Discover your soul's karmic mission
Judith Hill: The lunar nodes

Retrograding Planets
The importance of understanding the influence of a retrograding planet in a house (and in a zodiac sign) can be very powerful, so it is very important to include the influence on the client of a planet in retrograde in a horoscope interpretation. A planet 'in retrograde' means a planet is doing one of its backwards 'loops' - viewed from the Earth, not the sun, of course. This retrograde motion in the horoscope is occurring not only in the house in which it is placed, but also in the zodiac sign.

The influence of a retrograding planet does not result in a set, predictable pattern, unlike the lunar nodes; it produces a wide variety of effects, often negative, but sometimes positive. To learn about these influences, I recommend that you acquire a copy of Martin Schulman's book, *Karmic Astrology: retrogrades and reincarnation*. It is an outstanding achievement. On the printed horoscope, a planet in retrograde is shown with a modified form of the letter R (see illustration 9).

Some of the striking examples of retrograde planets which we can note here as examples, include **Mars in house Seven**. This indicates an abusive relationship in the past life, which, if its impact is strengthened by other aspects, leaves the scar of detesting or fearing a partner, and yet also yearning for closeness from someone. Then there is **Venus in house Nine**, which hinders a good relationship to others, and impels the person towards solitary inner contemplating or skilled solo work. **Saturn in house Four** brings a lot of emotional tensions and phobias (one client had claustrophobia inherently as a child) and a persistent living in past events.

Uranos in house Five creates a huge urge to be unrestricted by anything; the person is always on the ready, to dodge any 'imprisoning' demand by others. **Pluto in house Three** can powerfully trigger off a clairvoyance (or at least a psychic ability), and if other features in the horoscope are helpful, a real skill in counselling. Naturally, if a person seeks personal development, then as with any other negative factor in the horoscope, the challenges caused by a retrograding planet can be effectively worked with.

With all of these examples, the counsellor should be able to understand how they have arisen organically, or belong inherently to, the chart. In other words, it should be clear from the other features of the horoscope, just why these dynamics, created by a retrograding planet, are there. The horoscope is a very closely interrelated entirety, like a mandala, as the zodiacal and planetary energies 'speak forth' the being of the incarnating person, as a unified, interlinked reality, as the time for rebirth draws near.

The Part of Fortune
You will need to acquire a book on this subject, to become really knowledgeable about the lunar nodes and the Part of Fortune. There are only a few books on this topic; Martin Schulman's book, *Karmic Astrology: Joy and the Part of Fortune*, is very good. Here we can note the core significance of the Part of Fortune in the houses. As we noted earlier, the location of the Part of Fortune indicates what goals or activity gives the deepest fulfilment to a person.

The Part of Fortune in the Zodiac Signs

Aries
Achieving goals through being an active, capable person brings happiness.

Taurus
Finding ways to be a relaxed, reliable person whose work and recreational habits create a dependable basis for life brings happiness.

Gemini
Achieving skills in interpersonal communicating, specifically through dialogue, but also in writing, brings fulfilment.

Cancer
Being a kind of mid-wife, bringing into reality new beginnings, nurturing new things into life, brings happiness.

Leo
Accomplishing goals, especially ones that allow other people to blossom, and being recognized for this, brings fulfilment.

Virgo
Organizing one's work in a capable way, bringing solid results that help the world, brings happiness.

Libra
Finding a way to integrate oneself into a social context, by relating to others in an harmonious way, brings fulfilment.

Scorpio
Participating in activity that leads to a renewal of oneself, or others, is deeply satisfying.

Sagittarius
Actively seeking out challenging projects, and feeling a sense of freedom in the tasks involved, brings fulfilment.

Capricorn
Experiencing the accomplishment of goals that oneself has set, perhaps long ago, yet in this process, acknowledging one's emotions, brings happiness.

Aquarius
Finding meaningful connections to others, and being free to interact socially as the urge arises, brings happiness.

Pisces
Feeling that one is inwardly attuned to a larger, higher reality, yet maintaining one's own sense of self, affirming one's rights and individuality, brings happiness.

****

We also need to consider the effect of the Part of Fortune, from its position in the houses of the horoscope.

The Part of Fortune in the Houses

House 1
Inner fulfilment is attained by acquiring a strong sense of self, which leads to having ideas and viewpoints or carrying out of actions through one's own initiative.

House 2
Inner fulfilment is attained by clearly seeing what one's talents and abilities really are, and also what one's life values are (reflected in life priorities.)

House 3
A deep happiness is attained by striving towards skills in thinking and speaking clearly, and thereby becoming a good communicator.

House 4
Inner fulfilment is attained by establishing a stable, balanced emotional life, and a sense of being at home with oneself.

House 5
A deep happiness is attained by being in touch with one's creative abilities, and bringing something notable into being.

House 6
Inner fulfilment is attained by applying oneself to daily life and work in a manner that leads to a productive, capable outcome.

House 7
A deep happiness is attained by achieving a genuine, meaningful relationship to significant other people in one's life.

House 8
With this house there is a much more subtle dynamic. Inner fulfilment is attained usually by being open to understanding a partner's contribution to a close relationship. In a fine chart, inner fulfilment is attained by responding to in-flow of influences from spiritual sources.

House 9
Inner fulfilment is attained by effort made in understanding life-questions through effort at study or by absorbing the lessons in life-experiences.

House 10
A deep happiness is attained by actually attaining a position socially (either vocational and/or the marital status) which one has set out to achieve.

House 11
Inner fulfilment is attained by the right choice friends, especially groups of friends, and by determining clearly one's goals in life.

House 12
A deep happiness is attained by becoming more aware of the veiled dynamics in the soul-life, and working with these. In a fine chart, by seeking to let a wise spiritual guidance be present in oneself, from beyond the conscious mind.

****

In conclusion

Aspect patterns
There is also a way of looking at the Aspects that takes into account angles from between three or more planets to each other; these are known as 'aspect patterns'. These are called for example, the grand cross, the T-square, the grand trine, the kite, and the finger of fate. These multiple planetary aspects derive only from medieval times, and I have not found them to be so important. But you may like to explore these, and see if you find them of value. There are websites and books that comment on them, but actually the interpretation of them varies considerably.

The Decans
There are two sides to this topic. In practical modern astrology a zodiac sign is viewed as being subtly divided into three sections, the first, the, middle and the last third. Each of these is called a decan. It is said by some astrologers that those born in the first third (the first decan) have some of the qualities of the previous zodiac sign. Those born in the middle third are purely influenced by their sign; and those born in the last third have some qualities from the sign ahead.
This idea does not seem to have much basis to it. It appears to be a relatively recent idea, and not one originating in an ancient esoteric wisdom.

The second definition of a decan refers back to a division of the sky by into 36 sectors ancient Egyptians, called decans. This has nothing to do with the above idea, even though the above theory probably has somehow been derived, incorrectly, from this older, quite unrelated idea. The ancient idea of decans was related to the rulership of star deities in the flow of the 24 hour day/night cycle.

Finally, it is important to realize that a detailed discussion about the negative aspects in a chart provides the greatest help for any client who is dealing with difficult life-issues. But these negative aspects can be there for several reasons. One is because the soul has those imperfections, and karma ensured that this is their reality. But another reason can be that the soul, in contemplating those imperfections before birth, experienced the lofty intention to make these problems clearly presenting this life, in order to get to work on the task of overcoming them. So a chart with mainly negative aspects can indicate a person who has made the decision, before their descent to birth, to really 'clean up the stables', and thereby speed up their evolution.[34]

Concluding the interpretation process
The process described in this book will take about one hour and will provide a sophisticated, profoundly accurate description of the client's psychology – once the practitioner has gained the experience from doing some dozens of charts (so maybe practise on your friends and family). And of course it is the case that the practitioner needs to have some life-experience and a deeper, insightful mindset. I recommend studying the core texts of Rudolf Steiner, to acquire the essential deeper viewpoint on the nature of the soul which gives an invaluable deepening to one's understanding of life and people. My book, the Rudolf Steiner Handbook, is designed to help readers find a way to begin to understand Steiner's books. Naturally, there is also much of value to learn from studying mainstream psychology and counselling texts.

Solar Returns
There is a very valuable service which clients can receive, concerning how their next year of life will unfold for them; that is, from their birthday in the current year to their next birthday. Every astrology software program can calculate this 'solar return' chart (often called a 'return chart'). It finds the day and time in the current year when the sun returns to the exact position in the zodiac it was located on the day of birth. This date may be one day before, or one day after the birth date. The leading authority on this subject is Mary F. Shea, whose brilliant book, Planets in Solar Returns is essential for this work.

The solar return is not superstitious, it does not make prophecies, it simply – and very accurately – informs the astrologer as to what dynamics will be operative in each of the houses of the Solar Return chart, where planets are located. People are unaware that this pattern is very, very influential for their life-year; and if they were to relocate, a great distance east or west, then their coming year would be very different indeed. Because then the planets on their birthday would be located in very different houses.

---

[34] Possibly, any eclipses that occur during the time the baby is in the womb, may slightly impair the energies from the Sign where the moon or sun is located; Spiller and K. McCoy, *Spiritual Astrology: your path to self-fulfillment* write about this.

The Arctic Circle
Returning to the question of which house system to use, there is one problem with the Placidus system, but this problem is true of most other systems, too. Namely, when it comes to doing horoscopes for people born in the very high latitudes, especially in the Arctic Circle, there is a problem. Owing to the complex mathematics involved in calculating the division of the houses on the top of the world, so to speak, various distortions occur. In most house systems, some of these signs are not able to be placed in a house at all for a birthplace in the Arctic Circle, as some zodiac signs are never seen above the horizon.

So this can mean for example, that the person's sun-sign may not be located in their chart. (!) Now, you may not have many clients born in extreme latitudes of north (there are virtually none in south), but if you have, even the excellent Placidus system will not work. This is a severe problem still in astrological circles. Much effort has gone into designing software that can produce a meaningful chart. This software is referred to as creating 'topocentric' horoscopes. The Sirius 1 and the Kepler 7 programs incorporate this, and give similar results to the Placidus system, whilst ensuring that a horoscope for someone born in the Arctic Circle does factor in the entire zodiac.
(For more about see, www.astrowisdom.net/articles/astrology-for-all-latitudes-new-topocentric-houses.)

Mean nodes or true nodes
As with most astrologers, I use the 'mean nodes' and not the 'true nodes' as I found the so-called 'mean nodes' to be correct to the person (you just choose this in the menu of the horoscope software); it gives you the two options. These two terms are about astronomical factors involving the speed and position of the moon regarding this intersection point in space.

The two hemispheres and the lunar nodes
The south node invokes the past of the person, and the north invokes the future potential. It is clear that the moon on its downwards journey, crosses the equator, heading south; whilst on its upwards journey, as it crosses the equator, it is heading north. From this fact, astrologers, the vast majority of whom live in the northern hemisphere, have concluded that the negative, old karma is invoked by this <u>downwards</u> journey, and the positive good karmic potential is invoked by the <u>upwards</u> journey.

But from the viewpoint of the southern hemisphere, the direction of the moon is in reverse: going down over the equator towards the north pole, but rising up in our skies towards the south pole. A colleague suggested to me that this could mean that for a southern hemisphere chart, the lunar nodes have to be interpreted in reverse. That is, the south node brings the future positive qualities, the north node brings the old negative material. But in my experience of clients, this is not actually the case. So the south node remains the past negative, and the north node remains the future, positive indicator.

This means then, it is not the descent downwards or the ascent upwards, which are the relevant factors with regard to the nodes. Some other factor must be effective here. That factor may be linked to the discovery by Rudolf Steiner that the southern third of the globe has a relation to the human will, and the northern third to the head, the thinking capacity. The old qualities of the past, invoked by the south lunar node, do reside in the subconscious, and could be seen as manifesting in the will or intentions of the person, so not consciously thought out or decided upon. So the lower or southern part of the globe represents on a large global scale, the veiled or subconscious will of the human being. (In this way of correlating the Earth to its offspring, the human being, the equatorial area relates to the feeling capacity of human beings.)

****

APPENDIX

The Life and work of Rudolf Steiner

Rudolf Steiner was born in February 1861 into an Austrian family, living in a village near the then Austrian-Hungarian border (present day Croatia). His father worked for the railways, which were being extensively developed at that time. The family had a daughter, and another son, who was severely speech and hearing impaired. The father, a stationmaster, was transferred to various villages in the vicinity of Vienna. The teenage Steiner, at 14 yrs, took up the study of Emanuel Kant's Critique of Pure Reason, a decidedly difficult philosophical text, which examines cognitional processes, that is, the study of how we perceive and know anything, often called 'epistemology'. However, already at 10 years the young Steiner showed artistic gifts too; a portrait he made then, found in the Steiner archives in the 1970's, is extraordinary for its skill and sensitivity.

At university, (from 1879) Steiner's intellectual brilliance allowed him to study more than a full curriculum of scientific subjects, and he coached fellow students to finance his own studies. His academic achievements led to him being appointed to the editorial team producing the first edition of Germany's greatest literary figure, the scientific writings of Johann Wolfgang von Goethe. From the 1880's to 1900 he undertook a vast and arduous project to study all major philosophical streams and pivotal scientific research of his times. During this phase of his life he attained the degree of Doctor of Philosophy, for a thesis examining cognition, and arguing against aspects of mainstream philosophy, which were strongly influenced by Immanuel Kant. Steiner did not teach nor write about spiritual subjects until 1900, when he entered his fortieth year. He was active as editor of a literary journal and as a philosopher, until then.

In 1890 he moved to the German city of Weimar, where he remained until 1897, where he worked as co-editor of Goethe's complete works. Johann Wolfgang von Goethe. Steiner found many observations in the works of Goethe, which stimulated him towards his own holistic attitudes to life. Steiner found in Goethe a great help in formulating his philosophical and his spiritual worldview with respect to cognition, that is the process whereby we perceive a sense object or have an 'inner perception' of an idea.

A particularly nihilistic attitude had developed in philosophy with regard to this process of knowing, in its most direct manifestation - sensory perception and having insights (rather than laboriously elaborated concepts). Philosophers had come to regard sense perceptions as illusions – that is, we may not be really seeing, hearing, smelling, touching, what we think we are. And therefore as for spiritual perceptions, since sense perceptions are an illusion, no one can possibly defend spiritual perceptions at all, since the way we experience those are even more subtle. In his time at the Goethe archives Steiner combated the philosophical theories which cast a nihilistic shadow over our sensory capacities.

In 1894 his book, "The Philosophy of Freedom" was published. It was precisely because of his deep interest in cognition, that Steiner was in a position to assess the inherent validity of his spiritual perceptions, and pioneer the capacity to bring procedural integrity to spiritual insights; hence as from 1902 he would refer to his research as 'spiritual science'. He was acutely aware of the objections to spiritual experiences as illusory or subjective, but his intense engagement with philosophical studies had given him an expertise in this area, for example, he was the editor of the definitive 12-volume edition of the complete works of the philosopher Arthur Schopenhauer.

He saw his task to bring the fuller, spiritual aspect to life into the area's of interest to humanity at large. This can only arise from a through knowledge of the interweaving of subtle energies and spiritual realities within material processes. This is turn demands a capable and reliable capacity for higher perception. Although Steiner did not refer publicly to holistic and spiritual matters in his twenties and thirties, he was already endowed with a personal knowledge of lofty and spiritual realities. But it was not his wish to publicly disclose this. A private document about Steiner's worldview as a young man, discovered some decades after his death, written when he was 27, reveals his profound spirituality,

> The origin and sustaining Principle of all Existence is the realm of archetypal Thoughts. In it is never-ending harmony and joyous tranquillity. If any part of Creation were not illumined by this realm, it would be something dead and without being, and would have no part of the life of the universe......
> Devout, truly spiritual Love ennobles the innermost fibre of our being, it refines and uplifts everything that lives in us. This pure, devout love transforms the entire soul-life into something that is akin to the Universal-Spirit....One must first know something of the holiness of Love, before one can speak about Spirituality (piety)....

At first it is a puzzling fact that Steiner would devote so much of this life to mastering scientific and non-spiritual philosophical analysis. One might think that a person who would later bequeath a vast heritage of spiritual teachings, obtained by first-hand spiritual experience, may find such studies of little interest. In effect Steiner was mastering the intellectual currents of the times, when the prominent thinkers of the dawn of modern science were almost totally materialistic, indeed atheistic. In 1897, his work at the Goethe archives completed, he moved from Weimar to Berlin, a thriving hub of European culture, where he lectured in Adult Education. He was also extensively involved in the literary and artistic culture of the times, worked as a school teacher for a year, and contributed to a literary magazine, writing some 270 articles on theatre.

Reflecting on the life of this remarkable man, it becomes clear that the reason for Steiner being involved in such a comprehensive study of modern thinkers is that he was aware that the modern materialistic attitude was devoid of a feeling for the living environment and for inner nature of the human being. He concluded that this modern spirit-estranged attitude would gradually join with an increasingly powerful technological capacity. It was obvious to him that this dangerous liaison would have the power to not only lethally damage the eco-system, but to bring about changes in the very nature of human consciousness, by genetic manipulation, or the incorporation of electronic devices into everyday life, beyond the boundary of what remains healthy for the human being. This would lead to an increasingly artificial, unnatural, view of what it is to be a human being.

At the dawn of this new era, the beginning of the twentieth century, Steiner, like the solitary conscience of modern humanity, looked into the future and saw that it would be vitally important that humanity did not exclude the fuller, holistic side of life. He saw that scientific research, although accurate, and often very helpful, indeed immensely important for our civilisation, should be seen as only one side of the truth. He saw the need for an holistic perspective to be integrated into modern scientific modes of thinking. Whilst he had been acquiring a competent knowledge of the newly emerging scientific research, he had also been mastering the processes which endow a person with higher consciousness.

He was pioneering a way to develop a form of spiritual wisdom and skilled exact clairvoyance, which he could use with scientific precision. He describes the path towards higher consciousness in his book, "Knowledge of Higher Worlds, how it is attained?" In effect

Steiner had discovered how to gradually gain perception of increasingly more transcendent realms and yet to maintain his self-awareness in this process, so as to monitor what was occurring, and to even be pro-active in the experience, testing, and assessing the perceptions.

Consequently, he had acquired a vast body of spiritual-holistic facts which constituted the 'other side' to the material facts of life. He made the decision to attempt to communicate his 'spiritual-scientific' research to those interested. Steiner set out to communicate his 'spiritually scientific' view of life, and endeavoured to bridge the yawning gap between materialism and his spiritual views. The term 'materialism' here does not mean the desire to have material possessions, but rather means an attitude to life which regards consciousness as deriving from chemical and nerve processes in the body, and the universe as originating in atomic reactions.

We need to pause here to realize just what an incisive change had come over modern humanity during the 19th century. In the 1860's, when Steiner was a school child, if a school teacher had tried to insist that Creation occurred through atomic processes happening at random, and not through God, then they would have faced dismissal. But by 1900, when Steiner was deciding whether to publicly communicate the spiritual teachings his research had given him, if a school teacher had insisted that God had created everything, and random chemical processes were not the primer mover, then that teacher would have faced dismissal.

This change in consciousness is also illustrated in the famous incident from ca. 1800, where the astronomer, Laplace, was explaining to Napoleon Bonaparte his idea that mechanical forces were the sole factor needed to explain creation, especially the movement of planets around the Sun. When Napoleon asked, "What about God?" The mathematician replied, "I have no need of that hypothesis." On a more ominous note, it was in the 19th century the Frenchman Claude Bernard introduced the horrific attitude of regarding the practise of vivisection as a scientific method; and at his death, his government contributed a eulogy to his funeral arrangements. The times had changed.

Steiner saw in the march of a one sided, and at times, unethical scientific attitude, the weakening of the influence of the spiritual aspect of human consciousness. He taught that the higher spiritual aspect to our being manifests as what we call our 'conscience'. He viewed the conscience as a special voice in the soul, deriving from the spirit of the person. He wanted to help strengthen the sensitivity to the conscience, and indeed to even offer a pathway to the development of spiritual faculties, that people might learn to be receptive to and to contemplate spiritual insights.

So in 1900 he began to seek avenues to commence this new task, and responded to a request to lecture on the subject of the medieval mystics. In the audience were some Theosophists, who eagerly requested more such lectures to their own organisation. In 1902 he agreed to join the organisation, which appointed him as the General Secretary of the German branch of the Theosophical Society. The international society was originally founded by Madam Blavatsky and colleagues in 1875, and had a keen interest in Oriental wisdom and traditions. Steiner insisted that he would only teach what he himself had ascertained to be spiritually true, from his own research, with its European and cosmopolitan Christian nuance.

He began his lecture work, and writing of books on spirituality, speaking on the nature of the human being. He explained how we have several primary aspects to our soul or consciousness - logical thought, emotion and will - and how these can be spiritualized to produce three distinct aspects to our spirit or higher self. He explained how our sense of self arises in the third year of life (as the child starts to say "I"), and how this ego-sense has been developing over the millennia. The result of this development has been a slow extinguishing of the holistic psychic sensitively of earlier humanity, but such a consolidation of this sense of self provides the foundation for individuals to develop from within their own ethical integrity.

He spoke of higher spiritual realms, and explained the difference between the soul worlds, and the divine spiritual worlds. The soul realms are intermediate realms where souls are found before birth and for a while after death. The spiritual realms, (referred to in his Credo), are the realms of Plato, where the archetypal Ideas, emerging from God are moulded and metamorphosed by divine beings.

Steiner also taught the inner aspect to cosmology and creation of the universe, how the universe condensed out of subtle ethereal energies, after being formulated in the Platonic realms. He spoke extensively about these subtle ethereal energies which maintain the eco-system of the planet, and the role of cosmic influences from planets and the zodiac in the life on our planet. He gave visual architectural expression to this interaction between cosmic forces and humanity in his great building, the Goetheanum (see below). Steiner also gave sessions about the way to develop spiritually through meditation, explaining what occurs as consciousness becomes spiritualized, and the student encounters the soul-spiritual realms; a process which he called, 'crossing the threshold'.

He also lectured on various religious themes, especially an esoteric approach to Christianity. He describes the Gospel narratives as indicating a union of a cosmic being of great significance, the Logos of St. John, to the soul of the Earth. He also lectured extensively on psychology – in a more holistic spiritual sense – and on history, showing the gradual evolution of humanity's inner life through the ages. Steiner also spoke on karma and repeated earth-lives, and how this was not incompatible with Christian teachings.

In 1913 his association with the leaders of the Theosophical Society ended, when this Indian-based Society, led by Annie Besant, announced that they had found the Indian boy who was the vessel for the returned Christ, and who was the same as the world-teacher Maitreya. Steiner cautioned people against this absurdity, but eventually a split became inevitable, and in February 1913 the Anthroposophical Society was founded. In 1929, (four years after Steiner's death) the young Indian man who had been touted as the returned Christ announced it was all humbug, and the movement around him collapsed.

Steiner as a lifelong advocate of the equality of women, and a close friend of Rosa Mayreder, a leading German feminist, appointed three women and three men to the executive of this Society. The word 'anthroposophy' is derived from the Greek language, and basically means the wisdom in the human soul, or as Steiner explains, expressing it more fully, "a knowledge which becomes born in the heart as wisdom, when the heart is raised to selfless love". On another occasion, Steiner defined anthroposophy as "a path of knowledge which seeks to guide the spiritual in the human being to the spiritual in the cosmos."

During his tenure as General Secretary of the Theosophical Society, Steiner had introduced the world of Art to his fellow members, who had never incorporated art into their esoteric-spiritual interests. But Steiner insisted that the wholesome spiritual life, and indeed the effective spiritualization of the soul, requires that we immerse ourselves in the beauty and wonder of artistic activity. As he told his listeners, in a 1907 Conference, "...indeed I am convinced that when the artistic element draws ever more into our ranks, then it shall also become more possible for our friends to overcome the difficulties in attaining to actual spiritual consciousness".

Steiner had been teaching for about a decade when the disastrous first World War began, severely restricting his lecture activity; he took a lively and concerned interest in the tragedy unfolding around about him, hoping to reduce the length and severity of the conflict. It was in these years that work had started in neutral Switzerland on the building of the magnificent international centre for his work, named in honour of Goethe, "The Goetheanum".

At that time, Marie von Sivers, a Russian woman, a Theosophist already in 1900, and Rudolf Steiner's foremost student and closest friend, was given the task of returning to the war zone, to reach Berlin and despatch their publications and office documents to Switzerland. To enable her to enter German territory, she and Steiner underwent a formal civil-wedding ceremony to give her Austrian citizenship. This was a legalistic arrangement; otherwise, Steiner's personal life was that of a spiritual seer, teacher and scholar.

This remarkable building, built from wood, was one of the greatest achievements in European architectural history. Its form was based on two large intersecting cupolas, one smaller than the other. These represented the emergence of humanity from the cosmos. Its hand-carved interior, extensively painted in plant-based water colours, was intended to embody the organic architectural feature of metamorphosing surfaces. Teams of people, whose nations were locked in deadly conflict, worked at this task in relative harmony, shaping the interior to remove any linear surfaces, and painting scenes from the spiritual history of humanity. In 1915, architects from around the world came to see the scaffolding removed, fully expecting it to collapse as the feat of joining two large domes, without the normal quota of support-columns in place, was regarded as impossible to achieve.

Steiner was also busy developing a new approach to the use of colour in art, emphasizing water colours in painting, to allow more subtle spiritual nuances to emerge, also creating a new art of dance called eurythmy. He created some 800 choreographic settings for this new art of dance, and also gave instruction as to how it could also be applied in a therapeutic manner. In eurythmy the dancer strives to make the moving, metamorphosing forms, with her or his arms, which in effect make visible, the extraordinary forms which musical sounds, and vowels and consonants form in the air and ether as we speak. He made 100 paintings or drawings, and designed 14 buildings in a superb organic architectural style.

From 1918, as the war and its aftermath devastated Europe, raising extremely serious questions about the nature of society, economics and government, Rudolf Steiner was approached by people who wished to find ways to work in their chosen vocation in a manner which would contribute to the future health and re-building of society. It was then that people found that Steiner's far-reaching knowledge of the interrelatedness of the earthly reality and the spiritual could be put to practical humanitarian use. His knowledge of the subtle ethereal forces at work in all living organisms enabled him to lay the foundation for immensely valuable organic farming known as bio-dynamics. This is an enhanced form of organic farming, which is a fully commercially viable system of agriculture which does not put poisons and synthetic fertilisers into the soil, but which also actually enhances the life of the soil, both the micro-organism and the subtle 'ethereal' energies which we need to take into our bodies through our food.

The bio-dynamic system of farming has spread to many parts of the Earth, with tremendous benefits to the eco-systems where it is practised. In 2000, some 50% of the Egyptian cotton crop was grown under the bio-dynamic method. This means that a large part of the Nile valley could be spared the high volumes of toxic, persistent insecticides normally used in the cotton industry. In the 1980's and 1990's large numbers of cattle were subject to the creutzfeldt-jakob disease, popularly called mad-cow disease. Huge number of animals had to be killed. Steiner had warned against feeding meat pellets to these naturally vegetarian animals, saying that it would bring epidemics of insane cows. If this one piece of advice had been taken seriously, these horrific effects would have been prevented. Similarly, in 1923, he warned apiarists that if they continue to harm their bee colonies by manipulating the breeding process for queen bees, then in about 100 years time, bees would die in vast numbers. His advice was ignored, and the bees are now dying in huge numbers.

Steiner's teachings on spiritual themes are not unclear mystical sentiments. They are exceptional in their logical clarity. Hence his spiritual insights can be applied to practical demanding tasks, such as medicine, education as well as agriculture. The practical application of Steiner's works in the medical field alone is astonishing; it would eventually include medical and pharmaceutical data which has resulted in many hundreds of medicinal products and medical therapies, used by family doctors around the world. He founded the Weleda Company, which now produces some 2,000 medicaments for doctors and health practitioners.

The spiritual research in health and medical therapy undertaken by Steiner translated into a body of lectures given to doctors and medical students, which laid the foundation for a deeply needed holistic model of health and illness in the allopathic medical world. Steiner gave detailed guidelines for the understanding of the origin of illness, namely in disturbances to the interface between the physical body, the subtle life-force organism which maintains our body, and lastly, our consciousness (or soul).

Although anthroposophical doctors and therapists do use allopathic medications and procedures when necessary, they have a large body of other, non-toxic medicaments, therapies and above all, an effective new model of how to treat illness, at their disposal. Another aspect to Steiner's pioneering work in developing a new perspective towards illness and health is the application of his ideas to counselling, to the care of people with disabilities, to drug addiction and to personal development issues.

Steiner's educational principles are based on his direct knowledge of the consciousness of the growing child, how it gradually 'grows down' into earthly consciousness, leaving behind its innocent and highly imaginative 'pre-incarnate' condition. His practical advice to teachers was delivered in dozens of lecture cycles, and is now practised in over 800 schools worldwide. These are the well-known "Steiner schools" (also referred to as Waldorf schools, after the name of the company to finance the first Steiner school, in Stuttgart). The Steiner schools became more widely known after an international Steiner School exhibition travelled the world in the 1990's, under the auspices of UNESCO.

The Stuttgart school – and the Anthroposophical Society – were forced to closed in the late 1930's when the Nazi party came to power in Germany. Rudolf Steiner's work was high on their list of hated movements, and leading members of the movement were placed in concentration camps. Already in the 1920's Steiner had to experience Nazi thugs attacking the people gathering to hear his lectures. He had begun to speak on urgent social issues, on the governance of society, including the role of money. He set out to explain how "the body social" is triune, that is, it consists of three independent but interrelated spheres, just as our consciousness has three faculties, namely logic, emotion and will. By 1919, Germany was in a disastrous situation, with huge war losses, mass unemployment, a ruined economy and sinister political forces on the move.

Steiner did not give a utopian prescription for solving society's ills, rather he urged people to allow the various aspects of society to function healthily. He called his approach to social renewal, 'the threefolding' of society, by which he meant that people would be well advised to recognize the inherent triune nature of society, and let it come to expression. Once that was done through activity undertaken widely across the social spectrum, economics would cease to have its current dictatorial role which is so damaging to our lives.

Steiner saw how the way in which money is understood, or rather misunderstood, and consequently how it is used by powerful financial institutions, is perpetrating immensely harmful influences upon the rest of society. He explained that society consists of the economic sphere, the political sphere (that is, legislation) and also, as the third sphere, all other activity undertaken in society. This third sphere includes schools, tertiary education, the defence forces, religion, medicine, entertainment, the Arts, activity which furthers spirituality, and so on. He pointed out that these three spheres should have their own independent parliaments; and politicians would draw up laws, and their keynote would be equality of rights. This would be enshrined in legislation designed to minimize the infringement of others' rights by the exercise of one's own rights.

Political legislation should not determine the activity of the education sector, or the Arts, or medicine, etc. The economic sphere's natural keynote is fraternity or ensuring the goods of the world are available to all, in particular to provide the income for the non-commercial third sphere; money should not accumulate in vast amounts to banks and individuals. The third sphere's concern is to encourage the 'freedom' of the individual, by which Steiner meant the potential inherent in every person to be able to find opportunities in life to come to expression. His lectures on economics have lead to the forming of wonderful banking institutions, such as the 'Gemeinschaft Bank' in Bochum (Germany), 'Triodos' in Holland, and 'Prometheus Foundation' in New Zealand. In these institutions the effort is made to create a healthy role for money in society, where interest is minimal and a fraternal concern for the initiatives of others is fostered.

Steiner's lectures from this period, and on into 1921, were in such demand that a professional agency had to be used to arrange his lecture tours, and he filled the largest venues in the great cities of Europe. Communist agitators prevented him speaking to the workers in large factories, and, as not only their hatred, but addition Nazi violence increased against his work, the police were unable to guarantee the safety of Steiner's audience (or of himself) and his lectures had to be cancelled. Prominent in the Anthroposophical Society founded in 1913, (including in its executive) were some wonderfully literate, spiritual Jewish people, who found Steiner's esoteric, inclusive Christianity quite acceptable, it seemed this fuelled the nationalist-socialists hatred of Steiner's impulse.

In 1921 Steiner had responded to requests from Christian clergymen and theological students to advise them on how they could bring a renewal to the role of the church. His lectures and ritual texts lead them to found a church, called the 'Christian Community', offering services with qualities midway between Protestant and the more liturgical churches. Steiner pointed out the great value of liturgy for baptisms, marriage, funerals and so on, for the wider community and for anthroposophists. But he also reminded his audience that the mediating work of the priesthood, linking a person to the divine, through the Sunday liturgical service, would not be needed by those souls who were ready to seriously undertake meditative exercises for their own spiritual development.

Meanwhile opposition to Steiner's broad, non-sectarian Christianity, was growing from narrow and vindictive religious circles. Religious zealots, making use of a person with intellectual disability, burnt down the magnificent Goetheanum in late 1922. The man tragically perished in the flames. Then, one year later, in early 1923 someone in circles close to Steiner caused him to be poisoned, during a social gathering. The effect of this poisoning and the destruction of the Goetheanum building started to take its toll on his health. After the abortive 1923 'Putsch' involving Hitler had occurred, Steiner transferred his activity to Switzerland, where land in the village of Dornach, near Basel, had already been donated in 1915. Here the construction of the Goetheanum was well underway.

In an effort to give his listeners a link to the deeper spiritual foundations of existence, Steiner spoke in 1923 on the subtle forces which maintain the planet's life-processes, and which could be celebrated in nature festivals, which incorporate spiritual elements, and link our everyday life to something higher and grander. But by now Steiner was internationally renowned, as a spiritual thinker of outstanding value, and as a spiritual teacher of impeccable integrity. Large numbers of people began to flock to Dornach for their own personal benefit, to receive personal help with their problems and yearnings.

Steiner was at the peak of his spiritual capacity, and perhaps sensing the end of his life may not be far away, was working at a super-human pace, delivering six lectures a day. Each of these lectures, in

1924, was in itself a work of genius, providing the foundations of his medical, agricultural, educational and artistic research. In the decades after his death this material would be used and explored, at first by hundreds, and now by thousands of people, seeking to help humanity by creating an holistic approach to their tasks in life.

The demands for personal advice began to take their toll, and as word spread that he was not so robust, many more people, fearing they might not get a chance to put their personal question to him, flocked to Dornach. On some days, up to 400 hundred insistent people would be lining the pathway leading to the venue where he was to speak, forcing his exhausted body to 'run the gauntlet' of their questions before even getting inside to deliver a lecture.

Finally in late September 1924, he was too ill to finish a lecture, and was forced to the sick bed, to undergo a period of convalescence. But his physician, despite being available solely to him, was unable to nurse him back to health. His condition mysteriously deteriorated, and on March 30th 1925 he died within a few hours of becoming gravely ill. The tragic, premature end to the life of this person, at the early age of 64, brings this booklet to a close. It only remains to note that Steiner's labours on behalf of humanity were to bear so many and varied fruits, alleviating the stresses produced by a one-sided application of modern technological-scientific achievements.

During his life he was not only poisoned and his audience subject to violent assaults, he was also the victim of smear campaigns which are occasionally raised even today by people incapable of assessing or feeling the integrity and goodness of the man. His last poetic text, found by his death-bed, expresses the drama of his life, and his yearning to see every human being find his or her inner truth, and to allow the spirit to enliven and ennoble the soul, despite the power of forces which this oppose this:

> I wish to enkindle every person, from the
> spirit of the cosmos,
> (so) that they may become a flame,
> and fierily unfold the essence of their being.
> The Others, they wish to take water from the cosmos,
> which quenches these flames, and by its dampness
> lames the inner nature of all being.
> O joy, when the human-flame
> is glowing, even there where it rests,
> O bitterness, when the human-creature becomes bound,
> there, where it wants to be consciously active.

Rudolf Steiner's condition deteriorated unexpectedly, and he died on 30th March 1925, in Dornach, at the age of 64. He was busy at the time designing the new Goetheanum, to be built in concrete. Steiner's impulse today is carried on by many groups, interested individuals, and formally by the world-wide "Anthroposophical Society". The international centre of the society is housed in the new Goetheanum, built of concrete in the 1920's, and constructed in a very different style to the first one. Branches of this Society are to be found throughout many countries around the world.

For an introduction to Steiner's teachings, which also assesses how his teachings relate to modern ideas, and gives a guide to how to reading Steiner's works, see my book, the Rudolf Steiner Handbook.

****

Recommended Books about the planetary Aspects
The most comprehensive volume is by Robert Hand, Planets in Youth, Para Research, 1977, followed by Robert Pelletier's, Planets in Aspect, Whitford Press, 1974.
These books are also useful:
Isabel Hickey, Astrology; a Cosmic Science, CRCS Pubs. 1992
Alan Leo, Astrology for All, the Astrologer's Library, 1978
Alan Oken, Complete Astrology, Bantam Books, 1980
J. McEvers & M. March, The only way to learn astrology, Astro-analytics Pubs., 1978

Software for creating charts
I have used the AstrolDelux system (www.halloran.com) for many years and found it excellent. The website, astrology-software-review.toptenreviews is a good site to visit, to see how they rate the best astrology software programs. It ranks Solar Fire as the best, followed by Janus, then thirdly, Kepler and in fourth place, AstrolDelux. These other programs offer much more than a counsellor-astrologer may need, and the AstrolDelux system by John Halloran, is half the price, or less, than the higher rated programs.

Epilogue

Any psychologist or counsellor who incorporates the interpretation of the horoscope into their sessions, will greatly assist their client's efforts for personal development and mental health.

Any person who seeks to learn about themselves from a mature, insightful astrologer-counsellor, for any reason, is strongly enhancing their personal development, and gaining profoundly useful self-knowledge.

I hope this book is a valuable contribution to these two endeavours !

INDEX

Alan Leo, 2, 54, 89, 331
Angular, 306
archetypal zodiac, 247, 249, 298, 299
Arctic Circle, 317
Aspect patterns, 315
atavistic clairvoyance, 209
Athribis, 21
Blanchini's Planisphere, 40
Cadent, 306
Cardinal, 306
choleric temperament, 75
clairvoyance, 291
Claudius Ptolemy, 8, 40, 54
claustrophobia, 219
cosmic Word, 299
Damien Pryor, 8
Dendera, 21
Dendera zodiac, 21
detriment, 220
ego-sense, 4, 34, 43, 47, 56, 58, 59, 61, 62, 66, 76, 77, 78, 97, 98, 99, 158, 159, 168, 172, 173, 174, 175, 176, 177, 178, 182, 203, 209, 216, 241, 261, 269, 276, 290
ether-body, 292
etheric body, 14, 45, 46, 60, 86, 88, 95
exalted, 220
fall, 220
fear of death, 204
Fixed, 306
Fortunata, 296
four primary features, 16
Four Temperaments, 55
Gavin White, 21
house location of the ruler, 245
imum coeli, 56
Intercepted Signs, 305
intuitive promptings, 149, 162, 163, 238, 239, 240, 241
Isabel Hickey, 72, 218, 331
Jeanne Avery, 254

karma-sensing, 148, 162, 163, 167, 292
Karmic awareness, 67
life-forces, 14, 32, 44, 45, 46, 52, 59, 60, 80, 81, 83, 86, 87, 89, 91, 94, 95, 98, 99, 100, 199, 221, 295, 299
loud noises, 221
lunar nodes, 16, 18, 56, 295, 296, 297, 310, 311, 312, 317, 318
Martin Schulman, 311
Mary F. Shea, 316
mean nodes, 317
Midheaven point, 56, 78, 79, 99, 100, 115, 116, 131, 132, 146, 156, 157, 178
Mutable, 306
Nadir, 56
Neptune, 50
Noel Tyl, 298
north lunar node, 297
opposite-gender parent, 247
Part of Fortune, 296, 312
Placidus, 12, 244, 305, 317
Placidus system, 244
psychosis, 163, 188
psycho-somatic illnesses, 198
quadrants, 6, 12, 13, 14
Quincunx, 53
retrograde, 217
Retrograding Planets, 311
Rising Sign, 56
Robert Hand, 54, 59, 68, 171, 174, 177, 296, 331
Rudolf Steiner, 1, 2, 3, 4, 6, 8, 10, 12, 13, 14, 16, 23, 25, 27, 29, 32, 33, 40, 43, 44, 45, 47, 48, 49, 50, 54, 75, 243, 298, 299, 316, 318
ruler, 220
same-gender parent, 249, 298
Saturn's influence, 237
self-sacrificing tendency, 289

sense of self, 3, 4, 13, 14, 16, 19, 23, 28, 34, 47, 56, 60, 77, 78, 98, 146, 147, 158, 159, 177, 179, 180, 181, 182, 183, 184, 185, 190, 227, 240, 244, 259, 290, 313
sensitivity to chemicals, 173
sevenfold human being, 45, 52
sidereal zodiac, 7, 10
sleep-talking, 134, 293
sleep-walking, 163, 179
solar return, 316
south node, 295, 306
spirit-intuitiveness, 121
Spiritual-self, 46, 47, 48, 52, 125, 126
spiritual-soul, 48
subconscious will, 49, 67, 107
Succedent, 306
Table of The Houses, 13
The Part of Fortune in the Zodiac Signs, 312
The Part of Fortune in the Houses, 313
The Ascendant, 56
The Decans, 315
The Origin and Nature Of The Tropical Zodiac, 8
The south lunar node in the Houses, 309
The south lunar node in the Signs, 307
threshold, 13, 110, 137, 139, 140, 169, 174, 175, 203, 204, 245, 252, 257, 260, 279, 286
transits, 300
topocentric, 317
triplicity, 3
tropical zodiac, 7, 8, 10
Uranian forces, 50, 70, 108
Uranos, 50
Vettius Valens, 4, 40, 54

Illustrations acknowledgements

The zodiac and planetary graphics, except Virgo and Libra are from:
http://www.fontspace.com/category/greek,zodiac,symbols

Virgo & Libra graphics: the author

Illustrations 1 - 5,7,9,11,12,13: the author
6: Wikimedia Commons
8: Wikimedia Commons
10: Wikimedia Commons

Cover design: Working Type Studio.com.au

www.ingramcontent.com/pod-product-compliance
Lightning Source LLC
Chambersburg PA
CBHW080728300426
44114CB00019B/2514